JOHNSON'S ISLAND (FEDERAL) CIVIL WAR PRISON
FOR CONFEDERATE OFFICERS, LAKE ERIE, OHIO

James L. Douthat

Heritage Books
2024

HERITAGE BOOKS
AN IMPRINT OF HERITAGE BOOKS, INC.

Books, CDs, and more—Worldwide

For our listing of thousands of titles see our website
at
www.HeritageBooks.com

A Facsimile Reprint
Published 2024 by
HERITAGE BOOKS, INC.
Publishing Division
5810 Ruatan Street
Berwyn Heights, MD 20740

— Publisher's Notice —
In reprints such as this, it is often not possible to remove
blemishes from the original. We feel the contents of this
book warrant its reissue despite these blemishes and

International Standard Book Number
Paperbound: 978-0-7884-7737-9

JOHNSON'S ISLAND FEDERAL PRISON DURING THE CIVIL WAR

BACKGROUND

In 1861, the Federal authorities needed to plan a prison camp for the officers of the Confederacy. Lieutenant Colonel William Hoffman was assigned the role of securing a location for the prison. He traveled over the Lake Erie section of the north and turned down a number of islands close to the Canadian border and instead chose the un-inhabited island within the Sandusky Bay called Johnson's Island. This island was about 300 acres in size with about half of the island under cultivation by the owner L. B. Johnson who was willing to lease half of the island for $500.00 per year to the purpose of the prison. The Federal Government has the right to cut timber for fuel and other purposes and this would clear the land for more cultivation following the war.

Johnson's Island was originally called Bull's Island because the locals turned their cattle loose on the island in the summer to forage. In 1852, L. B. Johnson purchased the island for cultivation. During the Civil War, a Federal Prison was constructed here to house the officers of the Confederacy who were captured.

In 1894 the Johnson's Island Pleasure Resort Company was opened on thirty acres where a pavilion, a skating rink and cottages were erected. In 1904 a second resort was built with a dancing pavilion and theater were constructed since the first one burned in 1897. In 1901, the island saw stone being quarried to build breakwaters for the Cleveland, Lorain and Cedar Point areas. Following this, in 1956, a Cleveland investment group purchased the island for development. When the causeway was completed in 1972, rights were acquired in 1977 for the public to visit the cemetery of the Civil War prisoners who are buried on the island. Those buried in the 206 graves are given later in this publication.

REMINISCENCES

The time period of interest to us is the time in which this was a Federal Prison for Confederate Officers. We want to hear from those who were there at the time.

Samuel Josiah Abner Frazier of Tennessee was one of those held captive on the island during this time. Before his death in 1921, Mr. Frazier spoke to a local chapter of the Daughters of the Confederacy and gave an account of his nineteen months on the island.

"A few weeks after I reached there I took chills and fever, a remnant of the Mississippi campaign. A companion of mine from South Carolina, who accompanied me to the island, delicate and refined, also took chills. He was taken to the hospital and died. We had one heating stove for forty men. There was dirt a foot thick on the floor, and ice six inches thick on the windowpanes. I had nothing to read. I could not hear from home nor companions. We had plenty to eat, but no place to cook except on a heater."

"Two cases of small pox developed and remained in the room several days after it appeared. There was no ray of sunshine that broke the dark cloud. These conditions were those of the first three months. Most of those who were there with me are gone. Col. Aiken, who resided in Chattanooga, alone is left. Frank Gardenhire, Warren Hooper, Dan Kennedy and other of Chattanooga; Hugh White, Lip Taylor and Frank Blair of Knoxville, former schoolmates of mine, are all dead."

"Five cannon were kept at the entrance, trained on the prison, ready for instant use in the case of an uprising, which they constantly feared. They also kept paid informers in them to watch and report. Prisoners were searched on their arrival for money and arms. I gave them $10 in greenback, which was placed to my credit and afterwards checked out. In the sutler's tent I kept $200 in Confederate money, which I afterwards sold for $10 in greenback."

"Whenever a fresh batch of prisoners came the cry of 'fresh fish' was raised, and men of the whole prison flocked around them to see if there were any they knew from whom they could get information from the front and from their companions in arms and possibly from loved ones at home. They were eagerly questioned as to what was going on down south, as to who was killed and as to whether old 'Bob' Lee and others were whipping those Yankees."

"The best blood of the south was represented there, the soldiers being from every state and territory. They were high strung and proud. Their demeanor was more like that of captors than prisoners. They would brook no insult even from armed guards, and they strike even at the risk of life."

"The prisoners were of all ages, from the youth of 21 to gray beards of 50 years. They were mostly young and unmarried men, and in the vigor of youth. Those inside the lines, accessible to friends, were well dressed. Those outside were not so much so. Many wore their battle stained uniforms of gray. The drum beat at 9 o'clock p.m. for lights out; no fires were allowed before daylight, and a violation of those orders brought a bullet from a sentry, so in those long winter nights we could only lie in bed on cots inside the walls and dream of hog and hominy, big corndodgers and buttermilk away down at our homes in Dixie. We did our own cooking and washing, which most of us were not accustomed to doing. A negro boy Tom performed those duties before my capture."

"As long as the sutler was allowed to sell provisions and boxes were allowed to come in from friends, provisions were abundant. Those who got boxes let their rations go to the others. But when all boxes containing provision were cut off and the sutler was not allowed to sell anything to eat, the starvation commenced. This condition lasted about six months. It was not so at first or at last. I got a box in on a doctor's certificate. This was because I looked so pale and thin, caused only by want of nourishing food."

From the Confederate Veteran, Volume sixteen page 168 L. H. Kemp, Captain Co. F, 11th Arkansas Infantry writes, "In the Veteran for February, I note the list of Confederates buried on Johnson's Island. I was a prisoner there from April till sometime in September, 1862, at which time there was a general exchange. The death rate was very small in 1862, but among the number was Lieut. E. Gibson, a most excellent young man about twenty-two or twenty-three years of age. I loved and admired him. It was a bright moonlight night, and Friend Gibson was at my room for a few hours; he was in perfect health. Starting to his own quarters, nearly opposite mine, the sentinel on a near beat ordered him back, at the same time drawing his gun and shooting him dead on the spot, as cold-blooded a murder as was ever committed."

"There were officers at Johnson's Island from almost every Southern State, as it was for officers. Our regiment was surrendered at Island No. 10 [a battle in the Mississippi River in present Lake County, Tennessee] just after the battle of Shiloh. The Fort Donelson prisoners had preceded us. Many officers from Nashville were there, and among the names I remember General Battle - a fine, portly looking old gentlemen he was. I should be glad to know how many are yet living [written in 1908] who were exchanged in September, 1862. Nearly all my comrade officers are dead. I also saw in the February number that my old friend, Maj. Thomas J. Reid, of the 12th Arkansas Regiment, has gone to his reward. He was a gallant soldier."

In the 1908 issue of the Confederate Veteran a Federal officer writes in response to a request to hear from their side of Johnson's Island. Captain H. A. Smith of the 128th Ohio Infant writes, "A subscriber to the Veteran called my attention to article relating to the care of the prisoners at John's Island. I was stationed at the island for about two years. The conditions as described by your correspondent were not possible. The quarters (barracks) occupied by prisoners were just the same as used by the soldiers doing guard duty. The water from the wells was the same as all of us used. Ticks were filled with straw and blankets were issued to all alike, and the prisoners had all the wood they wanted. Inside the bull pen was a small grocery, where the prisoner's could purchase tobacco, fruit, eggs, etc. Clothing was issued when needed, as were also socks and underwear. The rations were just the same as the soldiers had. I never heard a complaint while there. I often asked the question: 'Can I do anything for you?' But only in a very few instances could I render help in that way."

"My brother was a prisoner in various prisons in the South, winding up with nine months in Andersonville. He visited me at the island, and met there a Mr. Jones, who captured him at Rocky Face. They had a very pleasant visit together. Brother Frank asked Mr. Jones if there was anything he needed that he could get for him. He said: 'I have all I need except my freedom. Your brother has treated me well here, and I have no complaint to make.' Brother Frank went through the hospital and sick quarters with Jones. When in the kitchen, he saw a large tub filled with pieces of bread, potatoes, scraps of meat, etc. and asked: 'What are you going to do with this?' Jones replied: 'Throw it in the lake.' Frank said it would be a God send to the prisoners in Andersonville."

"I took prisoners South for exchange, and in many instances they expressed satisfaction in regard to their treatment as prisoners. All the prisoners on the island were officers and, as far as I knew, gentlemen. I have some very warm friends among them. And I know they did not suffer from cold or lack of plenty to eat. Quarters, bedding, and rations were the same as the army had."

Again in Volume thirteen of the Confederate Veteran we find another set of reminiscences by Captain M. W. Sims of Bryan, Texas. He writes:

"I see in the March Veteran, the article by Captain A. O. P. Nicholson of Columbia Tennessee who occupied the same room (No. 10, Block 2) in Johnson's Island Prison that I did. I was there in August and September 1863. I recall Col. Nixon, Col. Robertson, Maj. Bate, 'Bill' Minor, and Captain George Ralston. The last named and I were captured together at Natchez, Mississippi soon after the fall of Vicksburg."

"We were a *rich* mess - paid a Confederate Captain to cook for us. 'Bill' Minor had friends in New York, Hall and Hildreth, former lessees of the St. Charles Hotel in New Orleans, who sent him money and cases of liquors; Col. I O. Nixon's old partner had been lessee of the St. Charles Theater in New Orleans (Johnny Owens, the actor, was in New York, and kept him supplied with wines, etc.); while the writer had fifty dollars in greenbacks, sent him by a lady friend in Glasgow, MO - so that up to the time I left, the later part of September, 1963, we 'lived high.'"

"I was sent for by Major Hoffman, the commandant, and on going to his headquarters was notified to be ready to leave next morning, as I was to be sent to General Grant at Vicksburg for special exchange. All exchange of prisoners had been discontinued; but Gen. E. Kirby Smith had captured Gen. Grant's brother-in-law, Dent, who promised that if released he would have me released also; hence the order for me to report to General Grant for special exchange. On my arrival at Vicksburg, I found that I had been charged with shooting some prisoners at Milliken Bend, Louisiana, and had been sentenced to death - quite a change from my expected liberty. I was placed in a cell in the Vicksburg jail, where I was when the battle of Chickamauga was fought. Thomas called for re-enforcements, and all available troops in Vicksburg were hurried forward to Chattanooga. All the prisoners in Vicksburg including myself, were ordered to be sent to the 'Irving Block,' in Memphis. We were placed on a boat one dark, rainy night. About an hour before day I jumped overboard aft of the wheel room and swam ashore."

Not all was peaches and cream at the prison. Captain Frank Battle of Palmyra, Tennessee writes in the Confederate Veteran Volume nineteen page 138 the following story:

"In the winter of 1863, I was a prisoner on Johnson's Island. About three thousand prisoners were kept there. They were very restless and anxious for exchange. We were living on half rations, and the outlook was indeed gloomy. There was a deep snow on the ground and the ice was about two and half inches think. It was so cold that water thrown from the second story of the prison would be ice when it reached the ground."

"Someone proposed a snowball fight, and small parties would engage in the sport; then all the prisoners organized, and six blocks or wards, proposed to fight the other six. The first six blocks contained all the general officers except one, and he was not allowed to command in his department. A lad from Florida, I think, commanded in his stead."

"Major General [Isaac Ridgeway] Trimble and Brigadier General [William Nelson Rector Beall] Beal, of Missouri, Archer [James Jay Archer, Brigade General] of Texas, and Jeff Thompson, from Missouri, were in District No. 1 No. 2 had a colonel to command them. It took some time to get our regiments or brigades in fighting trim. Some of us had been out of the business so long that we were a little rusty; but when the war whoop was sounded and we had fairly gotten into the fight, we made the 'fur' fly, and we felt that we were at our old business again. The fight lasted about two hours, and wounded men were lying around thick. I was wounded in several places and taken prisoner, but was exchanged on the field."

"The fight was declared a draw, both sides being exhausted from hard fighting, and a truce was made to last until the next big snow. Our friends in blue took much interest in the fight and viewed it from the parapets of the prison."

In the first volume of the Confederate Veteran there is one of those interesting stories that can only come from one who was present at the time. Captain John Sargent of the Fourteenth Tennessee Regiment, CSA relates this story as told by B. F. Wilson, Jr.

"It was in the fall of '63, I think when the boys were worn in body and soul with the wariness of prison life. One day a regiment of Ohio volunteers were marched out amid much elation and beating of drums. Their bright new uniforms, fluttering flags, and glistening guns made a sad contrast to the boys inside the walls, who with a curiosity born of a long continued monotony, called out to them and asked them where they were going."

"It was in the days when the daring John Morgan had just escaped from the weary toils of the Columbus penitentiary, and had again with his undaunted spirit gotten together his famous command and was harassing the Yankees; and the boys had a sly notion of what was up; so when the answer was hurled back at them, in a preconceived triumphal derision, 'We are going to catch John Morgan and bring him back.' It was truly an inspiring sight to behold the gorgeousness and brilliancy of their departure, yet already in our minds eye we had bridged the lapse of time and beheld their triumphal (?) return. * * *"

"Of all the dilapidated, broken down sets of men ever seen, these surely were the worst. They appeared as if a 'cyclone had struck them.' From what had been the exultant departure, their dejected return made a pleasing contrast to the boys, and excited to no little degree their responsibilities. We called to them as they passed, and inquired kindly after the health of General John Morgan, but to none of our questions would they respond. I happened to notice a guard who I knew belonged to these Ohio volunteers. I asked him about their trip after general Morgan. To my inquiry, with an oath, he said: 'Why man, before we knew we were in his vicinity, he had us surrounded and captured us all at once; and then began the greatest race for fun (?) that you ever saw. He made us lay down our guns, and ran us up and down the country for ten or twelve miles, until we were completely worn out, and our clothes torn and covered with mud and dirt; and then giving us our parole, turned our faces toward home and told us to 'git,' and we 'got.'

Life within the prison was run by the desire to escape and survive at the same time. The following memory is shared by John Inzer Freeman of Ashville, Alabama in the Volume 21 of the <u>Confederate Veteran.</u> He gives the story as told by his grandfather Col. John W. Inzer of the 32nd and 58th Alabama Infantry as related to his time on Johnson's Island.

"In 1864, the Federal Government absolutely refused to exchange prisoners with the South, except in a few cases where the Confederate soldiers were unable to be of any service on account of wounds and various causes. In the early part of the year 1865 there were about three thousand prisoners on the island, and they were divided into thirteen blocks, or buildings. The buildings were built of wood, two stories high, fifty feet wide by about one hundred and fifty feet long, and were about two hundred feet apart. There was a total of thirteen blocks. They were divided into six on each side as you enter the prison and one in the extreme rear, each block represented one of the Southern States in the prison government."

"In February, 1965, the prisoners at Johnson's Island, coming to the conclusion that they would have to remain in prison for a indefinite period, began to form a government for their safety and welfare. They considered that a good form of government would be to let each block represent one of the Southern States; that each block should have its own government as the State government; that all the States should have a government with each State represented; that a president and all other officers to complete the Confederate government should be elected, and that they should hold meetings as the Southern Congress did. It was left with each State that they could withdraw if they referred, and generally the laws of the Southern States were carried out. It was a very complete form of government, and at this time the pres had many articles complimentary to it."

"The authorities never objected or interfered with any of these meetings. By the time of the surrender of the Confederate armies, in 1865, the State and Federal government of the Confederate prisoners was well organized and complete, having held elections, elected members and officers, and had many meetings. Minutes and records were kept of the meetings of this prison government. The writer has a number of these papers, but would be glad to hear if others can be found. The government meetings were held in building number four. The principal object was to make rules, laws, and regulations, and to be of benefit to all the Confederate prisoners there."

ESCAPES

The main thought of all prisoners, officers or enlisted men, was to escape their prison. Since the majority of the men at Johnson's Island were well educated and the elite of the south, their thoughts were sometimes more creative than others. S. J. A. Frazier of Chattanooga gives the following account of escape when he spoke to a chapter of the Daughters of the Confederacy.

"The prisoners made repeated efforts at escape, but were generally unsuccessful. In that cold January of 1864, the coldest ever known, the lake froze over. It was supposed that no southern man would venture out in such temperature. Over twenty prisoners scaled the walls, crossed over the ice to the mainland, but were compelled to go into farmhouses to warm. They were betrayed and recaptured."

"On one occasion, when some work was being done in prison, wagons and workingmen were coming in and out constantly. One rebel exchanged clothes with one of the workmen and accompanied the wagon out. Soon as it got out among the prisoners, blue coats were in demand at any price. And during that day and the next, about fifty prisoners had passed out as workingmen. Only about two got off the island, by forging an order, with the post commander's name, to pass them on boats. The others wandered around the island until next night, when the discovery was made, and drums were beaten to arms, and soldiers called out amid great excitement, as if a regular battle was expected. The Confederates, who were playing cards with, and making themselves agreeable to, Yankee soldiers, snatched up muskets, fell in line, and let the pursuit of those terrible rebels, who were not discovered until next morning, when their southern features betrayed them."

In Volume 5 of the Confederate Veteran Colonel B. L. Farinholt of Baltimore, Maryland recounts the following escapes:

"Well do we recall the Glee Club, with Col. Fite, of Tennessee, and the popular and brilliant Col. John R. Fellows - the late distinguished city attorney of New York, then from Arkansas, a member of Gen. Beal's staff when captured - as standing upon the stoop of his prison building leading with stentorian voice a chorus sometimes improvised for the locality and occasion, which would be joined by a thousand or more, and could be heard on a quiet afternoon over the smooth surface of the lake to Sandusky City."

"Quite a character was General Jeff Thompson, of Missouri, so indefatigable and versatile in resources that he might have been characterized as a good type of Yankee, but for his being so intensely Southern. And then came handsome Major Jack Thompson, of Kentucky, pleasing, and commanding a fund of humor and good nature, so necessary in prison to health and companionship. Also Major McKnight, so well known to the press of New Orleans and to the country at large as 'Asa Hartz,' a bright, genial soul; ex-Governor Nichols, the idol of his state, true to his allegiance, and now no less a patriot, warmly devoted to his state, with every reverence for the general government, a man whom Louisiana may feel proud to honor; Col. Lewis, the great Missouri preacher; Gens. Archer and Trimble, a part of the noble contribution from Maryland; and brave and enterprising Lieut. Grogan, who escaped the very week of our arrival at the island by secreting himself in some straw left in the bottom of a barge which was being towed back to Sandusky after another load to make beds for the prisoners. After reaching the mainland, being fertile in resources, he soon found his way back to his friends in Baltimore."

He continued, "Captain Robinson, of Westmoreland County, Virginia with two other brave officers, succeeded in making his escape during a fearful gale of snow and ice on a pitilessly dark night, and crossed the lake to Michigan, a good portion of the way on their hands and knees. Robinson finally reached Canada, where he was feted and given aid, going from there to Nassua, and by blockade to the Confederacy, where he resumed his command of the Westmoreland cavalry, as unassuming and superbly gallant after his wonderful and daring escape as before. His two companions were so frosted, hands and feet, that they had to seek shelter, and for a while passed as two shipwrecked sailors in farmhouses on the Michigan peninsula; but, being missed from the prison rolls, they were closely followed, and the next day brought back to prison. Their frozen feet and hands caused them to be much greater sufferers than before. Rigid punishment was meted out for such attempts by close confinement with ball and chain, with diet of bread and water, or a parole of honor never to make the attempt again."

"These failures, however, did not deter me from prizing liberty so highly as to make the attempt myself. I was to have been one of the party of three, with the quiet and intrepid Richard Ferguson, a prominent minister now of Virginia, and Captain McCullough of the Eighteenth Virginia; but being sick on the stormy night which suited their purpose, Col. John Timberlake, of the Fifty-Third Virginia, was given my place. They managed to elude the vigilance of the guards just over their heads by lying down and crawling in a small ditch which reached the stockade, beneath one of the many large reflecting lamps posted around within the prison, and with improvised knives and saws, made very sharp, soon succeeded in cutting a hole about 12 x 18 inches through the stockade, which in the pelting downpour of rain, they managed to plug up again; then, crossing the beach in the dark, Ferguson and McCullough waded into the lake, and would have escaped all guards and succeeded in building a raft of logs on which they proposed to drift to Michigan or Canada. Providentially perhaps - though they could not see it that way - Timberlake misunderstood the directions after getting out, and, instead of following the others into the water, he undertook to walk beneath the platform on which were the guards. Even then he might have escaped their observation, but lo and behold! The officer of the day, about to make his grand round of inspection, coming out of the blockhouse at the instant, ran full against Timberlake whom he grasped, and after a short struggle, turned him over to the guards. The garrison was immediately aroused, and several hundred men were stationed around the shore of the island. Ferguson and McCullough, hiding under a pile of brush, were discovered at daybreak. They were returned to our mess, the most disappointed and crestfallen victims of hard luck, muddy, wet, and in every way disgruntled."

Col. Farinholt continued his story, "The several wells within the stockade, from which our water supply came, were soon so impregnated with impure and most unhealthy acids and alkalies, which percolated through the earth into these wells form the sinks and refuse matter thrown into the ditches and yards as to be the foulest cesspools of intolerable liquid, to be shunned by us as would be a draught of deadly poison; so finally the authorities, through sheer necessity, granted us the right to obtain water from the clear and pure lake. O what a boon it was considered by those who for weeks and months had not waited at the opening of the large southern gate, which opened from the stockade upon the lake shore! Before the gate was opened in winter a semicircle of guards was stationed, facing inward, to watch our every movement. An officer stationed at the gate counted us, one by one, until one hundred prisoners with tubs, buckets, canteens, and other vessels had passed. Then the crowding, eager throng within halted, and no others were allowed to pass out until the fortunate first hundred had, after breaking the ice and filling their vessels, returned. Then another hundred were counted out and back."

"I noticed at times the inability of the officers to be entirely accurate in counting, and this determined me in the time and manner of a trial for liberty. I improvised a suit of Federal undress uniform by taking the black stripe off my Confederate officer's trousers. They made a very good substitute, although they showed a rent in the leg just above the knee, made by a bullet of no mean size

CAPT. JOHN S. LATANE.

received while advancing in that terrible charge of Picket's Division to what has since been correctly named the 'Bloody Angle,' at Gettysburg. My coat was simply a blue blouse and the hat a black slouch, done up in the jaunty, wide awake style, with a fancy black-and-gold cord around it - the style Federal officers usually wore. Under this suit I wore a citizen's suit, my plan being to pass as a citizen should I be fortunate enough to effect my escape. Over it all I wore loosely a Confederate gray shawl, to attract as little attention as possible to my make-up as a Federal soldier. My bed fellow and warmest friend, Captain John Latane, of Virginia, did all the sewing, and zealously helped me to adjust and fit both suits. The citizen's trousers had been worn out of prison by Colonel Luce, of Mississippi, who was fortunate enough to escape, but was recaptured near Alton, Ohio, and returned to prison. No fancy zephyr or embroidery on velvet wrought by woman's fingers has ever been watched with more earnestness or received from her hands with more loving pride by any fond devotee than was this needlework of my friend and fellow prisoner, a modest, whole-souled, brave fellow who survived the war; a man who made others around him happier and their lives brighter by doing many little irksome duties for them cheerfully and un-murmuringly."

CAMP MESS AT JOHNSON'S ISLAND PRISON.

"We had a long cold spell, freezing Lake Erie over solidly in the month of February. The provisions and other supplies had to be brought over to the island by means of sleds or ice boats, and all passing to and fro was done on the ice. On the 22nd of February the troops from Sandusky City and our guards on the island were to have quite a celebration. I determined on this day for my escape. I had kept my plans to myself, except to inform two or three whom it was necessary to take into my confidence in order to make preparation. It was a beautiful day, with the sun shining bright and the ice fields glistening in effulgence for miles away to the east. I determined to carry out my attempt, and communicated my intention to a few valued friends. Two of them helped me to secure a place in line early, so as to be counted out with the first hundred going after water that morning. They approached the circle of guards as near as permissible before cutting holes in the ice, then commenced an angry altercation with each other to attract a crowd of the Confederates, and as the guards closed in to disperse the crowd and drive them back into the prison (some even before they had filled their buckets, disorder of this kind being looked upon suspiciously and often punished), I quietly handed my gray shawl to Captain Latane, who was full in the secret of my intentions, and slipped through the line of guards and mixed with the number of Federals in undress uniform who were skating and sliding about on the ice outside the line of guards, several of whom rushed up to see the row between the Confederates. The Federals not on duty were ordered off by the officer in charge of the guards. I was only too glad to obey this order, and, with apparent indifference, began sliding about on the ice, gradually gaining toward the beach. I passed several of the guards along the shore without being challenged, and finally reached the apparent route for pedestrians to Sandusky, to be seen in the distance on the mainland of Ohio. At this point a watchful sentinel was impatiently pacing. I expected him to halt me, but as he walked up toward me I assumed the air of an officer and asked him how long he had been on duty. Upon his replying, 'It is about time for the relief,' I looked at my watch and remarked that the relief should be more prompt. He seemed well satisfied that I was one of their number, and I continued my walk on the ice, occasionally stopping to throw broken pieces of ice as far as I could and to slide about, all the while gaining distance from the hated prison, until I was half way to Sandusky and over a mile from the prison. Here I passed a number of Federal soldiers, members of our guard off duty, returning to the island from Sandusky. I politely touched my hat, and they saluted me in return. Looking back several times during this to me momentous but delightful walk of nearly three miles on the ice, I could see groups of my comrades - many of the most trusted being by this time informed of my escape - gathered at the windows of the prison buildings eagerly watching me and rejoicing at the success of my ruse. Reaching Sandusky, I avoided the principal streets of the city and the military parade. Willing to accord to Washington all the honors the civil and military could bestow upon his memory, I had before me other and more important work. With light and rapid steps, when unobserved, I made my way out of Sandusky to the Lake Shore railroad, and thence along its tracks, passing now and then a gang of laborers, until four miles out, in a thick piece of woods, when I divested myself of my soldier's clothes, hid them under a log, and returned to the railroad in my citizen's suit."

"I continued my journey until near a depot about eleven miles from Sandusky, then I waited in the woods near by until I heard an approaching train going east. I had secured in prison a copy of the timetable of the Lake Shore railroad from the Sandusky papers, and having with me this slip and a pretty well drawn map of the northern part of Ohio, I knew when to expect this train. Going to the depot just as the train stopped, I secured a ticket to Cleveland, and was soon bounding over the rails, my heart getting lighter and lighter as the distance increased. But my light heartedness was soon to be interrupted. A detective appeared upon the scene, took a seat by me, and remarked on the old-style interwoven stripe of my rather unusual citizen's trousers. He showed me his official assignment to duty on that line. However, he was under the influence of liquor and garrulous, or I might have had more trouble in eluding him. He had exhibited such strong indication of giving me trouble that I felt sure he would arrest me when the train reached Cleveland, not far ahead. Knowing that Colonel Luce, in his attempted escape, had been caught and returned to prison after just such an experience, I watched my opportunity for escape. I had taken the precaution to get in the rear coach, and when he went forward to talk with the conductor I jumped from the train. I had a hard fall and was much bruised and hurt, the worse as it renewed a very acute pain from an old wound received in front of Richmond. I scrambled up the embankment, and, placing my ear to the track, ascertained that the train had not stopped. It was late at night. I continued on down the track, arriving in Cleveland in about three hours without further molestation and in time to take th east bound train that night. From Cleveland I took the cars to Elmira, N.Y., spending the last money I had, except fifteen cents, for my ticket, and then via Tamaqua to Philadelphia with nothing of special moment to interest one, except that, having to wait several hours at Elmira, I endeavored to part with a valuable scarf pin in order to procure little money for food, having to that time spent only twenty-five cents for that necessity.

After my experience with that detective I made it a point, when practicable, to occupy a seat with some Federal officers in uniform on every train on which I traveled. This afforded me security from the intrusion of detectives and other disagreeable characters and added to my enlightenment as to army operations and the general thought at the North. Near Philadelphia I had a seat immediately behind two Canadians, who expressed themselves as warmly in sympathy with the South. While this was very gratifying to me, it suited me just then to be a warm Union man.

Reaching Philadelphia on the second day after leaving Johnson's Island, entirely destitute of funds and the cravings of hunger unappeased, I sought the residence of a lady friend, on whom I knew I would not call in vain for assistance. She extended to me the warmest hospitality, and sending for her husband, introduced me. That night, with several of their acquaintances, all sympathizers with the Southern cause, I spent a delightful time. I had provided myself with suitable clothing, with a refreshing bath, and super, and felt a different man, many degrees removed from the thoughts and discomforts of prison life. These friends advised me to return to the Confederacy via Canada, which might have been a safer route, but I determined to come directly South, crossing into Virginia from some place in Maryland.

After two days in Philadelphia I took the cars to Elkton, Maryland. Leaving Elkton that night, I returned to Wilmington, and it being Saturday, remained over there until Monday at the Indian Queen Hotel, when I hired a vehicle to take me ten or twelve miles by a country road across to the Seaford and Eastern Shore railroad. I talked with my driver about the Delaware crops and the country through which we were passing. The peach crop, then as now, came in for a large share of our attention and speculation. He told me some wonderful 'Mulberry Sellers" stories of fortunes that had been made in peaches. Dismissing my driver, I again boarded the cars, and arrived that night in Seaford, a small town in Southern Delaware. Within an hour after my arrival at Seaford I took passage on a small oyster sloop down the Nanticoke, and after an uneventful night spent on this boat in close sleeping quarters was landed by the captain in Fishing Bay, an arm of the Chesapeake. I hired a farmer to take me in his carriage six or seven miles to the house of a former friend, who joyfully greeted me. He had a son in the Confederate army, and his heart was with the South. I spent several days at his house. I passed among his neighbors, some of them active Union men, as a Philadelphian buying railroad supplies, and inspected such timer as might be suitable to purchase for this purpose. After many and various efforts while there to learn of some chance to cross the Chesapeake, and having been told by a former blockade runner whom I met that it was worth one's life to undertake it then, in consequence of some recent captures, my friend and I concluded that it would be better for me to reach his vessel, then about to load coal at Havre de Grace for Washington; so riding with him to Cambridge, I took passage on the steamer "Pioneer" - Captain, Kirwan - to Baltimore. On this trip I had the pleasant companionship of a Federal naval officer, who, ignorant of my being an escaped Confederate prisoner, seemed to take much interest in conversation with me. Upon arriving in Baltimore, at his suggestion, we went together to Guy's old hotel, then standing where the new Baltimore post office now stands. This was the 8th of March 1864, the day on which Gen. grant passed through Baltimore on his way to take charge of the Army of the Potomac.

There were a great many Federal officers in the city. My naval friend, who enjoyed the acquaintance of many of the officers then in Baltimore, introduced me to several, and that night at Guy's about eleven o'clock we had an oyster supper, and over sparkling champagne discussed the merits of General Grant's Western campaigns. To my edification and surprise, several of these officers did not like his appointment as chief commander. They criticized him closely and pronounced him inferior to many other generals. I was then pretty well posted on his Western campaigns, and warmly espoused his cause, aided by my naval friend and two other Federal officers of our party.

I did not make myself known to any Baltimore friends or acquaintances. I thought it best not to see them. On the third day after arriving in Baltimore I took the train for Havre de Grace, and, for my impatience, had to wait in that dull, inquisitive town two days before the vessel arrived and then another day for her to load. The captain gave me passage, ostensibly as a hand before the mast, but before going aboard I provided myself with a little skiff and ducking outfit, and was then prepared to leave the vessel any night after she entered the Potomac, when an auspicious hour should appear to make it possible for me to reach the Virginia shore.

We had favorable winds down to Point Lookout, when it began to blow a gale, and anchoring there, close ashore, for harbor, we could plainly see thousands of my fellow Confederate soldiers as they passed about the prison, surrounded by the ever watchful Federal sentinels. How thankful, when lying on the cabin, viewing this scene at Point Lookout, was I for the good fortune so far attending my escape! And how dearly I prized freedom no one can tell. I had no weapon but a pocket knife, but I felt that it would take a well trained and strong force to effect my recapture. So, free but not too secure in that freedom, I saw held up before my eyes, within a few hundred yards of where I lay, the counterpart of the loathsome prison, the scanty and coarse food, and the deprivation of home and family - in a word, the purgatory - in which for nine long, weary months I had been confined and from which I had been fortunate enough to escape, but were I recaptured, might never be able to accomplish again.

The storm finally abated, and it was a joyous sound to hear the anchor weighed. With a good breeze we went on up the Potomac. Several guard and gun boats passed close to us. Some hailed us, and I put on an oil cloth jacket, so as to pass as a sailor on duty if any inspecting officer should board us. However, none of them gave us any particular attention. On we went, and, when nearing a prominent point on the Virginia side, which could be distinguished in the dark, the captain and his mate assisted me to launch my little skiff. Though not an experienced oarsman, I committed myself and my all unhesitatingly to the dark waters of the Potomac. The crew being ignorant of the fact that I was a Confederate, I passed with them as going to visit a friend in Maryland; hence for the protection of the captain and the vessel, I rowed toward the Maryland shore until the vessel was some distance off, and then turned the prow of my little boat south. After a long and hard pull I struck the shore on the slope of a sandy beach. Getting out of my boat, with the painter clasped tight in my hand, I lay on the cold sand beach for some time to rest from the exhausting fatigue of my long row in a leaky boat. I was about to go fast asleep, when with difficulty I aroused myself and fervently thanked God that I was once more in old Virginia, again free, with the horrors of prison life behind me.

I clambered up the bank, and in crossing a field struck a path, following which I soon came to a negro's hut. He and his wife were very much alarmed when I aroused them. This was in Westmoreland County, the inhabitants of which section had been severely treated by the cavalry raiders of both Northern and Southern armies, so this darky knew not what to expect from a stranger calling him up at such an hor (about 3 a.m.) However, my most convincing argument to him was my little boat and oars, which had then served the purpose for which they were bought I gave these to him and helped him secure them.

From a neighbor he obtained a horse and vehicle, and carried me to the house of a gentleman named Bronson, about three miles from the river, who had two sons in the Confederate Army.

This man we aroused at four o'clock in the morning. Imagining that possibly his visitor was a spy or likely to give him trouble, he at first refused to take me in, although I frankly told him I was an escaped prisoner, that I had just crossed the Potomac, and had come to him after hearing that he had two sons in our army, feeling safe in so doing. Bronson was overcautious, and before consenting to take me in he desired that I should go with him upstairs to a room occupied by a blockade runner, a man from Richmond, who was in the habit of stopping with Bronson when near the Potomac. Bronson had questioned me quite closely, and I had told him my rank, brigade, and division in the army, also the place of my nativity. He now desired to confront me with this blockade runner, in whose shrewdness he placed much confidence; and if I could answer readily all the questions of this man and confirm that I had said, it would be satisfactory.

By this time Bronson's whole family were awakened, and as they gathered in the large hall of the comfortable, old fashioned house, peering to see me and what was going on, we went up the broad stairway and entered most unexpectedly the room in which the blockade runner lay snoring away, loud enough, it seemed to me, to have kept every one in the house awake. You should have seen the surprise and fright depicted on the countenance of this large, bald headed, but, blue eyed man as, when rudely awakened by Bronson, he sat bolt upright in bed and appealingly inquired what as wanted, expecting that he was already a prisoner, and that his team and chattels would be confiscated. It was some time before he could realize what was wanted of him, but when he did collect his frightened and scattered senses he became a fairly good inquisitor, glad, I suppose, to have the turn on me for such a fright as had been given him. I soon satisfied him that I knew more about the vicinity and the persons he asked concerning than himself. This seemed to thoroughly satisfy Bronson, so he asked me to a comfortable fire, and his servants soon prepared a palatable breakfast, for which my recent night's exposure and exertion gave me much zest.

After breakfast Mr. Bronson drove me over to Mr. Newton's, an ex-Congressman, near the Hague. Here I remained two days, as Mr. Newton and his wife feared that on the road I might be recaptured by some Federal Cavalry, then raiding the upper part of the county. But I was anxious to reach Richmond and learn from friends there the condition of everything concerning our cause. Then, too, my home being within the enemy's lines, I in a measure considered Richmond my home. However, much the word implies usually, it had a deeper significance to me as a returning prisoner of war.

Mr. Newton had a servant drive me twenty miles to the Rappahannock River, near Tappahannock, a straggling village on the south side of the Rappahannock, said to be as old as Philadelphia, but having then only about three hundred inhabitants, well-to-do, genial people, who, in the old families, yet retain the spirit of refinement and extend hospitality, as did their ancestors. There was a court house there and pleasant residences. From this place I went by stage to Richmond, paying $100 in Confederate money, with which I had now provided myself, for my passage, in a rickety stage with poor horses. Starting very early in the morning and changing horses on the road, we reached Richmond at ten o'clock Saturday night, a distance of about sixty miles. Here I met with a warm reception. Sunday morning I sent to a prominent tailor and obtained a suit of uniform which I had ordered ten months previous, when our division was encamped near Richmond. It came in most opportunely, as it saved annoyance from guards, who were diligent in requiring passports of all in citizen's dress; besides, when I ordered this suit I paid $250 for it, and now it would have cost me $1,000.

That Sunday was a happy and memorable day to me. In the morning I had an interview with President Davis regarding the condition of our officers in prison at Johnson's Island, and I can assert, from the great feeling and warmth he evinced for them, that I believe no one connected with our cause more earnestly desired the exchange of prisoners than Mr. Davis.

In the afternoon a large crowd had assembled on the Capitol Square to meet a small detachment of officers and privates just from Point Lookout, who were exchanged at City Point. I was delighted to met among these several of my old comrades and fellow sufferers of Johnson's Island, among them Dr. William Christian, who had been of great service at the prison as Confederate Medical Director, in general charge of the hospital and junior surgeons, in which capacity he was invaluable and helped to relieve much suffering and mitigate many hardships.

President Davis appeared on the square and cordially greeted each of the exchanged soldiers and again grasped my hand and congratulated me on having arranged my own cartel. Many lovely women and brave men met to greet the returned prisoners, whether known personally or not.

The day following was spent with friends in various departments, where I ascertained the loss of many a dear friend until then thought to be living, and learned of the disposition of the regiments, brigades, and divisions in which I had warm personal friends. In the afternoon I called on the Secretary of War and obtained a leave of absence for thirty days, the Secretary very kindly asking me to name the time I wished.

My home being on the peninsula between the York and the James Rivers, which singularly had been the scene of the chief strategic events and great battles in both the war of the Revolution and those fought in the first two years of the civil war, to say nothing of it being the section made historic long before either of these wars by the numerous conflicts of John Smith and his followers with the hostile Indians, and a little later of Nathaniel Bacon and his liberty loving but rebellious band against the irascible and haughty, though brave God. Berkeley, I was compelled in order to see my family to go not only outside of our lines, but very near the enemy. The Secretary cautioned me of this, but said he was not afraid of my recapture, when I had just risked so much to escape from prison.

Leaving Richmond on Tuesday, the 22nd of March, by the York River railroad for the "White House" - General William H. F. Lee's historic home on the Pamunkey - I took a private vehicle and reached my home, about twenty miles farther down the peninsula. Loving wife and child waited impatiently my return and welcomed me with the fervency which the fond heart of wife and mother can intensely cherish for the absent husband, and there was great happiness at our fireside that memorable night - just a month from the day I left Johnson's Island - yet our joy was tinged with sadness for the loss of a dear mother whose death was hastened by anxiety for her absent sons and the frequent rude searches through her house and premises for those sons by Federal soldiers stationed near. These searches were made upon the false reports of negroes, and thus a good Christian woman was harried to death by excitement and worry occasioned by soldiers in their almost brutal exercise of power to search every private residence. On one occasion, the whole household being aroused from sleep at midnight to permit a search of the house by a squad of cavalry, who had ridden up to the door firing off their carbines and pistols in every direction, like very demons, the officer in charge dismounted and entered my mother's chamber, followed by a number of his soldiers, who searched every closet and corner in the room, not forgetting even the bureau drawers. Of course they did not find either my brother or myself, for whom they professed to be looking.

While bravely undergoing such ordeals and showing no signs of anything but the coldest, most reserved equanimity on these occasions, either by speech or action, this devout Christian woman was usually sick for days afterwards.

My leave of absence passed quickly away without any interruption from the enemy, except an occasional cavalry raid, for which I was always on the alert, and absented myself in time.

When I returned to the now deservedly renowned Pickett's Division and met the survivors of that sanguinary charge at Gettysburg, and particularly the remnant of my old brigade (Armstead's), I felt that I was with brothers again, doubly and trebly tried in the very crucible of fire at the "bloody angle."

I was soon ordered to Richmond and detailed in charge of a number of picked men to proceed to the vicinity of Curl's Neck, on the north side of the James River, to watch the movements of the transports, and of General Butler on its south side.

While engaged in this service, one night upon crossing the main road I discovered to my great surprise that a large body of horses had just passed. I soon had my men under arms, and captured a number of the rear guard of Sheridan's Cavalry and ascertained and reported to Richmond, carrying my prisoners with me, the news of Sheridan's famous raid from Atlee's Station around and in the rear of General Lee's army.

From this time on to the end of the war I was engaged in strengthening the defenses along the Richmond and Danville railroad and improving the defenses at High Bridge, near Farmville, a timely precaution, as evidenced by the opportune and successful defense of Staunton River bridge from the attack made upon it by Generals Wilson and Kautz on the 25th of June, 1864, when General Lee's communications with Richmond and the entire rolling stock of the Richmond and Danville railroad were saved only by the most obstinate defense of this point. Had this point been lost and the Richmond and Danville railroad been destroyed from Richmond to Danville, Lee's supplies from the south would have been entirely cut off, and consequently Richmond would have been abandoned ten months earlier.

An all-seeing Providence guided the destinies of our country to a different time and through many more trials. The conflict was finally closed by the surrender of Lee and Johnston; and the peace, then established, has been maintained inviolate by the soldiers of each army recognizing fully all their obligations, which were not for one side alone, but mutual.

[Col. B. L. Farinholt corrected a few errors that unwittingly made it into the article. He was not a colonel in Armistead's Brigade, only a captain for three years, but was promoted to a colonelcy and given a separate command in consequence of my escape and in recognition of my services while in command at Staunton River bridge in an engagement on the 25th of June, 1864. William R. Aylett was colonel of the Fifty-Third Virginia at the time of the Gettysburg battle, but Lieut.-Col. Raleigh Martin commanded and gallantly led the regiment in the charge. Colonel Farinholt's home as Baltimore was in error as he is "of Virginia."]

In the Volume 32 of the Confederate Veteran is an account of the escape of Colonel John R. Winston of North Carolina. Colonel Winston was born in Leaksville, Rockingham County, North carolina, a graduate of Trinity College and volunteered into the Confederacy, and was made captain of Company F 45th North Carolina Regiment, and later became its major, then colonel. He was wounded and captured at Gettysburg, July, 1863, and taken to Johnson's Island. Escaping from that prison, he rejoined his regiment and with it was engaged in many battles to the surrender at Appomattox. Here is his story.

In the southern part of Lake Erie, three miles north of Sandusky City, Ohio, is Johnson's Island, about three-fourths of a mile long by one-fourth wide. On the northeast side an old field was occupied by the Confederate prison, which was enclosed by a wall fifteen feet high, embracing a plot two hundred yards by two hundred and sixty. There were thirteen frame buildings or "blocks;" some were ceiled, but most were weather boarded only. During the winter of 1863-64 some 2,300 Rebels - 2,000 officers, the others private soldiers - and some citizens were domiciled in this delectable retreat for Southern fire-eaters. The prisoners whiled away the weary days, weeks, and months with chess and cards, in debating societies, and Christian meetings; but the one idea running under all was to get back to "Dixie." Various efforts to bribe or persuade the sentinels were made, and sometimes promised success; but up to the time this narrative relates not a prisoner had ever made his escape in this way. On one occasion, indeed, a gallant brigadier with four or five other officers did bribe a sentinel to let them over the wall;' but after they had handed over the gold watch and stipulated sum of money, a line of armed soldiers rose up around them and marched them back to prison, too poor to attempt bribing again. A great many plans to escape were attempted, but probably the one most assiduously followed was that of tunneling, or "gophering," in prison parlance. Five or six men would form a party to escape; after selecting a "block" as near to the wall as may be, they went to work under the floor, digging with case and pocket knives and any other instrument that came to hand. As but one man could work at a time, this took many days. Several parties escaped from the prison, but were invariably captured on the island, as they had no means of crossing the water. Such was the vigilance of the garrison and the nature of the difficulties to be overcome that every attempt to escape had failed up to January 1, 1864, except in the case of one young officer from Baltimore (I think he was), who, with others was sent into the hold of the island steamer for straw for bunks, and, instead of returning, went to the bottom of the straw, and that night when the boat was lying at the wharf at Sandusky City, he cautiously crept forth and, unperceived, went away.

New Year's day, 1864, was extremely cold'; that night the mercury fell to thirty degrees below zero. As the cold north winds beat with cruel violence against the thin weather boarding, the shivering prisoners, whose blood was unused to such rigorous climates, felt peculiarly sad. "If we could only get out of prison, we could leave the island on the ice; but it is too cold to live through the night in the open air." So thought most of the prisoners; but Major Stokes and Captains Stokes, Robinson, and Davis, of Virginia; Captain McConnell, of Kentucky, and Major Winston, of North Carolina (afterwards colonel of the 45th North Carolina Regiment), determined to risk a desperate attempt that night; for as soon as the authorities at Washington should hear of the ice connecting the island with the mainland they would strengthen the garrison so that there would be no hope of getting away. They came to the conclusion that the boldest was the best way to get out of prison - viz, by scaling the wall. So a rude ladder was extemporized by tying with clothes lines the legs of a bench across it at intervals of about three feet to answer for steps. Of course this was all done after dark to prevent any surprise. Our means of escape ready, we made such preparations as we could to protect ourselves against the weather; our chums were exceedingly kind in furnishing all the citizens' clothing they had. The next thing was who should go over first. The lot fell to Major Winston. Hush! Ten o'clock. Hear, "Post No. 1. Ten o'clock and all's well!" "Post No. 2! Ten o'clock, and all ish good!" (Dutch sentinel), and thus the usual cry goes the rounds in the various brogues of the English, German, Irish, and other European tongues. "Lights out!"

is shouted form the walls, and all is hushed in darkness and stillness. "The time has come; and affectionate good-by, friends," said Captain Davis and Major Winston, and promptly left the room, each placing himself flat on the frozen ground at his end of the ladder. Thus they drags the ladder up the sewer to the corner of the building, thence across toward the "dead line." This was a line of stakes twelve feet from the wall, so called because the sentinels had orders to kill any prisoners who passed it. "Hold, Davis!" Lie low. Don't breathe; the new relief is coming." They double quick on the wall and relieve the sentinel first above us, and double quick on, the new sentinel walking slowly to and fro on his beat. With great caution we crawled on over the "dead line," and, reaching the wall, stand our ladder against it. Davis holds while Winston mounts. Davis screams in whispers and jerks at the feet of Winston, who, fearing they were discovered, stooped down and asked; "What's the matter?" "Get off my thumb!" After complying with his friends earnest wish, Major Winston addressed himself to his critical situation. The ladder proved to be about four feet too short. It was no place to make noise climbing over, for the sentinel would be sure to detect it; however, Major Winston succeeded in pulling himself over on the parapet as silently as possible, and after looking to see if he was seen by either sentinel on his right or his left, he let himself down, first on a brace that supported the wall, and then on a large stump to the ground. Evading this line of sentinels (for there was one on the wall and one on the ground on the outside) he sat behind a large oak some fifteen steps from the wall. Captain Davis soon joined him; then came Captain Robinson; Next Captain McConnell, who very nearly lighted on the head of the man on the ground, but fortunately was not discovered. Finally, this sentinel on the ground saw Captain Stokes, but not until he had reached the ground, and took him to be a Federal soldier returning from a hen-roost expedition, and so failed to fire on him when he refused to halt. (Major Stokes, failing to get a sufficiency of clothing, had decided not to leave.) So our party was all out, and, to prevent discovery, Captain White very kindly took the ladder back to the dining room. Captain Stokes never got with us, but ran across the island, and, after great exposure and suffering, crossed the ice to the Ohio shore and remained for several days in the neighborhood, when he was betrayed and taken back to prison and committed to a dungeon for refusing to tell who had escaped with him. His feet and hands were badly frosted and he lost several of his fingers.

When the sentinel ordered Stokes to halt, the other four behind the tree ran across the island and, finding the ice firm, ventured on it. It was about one mile over to Ottawa County, Ohio. About half way across we found a large air hole, and in our heedless hurry came near being engulfed; but fortunately that night a thin snow whitened the ice, while the water appeared black. After an exciting run, slipping, sliding, and tumbling, we reached the shore almost breathless. It was half past ten o'clock, and we could hear the soldiers on the distant wall calling out the numbers of their posts and "All's well!" The officer of the day examined the wall with a lamp to see whether any rebel had dared to saw or cut out, doubtless deeming it impossible to elude the vigilance of the sentinels on the walls.

A short rest and we started on our long journey over fences and through fields toward the west. We observed lights in all the houses we passed, which gave us some uneasiness, as it might be a system of signals to show that our escape had been discovered. We soon concluded that in this cold climate it might be necessary to have fires all night. We had mapped out our course, and when we got to the Port Clinton road, took it. We found it much warmer in the woods. Two hours before day, footsore, chilled, and weary, we sought shelter in a straw stack; but it had been wet and was frozen. We went to a farmer's table and groping in the dark, found bridles and two large fat horses. This last condition was quite a consideration to men who expected to ride rapidly and bareback. While the honest man slept and slumbered, each of his spirited animals bore away two Rebels. On we sped over the level country, passing farmhouses and woods. When many miles had fled behind us, just as streaks in the east ushered in another gray, cold morning, Captain McConnell stopped his horse and complained that he was freezing, Major Winston who rode behind him, said: "I hope not." After going a little farther McConnell repeated, "I am freezing," and fell from his horse, groaning like a dying man. Winston tried by chafing to revive him, but to no effect, as he had on too much clothing. We tied the bridles over the horses' necks and turned their heads homewards; from their eyes to the head was white with frozen breath. They were in a trot the last we saw of them. Poor McConnell was straightened up and pushed along till his frozen hinges got in good working order again. Awhile before sun up we knocked at a door to warm and, if possible, to get breakfast. Mine host asked us in, and soon had the sheet iron stove roaring. We passed ourselves off as land speculators walking over the country prospecting, but our jaded looks, and especially the dilapidated condition of our apparel, excited his curiosity. He "guessed how" we were going to this, that and the other place, and a thousand other things about which we were disposed not to be communicative. After such fatigue and exposure to cold, we would go to sleep in spite of ourselves; we gratified our friend's curiosity "by reliefs," as soldiers say. Brad, strong coffee, and fat bacon were soon prepared and dispatched. We left the little man standing in the door wondering why land speculators should be too mean to pay for breakfast. Don't, kind reader, indulge the same reflection, for understand, three little gold dollars were to defray the expenses of four men three thousand miles.

For fear of being overtaken we shunned the highways. Painful feelings stole over our minds when we reflected on balls and chains and dungeons, and possibly death, in case those irate guards should ever lay eyes on us again. Moreover, though horse stealing may be punished by a long term in the Ohio penitentiary, yet the order of Judge Lynch is much more summary. Especially would this be the case with prowling Rebels; nor, we may presume, would our jurors be very inquisitive as to whether we had stolen the horses or a ride. The frost told badly on our ears, fingers, and feet and noses, though the skin did not peel off until we reached Canada. We heard large oaks bursting about in the woods, I suppose from the moisture in the trees crystallizing.

In the evening of January 2, we stopped at an Irishman's for rest. His person constituted his family, and he was not disturbed at our tumbling and snoring around his hearth and on the bed. Awhile before sundown, we wound our way to a troubled looking Dutchman's. We exhausted ourselves in endeavoring to talk his countenance smooth so we might venture to ask for super, but apparently to no effect. Finally we asked, "Well, sir, can we get supper?" He replied, "I'll ask my woman," and addressed a question in his knotty idiom to her who was ironing at the other side of the room. We had observed that her face seemed to be the counterpart of her lord's - his was troubled, hers the troubler. This parody on the gentler sex growled in the tones of distant thunder: "Nix." The poor husband cowered back to the fire and informed us that it was not possible to get supper that night. We often afterwards thought of the poor Dutchman in the woods. We left him to the tender companionship of his frau, and pursued our footpath through the woods, over a pond and marsh country. At ten o'clock we stopped to warm in a village. The people were stirring about, dropping in and going out; we spurred our drooping spirits to appear lively too. We were not "land speculators" this time, but "wood-choppers going to the pineries in Michigan," our appearance bore out our calling. After sitting and talking awhile, a soldier came in and joined the conversation. We thought our time had come, but tried to betray no uneasiness, as we expected every moment to see a squad of soldiers file in. To our great relief the soldier proved to be on furlough. The cold weather was the general topic. We carelessly observed that "those old Rebs on Johnson's Island must be enjoying the cool lake breezes." From their comments we concluded that they had heard nothing of our escape. We journeyed on, and a little after midnight Captain McConnell stopped at a house to get some soda for the heartburn. Several hours he continued to grow worse; before sunrise he gave out and begged to be left at the next house. We placed him on the doorstep and gave him one fourth of our money, and with much sorrow parted requesting him not to knock at the door till we were out of sight. Since the war, we learned that he recovered in a day or so and went to the next depot and traded off his watch for a ticket to Detroit. While on the cars he saw a man eyeing him suspiciously, and determined to leave the train when it stopped again. As he did so, the detective patted him on the shoulder and said: "Let's go back to Johnson's Island." Of course, he had to comply.

Our party, now reduced to three, stopped for breakfast at a house half a mile beyond the next village. We had traveled twenty-four hours on one breakfast and would not be hard to satisfy, but the prospect did look a little discouraging when we saw the landlord and lady and nine children all slept and ate in one room, "with no visible means of support." However, the brisk woman raised the lid of a box in the corner and was not long in setting before us cornbread, fat bacon, and gravy. We divided our mites with him, I forget in what proportion, but he seemed satisfied. We followed the railroad all that day, January 3. Near night we called at a hut where lived an old Irishman and little grandson. The old man said he could not accommodate us that night either with bread or bed, and a view of his surroundings had almost brought us to the same conclusion, but we were so tired and hungry and moreover it appeared to be a safe retreat, so we asked almost against hope for entertainment. At every settlement shelter was sought. The houses were generally occupied by Germans, who, from their bad English, we thought had been but a short time in this country. They seemed easily frightened. We knocked at a door where light and human voices gave some hope that rest might at least be found. They became silent. After listening awhile at the pounding on the door, an inmate ventured to inquire: "Vocht dat?" To our importunity for lodging, they sternly replied: "Nix." Some way farther on we sat on the side of the road to rest in the deep forest. The old oaks, whose giant arms must have defied the storms of centuries, groaned in the cold night winds. We sat and shivered and talked of the loved ones far away in the "Sunny South." Extreme exhaustion and feverishness caused shapeless images to flit over our minds. The glands in our groins had swollen nearly to the size of a hen's egg. We had been in motion continually forty eight hours, and except an hour the first evening, our eyes had not closed in sleep for sixty hours. Toward midnight one of our party asked admittance to a house larger than common on the road. To our great relief the door was opened, and we were invited to the fire. A few questions convinced us that we were in the hands of a shrewd Down Easter. He seemed to suspect something, and asked where we were from. "New Bedford, Mass.," replied Captain Robinson. "O! That's my old home," and he began by naming different residents of that place, to try Captain Robinson. But the Captain, who had been many years in the whaling service and had at least visited New Bedford, was posted. He soon lighted us upstairs to bed, all three huddled together. We retired quite uneasy; for might not this man have heard by telegraph of our escape and early next morning cause our arrest? After a few hours' sleep, we slipped into our clothing, and passing down thorough his room, gave him to understand that it would be quite agreeable to share his hospitality longer, but we must reach Toledo in time for the up train. We knew he was not then prepared to follow us and would make arrangements to overhaul us at the depot if he attempted anything. We crossed the river into Toledo about day and were in time to join the early workmen going to their places of labor.

After leaving the city we abandoned the railroad and bore away to the Lake Shore road. Some long legged boys were skating down the old canal; the ease, grace, and rapidity of their movements appeared to be caused by the wind. We remarked to each other that if we could only adopt that mode of travel as skillfully as those boys, we would not fear pursuit. At noon our treasurer, captain D., purchased some cheese and crackers at a country store, the first food we had eaten, I think, for thirty hours.

That night, January 4, we passed through Monroe during a snowstorm, and met people coming from church. We had walked a long day's journey, but it was about ten o'clock before we could find a hospitable roof. This was with a French Canadian, who had moved to Michigan a short time previously. We tumbled all three together on a pallet and were very soon asleep; had no supper, and left early next morning before breakfast. After going about half a mile, Captain Robinson discovered that he had left his pocketbook, probably on the pallet; it contained papers which showed that Captain Robinson was an officer in the Confederate army. Major Winston went back to the house, and the good woman handed him the pocketbook apparently unopened. Davis and Winston had left all their papers in prison and were provoked that Robinson had not done the same. We led people to believe that Detroit was our destination. We met an officer going to a depot just passed; we continued the Detroit road till out of his view, then turned to the right fifteen miles from that city and made for Trenton, a village on the Detroit River near its entrance to Lake Erie. About noon we stopped at a house for something to eat; the only person we saw was a woman, who invited us in to seats. I must stop to remark what we all observed to each other, that she wore the sweetest expression we had almost ever seen. She was not pretty, nearly middle aged, and rather pale; but she had evidently gone through enough of this world's trials in some form to mellow her soul. Her conversation evinced the same. She gave us a piece of light bread half as large as a man's hand and a good proportion of butter. We sat on a log on the roadside and enjoyed our lunch very much, we had not eaten anything since the cheese and crackers twenty-four hours before.

On the ice again, and now for Canada. After going about a mile, the ice became exceedingly troublesome. A storm a day or two before had broken and blown it about in waves. We clambered over the great blocks slipping and sliding at every pull. Major Winston felt the ice giving way, and remarked that we were approaching an air hole, and as he turned back one foot broke through, and he barely saved himself by leaning over on firm ice. Davis and Winston kneeled over and pulled him out, and almost instantly his trousers were frozen stiff. This treacherous hole had well nigh cut short our earthly pilgrimage. Had we done under, the current (this was the ship channel) would have washed us under the firm ice. The dark water in these places had before marked such contrast with the snow on the ice that we had little difficulty in avoiding them, but over this spray had been blown, and, freezing, became white as snow. Our situation was critical in the extreme. We would not return to the United States side and be captured, a step farther was fate, to remain in the sweeping northern wind equally fatal. Our only chance was to feel our way cautiously around this dangerous place. To avoid turning back in our confusion, Davis placed himself about ten feet in advance of the others, and under their direction made toward the north star. Poor Robinson was so worn out and stunned by his fall, he threw his arm over Winston's shoulder, who bore him on. When we felt that we could not dispense with our beacon, clouds suddenly shut out every star. Just then a light immediately before us in Canada rekindled our hopes. Davis said: "If we ever get there I'll kiss the ground." Near the shore another air hole obstructed our way. We concluded, after going up and down the beach trying for firm ice till we grew desperate, to run across one at a time, and if one broke in the others could save him. The ice did not let us in, but cracked. We were safe!

A few steps drew us to the door of a peasant woman, a Mrs. Warrior, half French and half Indian. They were glad to see us, gave us some pies, all they had cooked, and our extreme fatigue forbade more cooking then. They laid a pallet for us before a large fire and near a large stove, both of which they kept roaring all night. Our feeling of relief can be appreciated when it is remembered that this was ten o'clock at night of the 5th of January, four days and four nights to an hour since we left prison. We had been in almost continual motion, taking out six hours for sleep on each the third and fourth nights of the trip, for ninety-six hours, had traveled as nearly as we could ascertain about one hundred and twenty-five miles in the ninety-six hours, and this, too, when our limbs had been rusting since the battle of Gettysburg, six months before. In these four days and night we had eaten two regular meals and three snacks, counting the biscuit on the snow. Above all, we were safe under the protection of the British flag.

We arose next morning stiff, but much refreshed. Young Warrior and our party walked out on the beach before breakfast Captain Davis, point in the direct of our previous night's path over the broken ice, remarked: "That was a bad looking place for people to cross." Warrior replied:"People never cross there." When we beheld the broke, tangled ice and contemplated the ship channel slightly covered with treacherous spray, we involuntarily shuddered. I suppose any soldier who spent four years in active service can refer to scenes of thrilling interest, but I am ready to declare that this night's trials on the ice were the severest of my experience.

At breakfast we were informed that some refugee Kentuckians resided near Maiden, one mile down the river. Captains Robinson's and Davis's feet being sore from frost, Major Winston visited these people to get some information from them. They occupied a large brick building, three or four in number, strong hale looking young men, and apparently men of wealth, but the meanest Union and Confederate soldiers that met on the fields of Chickamauga or Gettysburg were too good to speak to the craven spirits who were forward in proclaiming their love of a country whose liberties they were too cowardly to defend. They were gloomy birds croaking over the prospects for Confederate people in Canada, and remarked that they would have remained on Johnson's Island. Major Winston indignantly returned to his companions. The good widow had two horses hitched to a sleigh to carry us to Windsor, thirteen miles up the river, without charge, and well so, for we had nothing with which to remunerate her. The trip was delightful to wearied pedestrians, gliding over the snow, and a good portion of the way on the river itself. We found Mr. Hiron, to whose hotel we had been recommended, a fat, chuffy Englishman, his appearance bearing marks of good living and his the countenance of an honest man. We honestly told him our situation: The Federal armies between us and our homes, we had no money, and the prospect of getting any soon quite gloomy, but we assured him that if he felt under the circumstances he could take us for some days, we would work - laborers there earning good wages - and repay him if we failed in getting means otherwise. He seemed to be touched with our story, and made us welcome to his house during our pleasure. We were much pleased to find the Hon. C. L. Vallandingham, then in exile, stopping at the same house. He invited us to his room several times, and on one occasion some toasts were proposed over wine - ours, "the happiness of the distressed South." He was happy, he said, to respond. He hoped the war might soon end, and peace make us all happy again, etc. One of our party went a little further and proposed: "General Lee, and the success of the Southern arms." He shook his head and set down his glass, saying "No, No! In that event the Union is gone forever," and in strains of the most touching eloquence gave his trials in struggling for the Union as our fathers left it to us. He wanted fraternal feelings restored, but war was not calculated to do it. He was afraid of the means, the same sword that conquers the South might subjugate the North as well. "For this cause," he exclaimed, "I am here today an exile from home, family, country." That man a traitor!

Major Winston road to a merchant in New York, requesting a check for two hundred dollars. He promptly replied that he did not know, and did not care to know, who he got to Canada, he was only glad to serve a kinsman of his old friend in North Carolina with whom in former days he had large dealings. Major Winston received the check in a few days, and went five hundred miles down to Montreal to solicit means among our many friends, refugees, and Canadian sympathizers in that city to bring the rest of our party that far on their way to the south. He arrived at the Donegana House in Montreal a little before day, and registering from North Carolina, retired to rest, but before breakfast received several visitors, and preparations for sending for his comrades were soon made, and they, together with some of General Morgan's scattered command, arrived next morning. We remained in the city about ten days and probably in all that time did not dine or take tea at our hotel more than twice, being invited out. People were exceedingly kind. When the time for our departure came, ladies and gentlemen, went with us to the depot, and gave us a purse of $1,350 in gold. On our way down the St. Lawrence we stopped over a day at Point Levi, opposite Quebec, to visit the fortifications of Quebec. They appeared indeed to be the Gibraltar of America. We went one hundred and ninety miles farther down the river to Riviere du Loup, all the way from Montreal by rail, as the river was frozen. At the Riviere du Loup we started on a long journey around Maine, through New Brunswick and Nova Scotia, to Halifax - five hundred miles. This part of our trip we traveled on sleighs. We went by Little Grand Falls down St. John's River many miles on the ice to St. John's City. In our eagerness to get home we remained in Halifax only long enough to witness the opening of Parliament and to be honored with a dinner at the rooms of the - - - Club (name forgotten). We took passage on Her Majesty's mail steamer the Alpha to St. George's Bermuda. As we sailed out of port the face of the earth was white with a thick covering of snow; a few days and nights we were winding our way among the hills and cliffs into the harbor of St. George's. Here early spring greeted us in all her loveliness, children were picnicking on the green sward, and lambs, and calves nibbling about on the grassy hills.

    In a day or so the North Carolina blockade runner, the Advance, was signaled. She came bounding over the billows, bearing aloft the beautiful banner of the South. The steamer made a very short stay and we were on our journey again. Many ships and steamers were seen, but we were quite shy of them until we could see that they were not armed. Indeed, there was but one feeling that detracted from the pleasure of this part of our trip; we felt as if we had stolen something. Fortunately, we did not fall in with the sea monsters, the ironclads, till we got in the network of the blockaders, and it was dark then, just before day. Our good and faithful steamer glided slowly among them, tacking this way and that. At one time she stopped and backed out of an encounter with a grim world warship, apparently asleep, not many waves ahead. Just as day began to dawn, the captain said; "Let her slide." She moved on the bay at the rate of ten knots; we were safe. Not yet! We struck on a sand bar within easy range of the blockading squadron, and every effort to get off was unavailing. We signaled distress to Fort Fisher. News was flashed to Wilmington that the Advance must be captured or sunk when it grew a little lighter. The lifeboats began to drop into the water to carry the escaped prisoners to shore, just then the steamer floated off, and, going around the sand bar, made for Fort Fisher. Then we were safe!!

LIST OF PRISONERS ON JOHNSON'S ISLAND FEB'Y 1ST, 1864.

Major-Generals	1
Brigadier-Generals	5
Colonels	51
Lieutenant-Colonels	44
Majors	58
Captains	623
Lieutenants	1,712
Chaplains	2
Privates	45
Citizens	72
Negroes	4
Total	2,617

A SKETCH OF THE MILITARY PRISON ON JOHNSON'S ISLAND, OHIO.

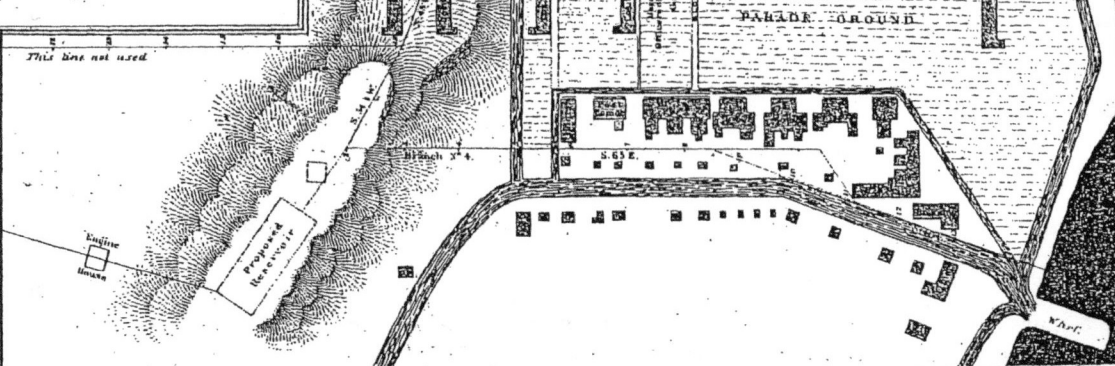

Prisoners of War at Johnson's Island, Lake Erie, Ohio,

FROM NOVEMBER 22D, 1862, TO SEPTEMBER 5TH, 1864.

Rank.	Name.	Regiment.	Army of	Residence.	Where & When Captured.
Lieutenant..	Alexander, J. M....	5th Texas.........	Northern Va..	Moscow, Texas.....	Gettysburg, July 3, 1863
"	Alexander, T. J.....	4th Alabama......	Tennessee...	Centre Store, Ala...	" " 3, 1863
"	Adams, W. H. H...	2d Tennessee......	"	Alton Hill, Tenn...	" " 3, 1863
Captain.....	Allen, H. A........	9th Virginia......	Northern Va..	Portsmouth, Va....	" " 3, 1863
Lieutenant..	Armstrong, G. W...	5th North Carolina..	"	Wilson, N. C.......	" " 1, 1863
Captain.....	Arrington, D.......	57th Virginia......	"	Glade Hill, Va.....	" " 3, 1863
Lieutenant..	Asbury, R. R......	51st Alabama......	Tennessee...	Talladega, Ala.....	Shelbyville, June 27, 1863
Captain.....	Alexander, D. G....	3d Tennessee......	Mississippi...	Campbellsville, Ten.	Raymond, May 12, 1863
Colonel.....	Adams, D.........	33d Tennessee.....	Tennessee...	Troy, Tenn........	Ohio, June 26, 1863
Lieutenant..	Allen, W. E.......	60th Tennessee....	Mississippi...	Newport, Tenn.....	Big Black, May 12, 1863
"	Adair, B. H.......	40th Georgia......	"	Dallas, Ga.........	Champion Hill, May 16, 1863
"	Armstrong, A. J....	46th Alabama......	"	Columbus, Ala....	" " 1863
"	Ashe, J. J.........	11th Mississippi....	Northern Va..	Memphis, Tenn....	Falling Waters, July 14, 1863
Captain.....	Adams, W. C......	3d Georgia........	Mississippi...	Independence, Mo..	Big Black, May 17, 1863
"	Alcorn, M. S......	1st Mississippi.....	"	Frear's Point, Miss..	Port Hudson, July 9, 1863
Lieutenant..	Askew, R. M. G...	51st Georgia.......	Northern Va.	Fort Gaines, Ga....	Gettysburg, July 2, 1863
"	Adams, R. M......	5th Florida........	"	White Springs, Fla.	" " 3, 1863
"	Apperson, W. W...	5th Texas.........	Mississippi...	Austin, Texas......	Fort Butler, June 20, 1863
"	Avant, W. R......	61st Georgia.......	Northern Va..	Macon, Ga.........	Gettysburg, July 4, 1863
"	Asbury, S. L......	54th Mississippi....	Tennessee...	Salem, Miss.......	Murfreesboro, Jan'y 4, 1863
Captain.....	Ash, V. (Chaplain)..	2d Kentucky Cav..	"	Chaplinton, Ky. ...	Kentucky, August 16, 1863
"	Asbury, A. Edgar..	6th Missouri Cav...	Mississippi...	Pittsburg, Ark.....	West Pt., Mo., April 20, 1863
Lieutenant..	Adams, J. J.......	16th Arkansas.....	"	"	Port Hudson, July 9, 1863
"	Alexander, C. C....	62d Tennessee.....	"	London, Tenn.....	B. Black River, May 19, 1863
Brig.-Gen...	Archer, J. J.......	....	Northern Va..	Maryland.........	Gettysburg, July 1, 1863
Captain.....	Archer, R. H., A A G	....	"	"	" " 1, 1863

Rank.	Name.	Regiment.	Army of	Residence.	When & Where Captured.
Captain	Allen, R. H.	12th Mississippi	Mississippi	Baldwin, Miss.	Tupelo, May 4, 1863
"	Allerson, W. H.	Cockrell's Mo. Cav.	Trans-Miss.	Arrow Rock, Mo.	Marshall, Mo., Jan'y 12, 1863
Lieutenant	Allen, Thomas J.	1st C. S. Cavalry	Tennessee	Memphis, Tenn.	Laurensburg, May 2, 1863
Captain	Abbey, G. F.	1st Mississippi Art.	Mississippi	Fort Gibson, Miss.	Port Hudson, July 9, 1863
Lieutenant	Barton, A. J.	55th Georgia	Tennessee	Colquitt, Ga.	Cumberl'd Gap, Sept. 9, 1863
"	Bryson, W. H.	62d North Carolina	"	Webster, N. C.	" " 1863
"	Bayless, B. J.	2d Cavalry	"	Morgan, Tenn.	Farmington, Oct. 7, 1863
"	Brown, D. F.	62d North Carolina	"	Webster, N. C.	Cumberl'd Gap, Sept. 9, 1863
"	Blaydes, F. M.	1st Kentucky Cav.	"	Dover, Ky.	Shelbyville, Oct. 7, 1863
"	Barr, A.	1st Tenn. Battalion	"	Smytheville, Tenn.	Chattanooga, Nov. 23, 1863
"	Bekk, J. T.	8th Tenn. Cavalry	"	Gainesboro', Tenn.	Sparta, August 9, 1863
"	Brooks, A. W. W.	4th Tenn. Cavalry	"	"	Chickamauga, Sept. 20, 1863
Captain	Bethel, R. L.	3d Arkansas	"	Athens, Texas.	Fountain Head, June 17, 1863
Lieutenant	Byrne, J. P.	17th Tennessee	"	Byrne, Tenn	Chickamauga, Sept. 20, 1863
"	Bradley, T. E.	23d Tennessee	"	Gallatin, Tenn.	" Sept. 17, 1863
"	Batson, W. A.	8th Louisiana Art.	"	New Orleans, La.	Port Hudson, July 9, 1863
"	Brown, R. A.	44th North Carolina	"	Cartecay, Ga.	Cumberl'd Gap, Sept. 9, 1863
Captain	Ball, T. J.	55th Georgia	"	Cuthbut, Ga.	" " 1863
Lieutenant	Boswell, J. C.	" "	"	Penfield, Ga.	" " 1863
"	Boswell, W. J.	" "	"	"	" " 1863
"	Bills, J. D.	23d Mississippi	"	Holly Springs, Miss.	Chattanooga, Sept. 10, 1863
"	Boten, J. M.	64th Virginia	"	Hickory Flat, Va.	Cumberl'd Gap, Sept. 9, 1863
"	Baldwin, W. D.	55th Georgia	"	Cold Water, Ga.	" " 1863
"	Brown, A. J.	64th North Carolina	"	Marshall, N. C.	" " 1863
"	Bird, W. J.	16th "	Northern Va.	Brownsville, N. C.	Gettysburg, July 3, 1863
"	Barthelemy, J.	20th Louisiana	Mississippi	Cartrell's, La.	Port Hudson, July 9, 1863
"	Bently, C.	1st. Md. Bat. Cav.	Northern Va.	Baltimore, Md.	Brandy Station, Oct. 11, 1863
"	Bloodworth, J. H.	4th N. C. Cav.	"	Bergen, N. C.	Catlett's Station, Oct. 14, 1863
"	Brown, J. H.	30th North Carolina	"	Longstreet, N. C.	Rappahannock, Nov. 7, 1863
"	Bryant, James	8th Louisiana	"	Winnsboro, La.	" " 1863
"	Brinkley, H. G.	41st Virginia	"	Norfolk, Va.	Nansemond co., Sept. 1, 1863

Rank	Name	Regiment	Army	Residence	Place and Date
Lieutenant..	Allison, W. B......	62d North Carolina.	Tennessee...	Webson, N. C......	Cumberl'd Gap, Sept. 9, 1863
"	Arrington, J. V.....	32d "	Northern Va.	Hilliardston, N. C..	Gettysburg, July 4, 1863
"	Anderson, A......	2d Tennessee Cav..	Tennessee...	Rogersville, Tenn..	Shelbyville, Oct. 7, 1863
"	Adams, R. H......	Engineer Corps....	" ...	Farmdale, Ala......	Mt. Pleasant, Sept. 24, 1863
"	Anderson, L. G.....	11th Texas Cavalry.	"	McKinney, Texas..	McMinnsville, Oct. 4, 1863
Captain.....	Ashton, John D....	18th Kentucky......	"	Hopkinsville, Ky...	Yellow Creek, Sept. 20, 1863
"	Allen, D. W......	Virginia Cavalry....	Western Va..	Applewood, Va.....	Gloucester Pt., July 20, 1863
"	Alexander, W. J....	37th North Carolina.	"	Memphis, Tenn.....	Gettysburg, July 3, 1863
"	Amacker, O. P.....	9th Louisiana Cav..	Mississippi...	Tangissahoe, La....	Port Hudson, July 9, 1863
Lieutenant..	Armstrong, S S.....	5th Tennessee......	"	Ococe, Tenn.......	Paris, Ky., July 29, 1863
"	Atwood, E........	15th Arkansas......	"	Fayetteville, Ark...	Port Gibson, May 1, 1863
"	Anderson, J. H.....	Wheeler's Scout....	Tennessee...	"	Perry, Tenn., Oct. 17, 1863
"	Allen, W. H.......	49th Alabama......	Mississippi...	Gainesville, Ala....	Port Hudson, July 9, 1863
"	Allen, L. B........	" "	"	"	" " 1863
"	Allen, H. J........	23d "	"	Arkadelphia, Ark...	" " 1863
"	Andrews, J. S......	" "	"	Amosburg, Ark....	" " 1863
"	Alston, T. B.......	32d "	Tennessee...	Greenhill, Ala......	Miss'y Ridge, Nov. 25, 1863
"	Arnett, V.........	" "	"	Rogersville, Tenn..	Hawkins, Nov. 12, 1863
"	Andrews, J........	15th Arkansas......	Mississippi...	De Witt, Ark.......	Port Hudson, July 9, 1863
"	Adams, N. K......	1st Alabama.......	"	Montgomery Ala...	" " 1863
"	Ashley, L. R.......	18th Arkansas......	"	Richmond, Va......	" " 1863
"	Archer, J..........	12th "	"	Princeton, Ark.....	" " 1863
"	Archer, A. G......	" "	"	"	" " 1863
Captain.....	Arbuckle, D. A.....	17th "	"	Fort Smith, Ark....	" " 1863
"	Argell, J. S........	5th Louisiana......	Northern Va.	New Orleans, La...	Rappahannock, Nov. 7, 1863
Lieutenant..	Alderson, W. H....	1st Tennessee Cav..	Tennessee...	Columbus, Tenn...	Columbia, Oct. 10, 1863
"	Allerson, J. R......	12th Bat. La. Art...	Mississippi...	New Orleans, La...	Port Hudson, July 9, 1863
Captain.....	Allerson, S. R......	13th Alabama......	Northern Va.	Burksville, Ala..,..	Gettysburg, " 1, 1863
Lieutenant..	Allen, J. J.........	10th Kentucky.....	Tennessee...	Henderson, Ky.....	Henderson, May 9, 1863
"	Adams, S. F.......	45th North Car.....	Northern Va.	Troublesome, N. C.	Gettysburg, July 4, 1863
"	Alexander, W. E...	53d "	"	Charlotte, N. C.....	" " 1863
"	Anderson, G. P.....	4th Missouri Cav...	"	Forsythe, Ga.......	" " 5, 1863
"	Arrington, J. D.....	32d North Carolina.	"	Battleboro, N. C....	" " 4, 1863
"	Aske, S...........	12th Louisiana......	Mississippi...	New Orleans, La...	Port Hudson, " 9, 1863

Rank.	Name.	Regiment.	Army of	Residence.	Where & When Captured.
Captain	Anderson, J. F.	16th Virginia Cav.	Northern Va.	Louisa, Ky.	Wayne co., Va., June 17, 1863
Lieutenant	Allen, C. N.	2d Arkansas	Mississippi	New Orleans, La.	Cold Water, Nov. 3, 1863
Captain	Archibald, A. B.	8th C. S. Cavalry	Tennessee	Pleasant Ridge, Ala.	Shelbyville, June 27, 1863
"	Allen, John	7th Tennessee Inf'y	Northern Va.	Carthage, Tenn.	Gettysburg, July 3, 1863
Lieutenant	Allen, J. W.	10th Arkansas	Mississippi	Quitman, Ark.	Port Hudson, " 9, 1863
Captain	Arnold, T. P.	1st Tennessee	Northern Va.	Georgetown, Tenn.	Gettysburg, " 3, 1863
Lieutenant	Archer, J. M.	15th Texas	Tennessee	Springfield, Texas.	Ringgold, Ga., May 21, 1863
"	Anderson, C. B.	49th Texas	"	Springfield, Texas.	Died Aug. 25, 1862.
"	Allen, P. F.	6th Kentucky Cav.	"	Harrodsburg, Ky.	Kentucky, July 16, 1863
"	Alcorn, A. S.	6th Kentucky Cav.	"	Somersett, Ky.	Ohio, " 14, 1863
"	Allensworth, S. P.	2d Kentucky Cav.	"	Haydensville, Ky.	" " 26, 1863
"	Armburg, W. M.	10th Kentucky Cav.	"	Brashearsville, Ky.	" " 2, 1863
"	Anderson, Pat	2d Texas	Northern Va.	Lake Providence, La	Vicksburg, June 12, 1863
"	Agnew, J. W.	5th Virginia Cav.	"	Lisbon, Va.	Aldie, Va., " 17, 1863
Captain	Anderson, James	35th Virginia Cav.	"	Rockville, Md.	Brandy Station, " 19, 1863
Lieutenant	Anderson, S. T.	1st C. S. Cavalry	"	Chester C. H., S. C.	Martinsburg, July 13, 1863
Captain	Adams, E. A.	2d Arkansas	Mississippi	Fort Smith, Ark.	Port Hudson, " 9, 1863
Lieutenant	Asmassin, M. P.	12th Arkansas	"	Fort Smith, Ark.	" " 9, 1863
"	Allen, W. B.	6th N. C.	Northern Va.	Carey, N. C.	Rappahannock, Nov. 7, 1863
"	Abernathey, F. S.	30th North Carolina	"	Forestville, N. C.	Kelly's Ford, " 7, 1863
"	Albright, G. N.	6th North Carolina	"	Melville, N. C.	Rappahannock, " 7, 1863
"	Armfield, B. F.	1st North Carolina	"	Monroe, N. C.	Catlett's Station, Oct. 14, 1863
"	Anderson, S. A.	Scout	Tennessee	Bondstown, N. C.	Tennessee, " 19, 1863
Captain	Anderson, R. M.	Scout	"	Bondstown, N. C.	Perry co., Tenn., " 19, 1863
"	Austin, A. B.	2d Kentucky Cav.	"	Charlotte, Tenn.	Duon co., Tenn., " 27, 1863
"	Allen, J. P.	55th Georgia	"	Dover, Georgia.	Cumberland Gap, Sep. 9, 1863
Lieutenant	Allen, Thomas W.	64th North Carolina	"	Marshall, N. C.	" " 9, 1863
Captain	Adams, E A.	17th Arkansas	Mississippi	Fort Smith, Ark.	Port Hudson, July 9, 1863
Lieutenant	Atkins, W. P.	5th Arkansas	"	Keysboro', Ky.	" " 9, 1863
"	Allen, J. M.	29th Mississippi	Tennessee	Grenada, Miss.	Chickamauga, Sept. 20, 1863
"	Anderson, D. C.	55th Georgia	"	Gold Mines, Ga.	Cumberland Gap, " 9, 1863

Rank	Name	Regiment	Army	Residence	Where/When Captured
Lieutenant..	Blue, J............	11th Virginia Cav...	Northern Va..	Romney, Va......	Catlett's Station, Oct. 4, 1863
"	Brandon, W. L.....	18th Mississippi...	Trans-Miss...	Vienna, Miss......	Oceola, Ark., Oct. 19, 1863
"	Brown, S. J........	6th Kentucky Cav..	Tennessee...	Mount Vernon, Ky.	Lebanon, Ky., July 5, 1863
Lieut.-Col..	Burke, R. E.......	2d Louisiana......	Northern Va..	Natchitoches, La...	Gettysburg, July 4, 1863
Captain.....	Brown, J. B.......	14th Arkansas......	Trans-Miss...	Oceola, Ark.......	Oceola, Ark., Oct. 19, 1863
"	Broughton, E. P. ...	7th Texas..........	"	Raufman, Texas....	Raymond, May 12, 1863
Lieutenant..	Burgess, W. L.....	Summer's Battalion,	Northern Va..	Raleigh C. H......	Fayetteville, Aug. 23, 1863
Captain	Blankenship, W. A.,	25th Virginia......	"	Petersburg........	W'msport, Md., July 13, 1863
"	Brown, N. P.......	1st So. Car. Cav....	"	Burch Island, S. C..	Upperville, June 21, 1863
Lieutenant..	Bracken, K........	10th Louisiana.....	"	New Orleans, La...	Gettysburg, July 5, 1863
Adjutant....	Bronaugh, W. T....	18th Arkansas.....	Trans-Miss...	Liberty, Miss.....	Port Hudson, July 9, 1863
Lieutenant..	Burruss, G. H.....	30th Mississippi....	Tennessee...	Yazoo, Miss........	Lookout, Md. Nov. 24, 1863
Captain.....	Brown J. B........	5th Virginia Cav....	Northern Va..	Gloucester, Va.....	Gloucester, Va., June 2, 1863
Lieutenant..	Barrett, W. L......	White's Bat. Cav...	"	Leesburg, Va......	Beverley's Ford, July 9, 1863
"	Belton, W H.......	11th Mississippi....	"	Crawfordsville, Miss.	Gettysburg, July 4, 1863
Captain.....	Brown, B. G.......	7th Virginia........	"	Orange C. H., Va...	" July 9, 1863
Lieutenant..	Brown, W. M......	Rockbridge Art....	"	Brownburg, Va.....	" July 5, 1863
"	Bartley, A. T.	7th Virginia Cav....	"	Orange C H., Va...	" July 3, 1863
Captain.....	Bell, D............	4th North Car. Cav.	"	Currituck, N. C....	Smithsburg, June 19, 1863
Lieutenant..	Bassinett, F. W....	12th Mississippi....	"	Orion Church, Miss.	Chester Gap, July 24, 1863
"	Brown, L. M.......	47th North Carolina,	"	Raleigh, N. C......	Bristoe Station, Oct. 14, 1863
Captain.....	Blanton, Z. A......	18th Virginia......	"	Farmville, Va	Gettysburg, July 5, 1863
Lieutenant..	Branch. H. K......	10th North Carolina,	"	Morgantown, N. C..	Falling Waters, July 14, 1863
Captain.....	Beall, J. C. A......	22d Georgia........	"	Warrenton, Ga.....	Gettysburg, July 5, 1863
Major	Bradford, H........	1st Florida Cavalry	Tennessee...	Tallahassee, Fla....	
Captain.....	Burroughs, R. M...	"	"	"	
Lieutenant..	Bryant, G. A......	5th Mississippi.....	Trans-Miss...	Bolivar, Miss......	
"	Britton, D.........	....			
"	Bledsoe, F. M.....	11th Georgia......	Northern Va..	Georgetown, Ga...	Gettysburg, July 4, 1863
"	Baslon, F. D......	7th Louisiana......	"	Covington, La.....	Rappahannock, Nov. 6, 1863
"	Brooks, A. M......	"	"	Campbellton, La...	" Nov. 6, 1863
"	Bell, R. H.........	48th Georgia.......	"	Calverton, Ga.....	Gettysburg, July 5, 1863
"	Basslitte, A. H.....	Print's Virginia Bat.	Tennessee...	Petersburg, Va	Morgan co., Va., Oct. 17, 1863
"	Bowman, A. L.....	2d Missouri Cav....	Trans-Miss...	Harrisonville, Mo..	Marshall, Mo., Oct. 13, 1863

Rank.	Name.	Regiment.	Army of	Residence.	Where & When Captured.
Lieutenant..	Bentley, A. R......	10th Kentucky.....	Tennessee...	Whitesburg, Ky....	Nashville, July 7, 1863
"	Bunham, P. B......	16th So. Car. Cav...	"	Greenville, S. C....	Graysville, Ga., Nov. 26, 1863
Captain.....	Brasher, L. B......	10th Kentucky.....	Northern Va..	Brasherville, Ky....	Gladesville, July 7, 1863
"	Burchfield, H. G....	26th Alabama	"	Tuscaloosa, Ala....	Gettysburg, July 5, 1863
Lieutenant..	Burton, J. F........	45th North Carolina,	"	Extra, Mo.........	Martinsburg, July 5, 1863
"	Bell, R. S..........	54th "	"	Norfolk, Va........	Rappahannock, Nov. 7, 1863
Captain.....	Berry, J. T.........	8th Kentucky......	Tennessee...	Louisville, Ky......	Ohio River, July 6, 1863
"	Blackman, F. H....	15th Tenn. Cav.....	"	Nashville, Tenn....	Salemville, O., Oct. 26, 1863
Lieutenant..	Bevill, J. M........	8th Kentucky Cav..	"	Springfield, Ky.....	" July 26, 1863
Lieut.-Col..	Baker, J. H........	31st Georgia.......	Northern Va..	Zebulon, Ga.......	Monterey, July 4, 1863
Lieutenant..	Banat, C. L........	31st Georgia.......	Mississippi...	Port Gibson, Miss..	Port Hudson, July 9, 1863
"	Branden, H C.....	42d Mississippi.....	Northern Va..	Jacinto, Miss......	Gettysburg, July 3, 1863
"	Bell, H. M.........	3d Tennessee......	Tennessee...	Rome, Tenn.......	Bern Post, April 4, 1863
"	Beard, T. R........	22d Texas Cav.....	Trans-Miss...	Richmond, Texas..	Arkansas Post, Jan'y 4, 1863
"	Bentley, ——......	22d Georgia.......	Northern Va .	Leathersville, Ga...	Gettysburg, July 2, 1863
Lieut.-Col..	Boyd, S. H........	45th North Carolina,	"	Troublesome, N. C.	Hagerstown, July 4, 1863
Lieutenant..	Baners, G. W......	1st Tennessee.....	"	Winchester, Tenn..	Gettysburg, July 3, 1863
"	Brannan, H........	1st Tennessee.....	"	"	" July 3, 1863
Captain.....	Bradley, A.........	9th Louisiana Bat...	Mississippi...	Ponchatoula, La....	Port Hudson, July 9, 1863
Lieutenant..	Breitz, E. A........	26th North Carolina,	Northern Va..	Salem, N. C........	Gettysburg, July 5, 1863
"	Birney, J. L........	49th Georgia.......	"	Goninton, Ga......	" July 2, 1863
"	Bonting, T. J.......	9th Louisiana......	"	Hornia, La.........	" July 5, 1863
"	Blackwolder, M....	1st Florida.........	Tennessee...	Lake City, Fla.....	Miss'y Ridge, Nov. 25, 1863
"	Bryan, N. L........	1st Florida.........	"	Blount's Ferry, Fla.	" Nov. 25, 1863
"	Bell, J. P..........	24th Alabama......	"	Shiloh, Ala.........	" Nov. 25, 1863
"	Barrett, J..........	9th Louisiana Bat...	Northern Va .	Fronctritis, La.....	Died Dec. 7, 1863
Colonel.....	Burbridge, ——....	4th Missouri Cav...	Trans-Miss...	Lonnana, Mo	Brownsville, Aug. 25, 1863
Major.......	Black, R. L........	23d Arkansas......	"	Helena, Ark.......	Port Hudson, July 9, 1863
Lieutenant..	Beck, W. J.........	36th Georgia.......	"	Woodsaun, Ga.....	Baker's Creek, May 16, 1863
"	Blackburn, J. G....	Wayde's Tex. Leg..	....	Fairfield, Texas....	Yazoo City, July 15, 1863
Captain.....	Barron, W. P.......	40th Tenn..........	Trans-Miss...	Jonesboro', Tenn...	Big Black, May 17, 1863

Rank	Name	Regiment	Army	Residence	Place and Date
Captain	Baker, H.	3d C. Cavalry	Tennessee	Fayetteville, Miss.	Chattanooga, August 26, 1863
"	Baker, J. H.	2d Tennessee	"	" Tenn.	Lancaster, Ky., Aug. 1, 1863
"	Buchanan, J. H.	2d Mississippi	Northern Va.	Ripley, Miss.	Gettysburg, July 5, 1863
Lieutenant	Byrne, H. H.	2d "	"	"	" " 1863
"	Baldwin, T. T.	40th Tennessee	Mississippi	Newport, Tenn.	Port Hudson, July 9, 1863
"	Barton, A. P.	55th Georgia	Tennessee	Gainesville, Ga.	Cumberl'd Gap, Sept. 9, 1863
"	Brear, J. R.	15th Alabama	Northern Va.	Newton, Ala.	Gettysburg, July 3, 1863
Captain	Blair, F. L.	60th Tennessee	Mississippi	Jonesboro', Tenn.	Big Black, May 17, 1863
"	Brantley, T. B.	Arkansas Cav	"	Grand Lake, Ark.	" " 1863
Lieutenant	Brindley, J. P.	4th Alabama Cav.	Tennessee	Blue Bond, Ala.	Shelbyville, June 27, 1863
"	Bunn, G. W.	1st Mississippi	Mississippi	Frankford, Ala.	Port Hudson, July 9, 1863
Major	Bate, H. C.	1st C. Cav	Tennessee	Gallatin, Tenn.	Shelbyville, June 27, 1863
Lieutenant	Bennett, W. H.	15th Tennessee	"	Hartsville, Tenn.	Chickamauga, Nov. 24, 1863
"	Britton, H. C.	9th Virginia Cav.	Northern Va.	Portsmouth, Va.	Gettysburg, July 3, 1863
"	Brooks, C. O.	11th Mississippi	"	Brookville, Miss.	" " 1863
"	Burks, C. C.	4th Virginia	"	Lexington, Va.	" " 1863
"	Bailey, P. R.	2d Mississippi	"	Gunn Town, Miss.	" " 1, 1863
Adjutant	Brown, W. W.	4th Texas	"	San Marcus, Texas	Chambersburg, July 6, 1863
Lieutenant	Boss, William	9th Mississippi	Trans-Miss.	St. Joseph, Mo.	Little Rock, Mo., Aug. 22, 1863
"	Bohart, J. M.	1st " Cav.	"	Savannah, Miss.	Big Black, Nov. 17, 1863
"	Bradshaw, A. M.	2d Tennessee	Tennessee	London, Tenn.	Lancaster, Ky., July 31, 1863
Captain	Buffington, W. H.	19th Arkansas	Mississippi	Lancaster, Ark.	Big Black, Nov. 17, 1863
Colonel	Bell, S. L.	Bell's Regiment	Trans-Miss.	Scarley, Ark.	Helena, July 4, 1863
Adjutant	Bell, S. H.	"	"	"	" 1863
Captain	Brarer, W. G.	26th North Carolina	N. Carolina	Goldston, N. C.	Green Castle, Pa., " 5, 1863
Major	Barkley, C. W.			Loudoun Co., Va.	Jefferson County.
Lieutenant	Bragg, J. G.	19th Virginia	Northern Va.	Bentivoglio, Va.	Gettysburg, July 3, 1863
"	Broughton, G.	26th North Carolina	"	Raleigh, N. C.	" " 1863
"	Brown, A. J.	38th "	"	Hallsville, N. C.	" " 1863
"	Brown, B. L.	59th Georgia	"	Fort Gaines, Ga.	" " 5, 1863
"	Baldrige, W. F.	31st Tennessee	"	Ellis Mills.	" Nov. 26, 1863
"	Bowers, S. C.	18th "	Tennessee	Goodletsville, Tenn.	Silver Springs, May 9, 1863
Captain	Boyd, W. M.	19th Virginia	Northern Va.	Massie's Mills, Va.	Gettysburg, July 3, 1863
"	Billingsley, J. A.	9th " Cav.	"	Hampstead, Va.	Hanover, Pa., July 30, 1863

Rank.	Name.	Regiment.	Army of	Residence.	Where & When Captured.
Captain	Burton, J. W.	6th Alabama	Northern Va.	Montgomery, Ala.	Gettysburg, July 4, 1863
Lieutenant	Bettell, G. A.	55th North Carolina	"	Staceysville, N. C.	" July 1, 1863
"	Branch, W. C.	45th Tennessee	Tennessee	Green Hill, Tenn.	Springs, May 9, 1863
"	Brockenbrough, M.	1st Louisiana	Northern Va.	Alexandria, La.	Gettysburg, July 2, 1863
Captain	Brown, B. C.	19th Virginia	"	Amherst, Va.	" July 3, 1863
Lieutenant	Ball, W. A.	2d Florida	"	Tallahassee, Fla.	" July 2, 1863
"	Barnes, F. C.	50th Virginia	"	Wilesburg, Va.	" July 5, 1863
Captain	Barzizn, D. W.	4th Texas	"	Owensville, Texas	" July 2, 1863
Lieutenant	Bedford, A. M.	Missouri Cavalry	Mississippi	Savannah, Mo.	Big Black, November 17, 1863
Captain	Bedford, F.	Morgan's Cavalry	Tennessee	Paris, Ky.	Shelbyville, October , 1863
"	Ballentine, W. W.	2d Florida	Northern Va.	Pensacola, Fla.	Gettysburg, July 2, 1863
"	Brown, R. G.	18th Mississippi	"	Terry Station, Miss.	" July 2, 1863
Lieutenant	Baxter, John	38th Georgia	"	Cross Keys, Ga.	" July 4, 1863
"	Burchell, W. D.	5th Florida	"	Lake City, Fla.	" July 2, 1863
Colonel	Bullock, Robert	7th "	Tennessee	Oceola	Miss'y Ridge, Nov. 28, 1863
Captain	Blount, T. W.		Mississippi	San Augustine, Tex.	Port Hudson, July 9, 1863
Major	Blackwell, C. C.	23d North Carolina	Northern Va.	Kittrell's Sp'gs, N C.	Gettysburg, July 5, 1863
Lieutenant	Baldwin, W. G.	20th North Carolina	"	Whitesville, N. C.	" July 1, 1863
Captain	Brunley, O. R.	" "	"	Oaktown, N C.	" July 1, 1863
Lieutenant	Bradford, W. B.	" "	"	" "	" July 1, 1863
"	Bond, W. R.	A. Q. C. (?)	"	Scotland Neck, N. C.	" July 4, 1863
"	Bryan, George P.	2d North Carolina	"	Hotel, N. C.	Ashby's Gap, Va., July 4 1863
"	Bridges, G. L.	8th Georgia	"	Hawkinsville, Ga.	Gettysburg, July 4, 1863
"	Breckinridge, J. C.	Staff	Tennessee	Lexington, Ky.	Tennessee, Nov. 25, 1863
"	Browder, D. H.	10th Kentucky	"	Danbridge, Ky.	Ohio, July 21, 1863
Lieut.-Col.	Berkeley, W.	8th Virginia	Northern Va.	Aldie, Va.	Gettysburg, July 5, 1863
Captain	Berkeley, N. M.	"	"	"	" July 5, 1863
Lieutenant	Boone, J. B.	12th N. C. Batt.	N. Carolina	Murfreesboro, N. C.	North Hampton, July 28, 1863
"	Barksdale, B.	23d Virginia	Northern Va.	Brooklyn, Va.	Gettysburg, July 4, 1863
Captain	Barnes, W.	9th Louisiana Batt.	Tennessee	Atlanta, Ga.	Cumberland Gap Sept. 9, 1863
Lieutenant	Boyd, J. W.	H. D. Scouts	"	Jackson, Tenn.	Tennessee, August 1, 1863

Rank	Name	Regiment	Army	Residence	Where/When Killed
Lieutenant	Benson, J. F.	1st Alabama	Mississippi	Allenton, Alabama	Port Hudson, July 9, 1863
"	Barker, J. L.	4th Mississippi	"	De Soto, Alabama	Big Black, May 17, 1863
"	Betsel, A. M.	2d Mississippi	Northern Va.	Baldwin, Mississippi	Gettysburg, July 5, 1863
"	Beckton, J. G.	21st Arkansas	Mississippi	Desarc, Arkansas	Champion Hill, May 16, 1863
"	Baird, W. B.	1st Arkansas Bat	"	Pocahontas, Ark	Port Hudson, July 9, 1863
Major	Blair, John A.	2d Mississippi	Northern Va.	Iuka, Mississippi	Gettysburg, July 1, 1863
Captain	Boston, R. B.	5th Virginia Cavalry	"	Union Mills, Va	Middleburg, June 17, 1863
Lieutenant	Bradford, J. B.	Adams' Cavalry	Mississippi	Lake Providence, La	Oakland College, May 16, 1863
Captain	Buckner, D. P.	Beall's Staff	"	"	Port Hudson, July 9, 1863
Lieutenant	Burton, W. D.	51st Alabama	Tennessee	Oxford, Alabama	Shelbyville, June 27, 1863
"	Ball, F. H.	8th Confederate Cav.	"	Pickensville, Ala	" June 27, 1863
Colonel	Bulger, W. L.	47th Alabama	Northern Va.	Dadeville, Alabama	Gettysburg, July 2, 1863
Lieutenant	Blackwood, W. L.	5th Arkansas	Tennessee	Austin, Arkansas	Perryville, Ky., Oct. 8, 1863
"	Burks, H. C.	2d Virginia Cavalry	Northern Va.	Big Island, Virginia	Westm'ster, Pa., June 30, 1863
Major	Burnett, W. K.	A. Q. M	Mississippi	Brownsville, Tenn	Port Hudson, July 9, 1863
Brig.-Gen.	Beall, W. N. R.		"	Little Rock, Ark	" July 9, 1863
Captain	Beardon, W. M. J.	58th North Carolina	Tennessee	Asheville, N. C.	Cumberl'd Gap, Sept. 9, 1863
Adjutant	Beardon, R. M.	2d Tennessee Cav.	"	Macon, Georgia	Kentucky, August 1, 1863
Lieutenant	Barton, R. R.			Warren, Arkansas	
Colonel	Brown, Jack	59th Georgia	Northern Va.	Tallerton, Georgia	Gettysburg, July 2, 1863
Captain	Bailey, W.	51st Florida	"	Tallahassee, Florida	" July 4, 1863
Lieutenant	Brice, H.	8th Florida	"	Quincy, Florida	" July 4, 1863
"	Bryant, F. M.	8th Florida	"	Alafin, Florida	" July 4, 1863
Captain	Betts, T. Edwin	40th Virginia	"	Heathsville, Va	" July 5, 1863
"	Bingham, Robert	44th North Carolina	"	Oaks, N. C.	Hanover Junc., June 26, 1863
Lieutenant	Blackwell, T. E.	40th Virginia	"	Heathsville, Va	Falling Waters, July 14, 1863
"	Bolling, R. P.	61st Louisiana	"	Summersville, La	Philadelphia, Oct. 20, 1863
"	Bryan, J. W.	43d Tennessee	Tennessee	Henry's X-R'ds, Ten	Jefferson co., Ten., Oct. 2, 1863
"	Branch, T. J.	13th Tennessee	"	Summersville, Tenn.	Germantown, Nov. 15, 1863
Captain	Ballenger, C. E.	7th Louisiana	Northern Va.	Jackson, Mississippi	Rappahannock, Nov. 7, 1863
Lieutenant	Banner, W. O. T.	2d North Carolina	"	Mount Airy, N. C.	Kelly's Ford, Nov. 7, 1863
"	Ball, R. C.	—— Kentucky	Tennessee	Flat Lick, Tenn	Cumberl'd, Ten. Nov. 11, 1863
"	Blount, J. B.	55th North Carolina	No. Ca.		Died, Dec. 20, 1863
"	Black, J. A.	4th Florida	Tennessee	Quincy, Florida	Murfreesboro, Jan. 5, 1863

Rank.	Name.	Regiment.	Army of	Residence.	Where & When Captured.
Captain	Bedford, P. P.	50th Georgia	Northern, Va.	Waynesboro', Ga.	Cashtown, Pa., July 5, 1863
"	Bruce, H. G.	20th Texas	"	Buchanan, Texas	" July 17, 1863
Lieutenant	Brady, J. B.	20th Texas	"	Alexandria, Texas	" July 17, 1863
"	Bowen, J. C.	8th Missouri	"	Nevada, Missouri	Bentonsv'e, Ark. May 22, 1863
Captain	Bowen, J. H.	Hampton Legion	"	Arnold's Mills, S. C.	Lookout M't'n, Oct. 29, 1863
Lieutenant	Boyles J. R.	12th South Carolina	"	Ridgeway, S. C.	Gettysburg, July 5, 1863
Captain	Bradford, N. G.	26th North Carolina	"	Lenoir, N. C.	" July 5, 1863
Lieutenant	Bradborn, M. S.	16th Arkansas	Mississippi	Huntsville, Ark.	Port Hudson, July 9, 1863
"	Blue, M.	18th Virginia Cav.	Northern Va	Springfield, Va.	Hampshire co., May 30, 1863
"	Burton, S. M.	2d North Carolina	"	Jackson, N. C.	Hanover C. H., June 30, 1863
"	Bentley, C. F.	8th Virginia Cavalry	"	Aldie, Va.	Gettysburg, July 3, 1863
"	Boyd, J. W.	H. D. Scouts	Tennessee	Jackson, Tenn.	Tennessee, August 1, 1863
"	Brown, L.	9th Mississippi	Mississippi	Hernando, Miss.	Died Nov. 22, 1862
"	Barton, W. D.	2d Mississippi	Northern Va.	Tupelo, Mississippi	Tupelo, May 4, 1863
"	Bryan, P. C.	18th Mississippi Cav.	Mississippi	La Grange, Miss.	Mississippi, April 25, 1863
"	Bonner, M.	29th Mississippi	Tennessee	Yazoo City, Miss.	Miss'y Ridge, Nov. 24, 1863
"	Bergen, J. M.	22d North Carolina	Northern Va.	Marion, N. C.	Gettysburg, July 3, 1863
"	Bean, P.	51st Georgia	"	Blakely, Georgia	" July 3, 1863
"	Brown, C. A. C.	Washington Art'y	"	New Orleans, La.	" July 5, 1863
"	Bateman, P. H.	14th Tennessee	"	Cumberland, Tenn.	" July 5, 1863
"	Bryan, J. D.	49th Georgia	"	Burkland, Georgia	" July 1, 1863
Captain	Butler, A. L.	8th Georgia	"	Savannah Georgia	" July 4, 1863
Lieutenant	Barnes, P.	Miles' Legion	Mississippi	Natchez, Mississippi	Port Hudson, July 9, 1863
Captain	Barnes, N. D.	10th C. S. Cavalry	Trans-Miss.	Pinckneyville, Ala.	" July 9, 1863
Lieutenant	Burgess, W. A.	13th Alabama	Northern Va.	Lamar, Alabama	Green Castle, July 5, 1863
"	Barton, M. W.	10th Missouri	Trans-Miss.	Huntsville, Missouri	Helena, Ark., July 4, 1863
"	Burroughs, J. J.	13th Tennessee Cav.	"	Woodville, Texas	Ponchartrain, Jan. 10, 1863
"	Bridges, D. L.	2d Georgia	Tennessee	Cuthbert, Georgia	Fort Donaldson, Feb. 4, 1863
"	Baker, S. W.	10th Missouri	Trans-Miss.	Huntsville, Missouri	Helena, Ark., July 4, 1863
"	Bowles, G. M.	10th Missouri	"	St. Louis, Missouri	" July 4, 1863
Captain	Barnes, W. F.	10th C. Cavalry	Tennessee	Pinckneyville, Ala.	Lancaster. Ky., July 31, 1863

Rank	Name	Regiment	Command	Residence	Where Captured	Date
Lieutenant	Bradford, W. J.	10th Missouri Cav	Trans-Miss	Rollo, Missouri	Helena, Ky.,	July 4, 1863
"	Benton, P. G.	8th Missouri	"	Cassville, Missouri	"	July 4, 1863
Captain	Blake, W. J.	Beale's Regiment	"	Caney, Arkansas	"	July 4, 1863
Lieutenant	Bishop, W. F.	16th Alabama	Tennessee	Benon, Alabama	Benon, Ala.,	June 20, 1863
Captain	Bell, A. E.	15th Tennessee	"	Gallatin, Tenn	Gallatin.	
"	Butterman, M. E.	18th Mississippi Cav	Mississippi	Mt. Pleasant, Miss	Mt. Pleasant,	Oct. 12, 1863
Lieutenant	Brooks, S. H.	37th Alabama	Tennessee	China Grove, Ala	Lookout M't'n,	Nov. 24, 1863
"	Blakeney, ——	40th Alabama	"	Livingston, Ala	"	Nov. 24, 1863
Captain	Bibb, L.	Forrest Cavalry	"	Monroesville, Ala	Athens, Ala.,	Dec. 1, 1863
Lieutenant	Brown, C. H.	11th Mississippi	Northern Va	Macon, Mississippi	Lucas Ferry,	Dec. 1, 1863
"	Bennett, W.	1st Arkansas Batt	Mississippi	Powhatan, Arkansas	Port Hudson,	July 9, 1863
Captain	Brent, J. L.	18th Arkansas	"	Louisville, Ky	"	July 9, 1863
Lieutenant	Blackburn, J. C.	14th Arkansas	"	"	"	July 9, 1863
Captain	Blackburn, J. W.	"	"	"	"	July 9, 1863
Lieutenant	Birdsong, J. C.	21st Virginia	Northern Va	Lynchburg, Va	Gettysburg,	July 4, 1863
"	Bailey, O. G.	21st Tennessee	"	"	"	July 4, 1863
Captain	Brewer, J. C.	12th Arkansas	Mississippi	Chambersville, Miss	Port Hudson,	July 9, 1863
Lieutenant	Bentley, T. J.	"	"	Princeton, Ark	"	July 9, 1863
"	Bowers, A. M.	14th South Carolina	Northern Va	Newberry, S. C	Gettysburg,	July 5, 1863
Captain	Braswell, W. D.	1st Arkansas	Mississippi	Powhatan, Ark	Port Hudson,	July 9, 1863
Lieutenant	Banks, J. F.	13th South Carolina	Northern Va	Frog Level, S. C	Gettysburg,	July 1, 1863
Captain	Boyd, Thomas	1st Mississippi	Mississippi	Moorish, Mississippi	Port Hudson,	July 9, 1863
"	Benson, W. B.	49th Alabama	"	Duck Spring, Ala	"	July 9, 1863
Lieutenant	Benson, H. H.	23d Arkansas	"	Harrisburg, Ark	"	July 9, 1863
"	Baxter, J. B.	"	"	Clarendon, Ark	"	July 9, 1863
"	Black, J. S.	49th Alabama	"	Guntersville, Ala	"	July 9, 1863
"	Borrum, W. J.	4th Alabama Cav	Tennessee	Huntsville, Ala	Shelbyville,	Oct. 10, 1863
"	Brand, G. C.	2d Missouri Cavalry	Mississippi	Boonesville, Mo	Holly Springs,	May 3, 1863
"	Bradford, W. B.	20th North Carolina	Northern Va	Oak Lawn, N. C		
Lieut.-Col.	Burkley, ——	8th Virginia	"	Loudoun co., Va	Gettysburg,	July 5, 1863
Captain	Bacon, M.	16th Tennessee				
Lieut.-Col.	Bowman, C. C.	1st Kentucky Cav				
Colonel	Baxter, G. L.	Baxter Battalion		New Orleans, La		
Captain	Burton, H. L.	Surgeon		Little Rock, Ark		

Rank.	Name.	Regiment.	Army of	Residence.	Where & When Captured.
Lieutenant.	Cross, J. F.	5th North Carolina.	Northern Va.	Gatesville, N. C.	Gettysburg, July 5, 1863
Colonel.	Candill, B. T.	10th Kentucky.	Tennessee.	Whitesburg, Ky.	Gladesville, July 7, 1863
Lieutenant.	Crawford, J. A.	57th North Carolina.	Northern Va.		
"	Crisp, A. J.	4th Tennessee.	Tennessee.	Bolivar, Tenn.	West Tenn., Oct. 26, 1863
"	Coselam, F. B.	5th Kentucky Cav.	Northern Va.	Trenton, Ky.	Sugar Creek, Oct. 9, 1863
Ex-Lieut.	Clopton, W. E.	3d Virginia Cavalry.	"	Tunstall's, Va.	Gettysburg, July, 3, 1863
Lieutenant.	Cleveland, J. B.	Alabama Artillery.	Mississippi.	Mobile, Ala.	Port Hudson, July, 9, 1863
"	Coleman, H. W.	Miles' Legion.	"	Delhi, La.	" July, 9, 1863
Captain.	Chinney, B. R.	9th Louisiana Bat.	"	Lobden Parish, La.	" July, 9, 1863
Lieutenant.	Conetoe, F. M.	1st Georgia Cavalry.	Tennessee.	Rome, Ga.	Mitchell, Ky., May 28, 1863
Captain.	Chichester, A. M.	Engineer Corps.	Northern Va.	Leesburg, Va.	Leesburg, June 12, 1863
Lieutenant.	Cross, J. T.	5th North Carolina.	"	Statesville, N. C.	Gettysburg, July 5, 1863
Colonel.	Candell, B. E.	10th Kentucky.	Tennessee.	Waltonburg, Ky.	Gladesville, July 7, 1863
Lieutenant.	Crawford, J. A.	57th North Carolina.	Northern Va.	Bethany Ch., N. C.	Rappahannock. Nov. 7, 1863
"	Crisp, A. J.	4th Tennessee.	Tennessee.	Bolivar, Tenn.	West Tenn., Oct. 26, 1863
"	Castleman, B. F.	8th Kentucky Cav.	"	Trenton, Ky.	Sugar Creek, Oct. 9, 1863
"	Clopton, H. E.	3d Virginia Cavalry.	Northern Va.	Tunstall's, Va.	Oct. 4, 1863
"	Carpenter, H.	9th La. Battalion.	Mississippi.	Camp Moore, La.	Port Hudson. July 9, 1863
"	Cleveland, J. B.	1st La. "	"	Mobile, Ala.	Vicksburg, May 18, 1863
"	Coleman, H. W.	Miles' La. "	"	Lobden Parish, La.	Port Hudson, July 1, 1863
Captain.	Chenney, W. R.	9th La. "	"	Delhi, La.	" July 1, 1863
Lieutenant.	Coulter, T. W.	1st Georgia Cavalry.	Tennessee.	Rome, Ga.	Mitchell, Ky., May 28, 1863
Captain.	Chichester ——	Engineer Corps.	Northern Va.	Leesburg, Va.	Leesburg, June 12, 1863
Lieutenant.	Crawford, J. R.	46th Alabama.	Mississippi.	New Site, Ala.	Champion Hill, May 26, 1863
"	Conden, C. D.	46th "	"	Dadesville, Ala.	" May 26, 1863
"	Crawford, J. M.	62d North Carolina.	Tennessee.	Heinassa, Ga.	Cumberl'd Gap, Sept. 9, 1863
"	Culpepper, J. A.	55th Georgia.	"	Carroll, Ga.	" Sept. 9, 1863
"	Cole, J. M.	60th North Carolina.	"	Ineptan Spgs., N. C.	Miss'y Ridge, Nov. 25, 1863
"	Carpenter, J. C.	4th Mississippi.	Mississippi.	Carrollton, Miss.	Big Black, May 17, 1863
"	Coss, C. A.	12th Miss. Cavalry.	Tennessee.	Corinth, Miss.	Florence. May 28, 1863
Captain.	Chambers, C. E.	13th Alabama.	Northern Va.	Tuskegee, Ala.	Gettysburg, July 5, 1863

Rank	Name	Regiment	Army	Residence	Place	Date
Lieutenant	Campbell, Ira	31st Alabama	Mississippi	Randolph, Ala	Champion Hill	May 16, 1863
"	Chamberlain, H. W.	8th Virginia	Northern Va.	Loudoun Co., Va.	Upperville	May 27, 1863
Captain	Carter, J. R.	8th "	"	Morrisville, Va.	At home	May 27, 1863
Lieutenant	Caldwell, J. P.	Waters' Battery	Mississippi	Panola, Miss.	Port Hudson	July 9, 1863
Captain	Carlons, W. W.	Miles' Legion	"	New Orleans, La.	"	July 9, 1863
"	Carter, W. A.	A. Q. M.	Northern Va.	Scouts, Virginia	Gettysburg	July 4, 1863
Lieutenant	Carter, R. D.	30th Georgia	"	Walnut Grove, Ga.	"	July 2, 1863
"	Carter, R. B.	1st Ala. Artillery	Mississippi	Selma, Ala.	Port Hudson	July 9, 1863
"	Carter, R. B.	1st " "	"		"	July 9, 1863
"	Card, E. T.	1st " "	"	Lounchapola, Ala.	"	July 9, 1863
Captain	Carmichael, T. L.	Law's Staff	"	Clayton, Ala.	"	July 9, 1863
Lieutenant	Clements, F. T.	1st La. Cavalry	Northern Va.	Uniontown, Ala.	Gettysburg	July 2, 1863
"	Christian, T. L.	Law's Staff	"	"	"	July 2, 1863
Captain	Corker, S. A.	3d Georgia	"	Waynesboro, Ga.	"	July 2, 1863
"	Cussons, John J.	A. D. C.	"	Selena, Ala.	"	July 2, 1863
"	Campbell, G. R.	Wheeler's Scouts	Tennessee	Summerville, Tenn.	Giles' Creek	Oct. 4, 1863
"	Culberton, A. L.	39th Georgia	Mississippi	Lafayette, Ga.	Champion Hill	May 16, 1863
"	Couch, John	28th Alabama	Tennessee	Marion, Ala.	Miss'y Ridge	Nov. 25, 1863
"	Croft, D. L.	46th Alabama	Mississippi	West Point, Ga.	Champion Hill	May 16, 1863
Lieutenant	Collins, H. A.	2d Texas	"	Coffeeville, Texas	Raymond, Miss.	May 12, 1863
"	Cowan, F. N.	8th Tenn. Cavalry	Tennessee	Danville, Ky.	Kentucky	April 16, 1863
Colonel	Cravens, J. E.	21st Arkansas	Mississippi	Clarkesville, Ark.	Big Black	May 17, 1863
Captain	Clayton, S. S.	7th Alabama	Tennessee	Rome, Ga.	Shelbyville	June 27, 1863
Adjutant	Cushmond, B. C.	30th Louisiana	Mississippi	Evergreen, La.	Port Hudson	July 9, 1863
Lieutenant	Clark, J. B.	18th Mississippi	Northern Va.	Jackson, Miss.	Front Royal	July 20, 1863
"	Cartwright, H. J.	9th Alabama	"	Elkmont, Ala.	Gettysburg	July 2, 1863
, "	Chisholm, A. C.	9th "	"	Florence, Ala.	"	July 2, 1863
"	Cordray C. S.	Miles' Regiment	Mississippi	Galveston, Texas	Port Hudson	July 9, 1863
"	Coldman, M. D.	20th North Carolina	Northern Va.	Fair Bluff, N. C.	Gettysburg	July 1, 1863
"	Coggin, Jerry	23d "	"	Troy, N. C.	"	July 3, 1863
"	Chappell, J. H.	23d "	"	Rockingham, N. C.	"	July 4, 1863
Captain	Cahill, T. J.	7th "	"	Jacksonville, N. C.	"	July 3, 1863
Lieutenant	Cattingham, J. R.	3d Louisiana	"	Columbus, La.	Rappahannock	May 23, 1863
Lieut.-Col.	Critcher, John	15th Virginia Cav.	"	Oak Grove, Va.	"	May 23, 1863

Rank.	Name.	Regiment.	Army of	Residence.	Where & When Captured.
Lieutenant..	Carter, J. S.	7th Tennessee	Northern Va.	Lebanon, Tenn	Gettysburg, July 1, 1863
"	Coles, Isaac	6th Virginia Cav.	"	Pittsylvania, Va	Beverley Ford, June 9, 1863
"	Cason, J. R.	17th Mississippi	"	Holly Springs, Miss.	Gettysburg, July 2, 1863
"	Campbell, R. C.	53d Virginia	"	Aylett's, Va	Gettysburg, July 3, 1863
"	Chadbourne, H. R.	10th Alabama	"	Selma, Ala	Gettysburg, July 2, 1863
"	Cronin, S. D.	56th Virginia	"	Richmond, Va	Gettysburg, July 3, 1863
"	Coughton, C. D.	45th Tennessee	Tennessee	Lebanon, Tenn	At home, Feb. 6, 1863
"	Carr, R. B.	45th North Carolina.	Northern Va.	Magnolia, N. C.	Gettysburg, July 4, 1863
"	Covington, W. R.	38th North Carolina.	"	Bostick Mills, N. C.	Gettysburg, July 3, 1863
Captain	Christian, J. M.	9th Alabama	"	Florence, Ala	Gettysburg, July 2, 1863
"	Chrisolin, W. R.	4th Alabama Bat.	Tennessee	Florence, Ala	At home, Oct. 30, 1863
Lieutenant..	Cabaniss, J. A.	55th North Carolina.	Northern Va.	Shelby, N. C.	Gettysburg, July 1, 1863
"	Camp, J. A.	34th North Carolina.	"	Shelby, N. C.	Frankstown, July 12, 1863
Captain	Cunningham, J. M.	4th Alabama Bat.	Tennessee	Rogersville, Ala	Rogersville, Nov. 9, 1863
Lieutenant..	Cromley, R. M.	64th Tennessee	Mississippi	Bristol, Tenn	Big Black, May 17, 1863
Captain	Cox, W. B.	15th Tennessee	"	Nashville, Tenn	
Lieutenant..	Chesnut, A. T.	1st Missouri Cav.	"	New Market, Mo	Big Black, May 17, 1863
"	Clewell, F. C.	1st Missouri Cav.	"	Platte City, Mo	Big Black, May 17, 1863
"	Caldwell, O. H. P.	19th Arkansas	"	Magnolin, Ark	Big Black, May 17, 1863
Captain	Coulter, E. B.	12th Arkansas	"	Centre Point, Ark.	Port Hudson, July 9, 1863
Lieutenant..	Cage, F.	3d Virginia	Northern Va.	Pittsburg, Va	Gettysburg, July 3, 1863
"	Carter, W. B.	4th Virginia	"	Calhoun, Miss	Gettysburg, July 3, 1863
"	Clay, M. B.	9th Virginia	"	Martinsburg, Va.	Gettysburg, July 3, 1863
"	Crocker, J. O. B.	9th Virginia	"	Norfolk, Va	Gettysburg, July 3, 1863
Captain	Conner, T. B.	Martin's Staff	Tennessee	Natchez, Miss	Shelbyville, Jan. 27, 1863
Lieutenant..	Carr, T. F.	43d Georgia	Mississippi	Cole Mountain, Ga.	Champion Hill, May 13, 1863
"	Clark, O.	55th Georgia	Tennessee	Gainesville, Ga	Cumberl'd Gap, Sept. 9, 1863
"	Crouch, R. C.	Thomas' Cav.	"	Jonesboro', Tenn	Henderson, Sept. 11, 1863
Lt.-Col	Cameron, F. J.	6th Arkansas	"	Princeton, Ark	Murfreesboro' Dec. 3, 1863
Lieutenant..	Carter, J. L.	15th Arkansas	Mississippi	Dover, Ark	Big Black, May 17, 1863
Adjutant	Cumming, Julian	48th Georgia	Northern Va.	Augusta, Ga	Gettysburg, July 2, 1863

Rank	Name	Regiment	Army	Residence	Place and Date
Lieutenant.	Callin, J. W.	10th Kentucky			Died, Dec. 2, 1863
"	Coleman, F. W.	7th Kentucky			Died, Dec. 8, 1863
"	Crane, R. M.	11th Kentucky			Died, July 21, 1862
Captain.	Cauthorne, ——	Staff			Died, Nov. 22, 1862
"	Copass, R. D.	60th Tennessee			Died, July 15, 1863
Colonel.	Clarke, R. S.	8th Kentucky Cav.	Tennessee	Pine Grove, Ky.	Seleville, Ohio, July 26, 1863
Captain.	Campbell, W. M.	6th Kentucky Cav.	"	Lexington, Ky.	Seleville, Ohio, July 26, 1863
"	Cox, M. M.	15th Tennessee Cav	"	Nashville, Tenn.	Seleville, Ohio, July 26, 1863
Lieutenant.	Cromwell, R.	15th Tennessee Cav.	"	Monroe, Tenn.	Seleville, Ohio, July 26, 1863
"	Colger, J. M.	10th Kentucky Cav.	"	Somerset, Ky.	Buffington, Ohio, July 19, 1863
"	Craft, J. H.	10th Kentucky Cav.	"	Whitesburg, Ky.	Glansville, Va., July 7, 1863
"	Cline, James	4th Tennessee	"	Columbus, Tenn.	Hayway Co., Oct. 7, 1863
"	Candell, H. R S.	10th Kentucky Cav.	"	Whitesburg, Ky.	Glansville, Va., July 7, 1863
"	Cockerell, W. M.	36th Alabama	"	Pleasant Ridge, Ala.	
"	Cooper, R. A.	Frazer's Battalion	Northern Va.	Tebanville, Ga.	
Captain.	Calvert, J. J.	56th N. C.	"	Jackson, N. C.	
"	Coker, W. C.	8th S. C.	"	Society Hill, S. C.	Hagerstown, July 14, 1863
Lieutenant.	Cooke, A.	1st Maryland Bat.	"	Bettsville, Md.	Williamsport, July 14, 1863
"	Crown, J. B.	White's Bat.	"	Frederick City, Md.	Loudoun co., Va., Sep. 12, 1863
"	Cooke, S. G.	28th Mississippi	Mississippi	Bolivar, Miss.	Mississippi river, Sep. 9, 1863
"	Clarke, S. P.	4th N. C.	Northern Va.	Wilson, N. C.	Middleburg, June 19, 1863
"	Clempson, J. C.	C. S. A.	"	Spring Place, Geo.	Manassas Gap,
"	Combie, A G. M.	22d Georgia	"	Arkadelphia, Ark.	Manassas Gap,
"	Callowage, T. D.	1st Arkansas Bat.	Mississippi	Arkadelphia, Ark.	Port Hudson, July 9, 1863
Captain.	Cloud, J. B.	16th Arkansas	"	Antonie, Ark.	Port Hudson, July 9, 1863
"	Calvin, H. G.	5th Kentucky	"	Pikeville, Ky.	West Liberty, May 16, 1863
Lieutenant.	Cox, J. H.	12th Arkansas	"	Louisville, Ky.	Port Hudson, July 9, 1863
"	Charles, J. D.	Orr's S. C. Reg't	Northern Va.	Greenville, S. C.	Falling Waters, July 14, 1863
"	Crawford, J. H.	Orr's S. C. Reg't	"	Due West, S. C.	Falling Waters, July 14, 1863
"	Corley, W. L. J.	25th Virginia	"	Braxton Co., Va.	Williamsport, July 13, 1863
"	Cargill, C. N.	10th Arkansas	Mississippi	Quitman, Ark.	Port Hudson, July 9, 1863
Captain.	Cocke, W. N.	9th Missouri	Trans-Miss.	Oceola, Mo.	Helena, July 4, 1863
Colonel.	Christian, W. S.	55th Virginia	Northern Va.	Urbanna, Va.	Falling Waters, July 16, 1863
Lieutenant.	Christian, T. L.	4th Alabama	"	Uniontown, Ala.	Gettysburg, July 2, 1863

Rank.	Name.	Regiment.	Army of	Residence.	Where & When Captured.
Lieutenant..	Cherry, G. O......	4th N. Carolina Cav.	Northern Va..	Wilson, N. C......	Gettysburg, July 4, 1863
"	Clopton, W. E.....	3d Virginia Cavalry.	"	Tunstall's, Va......	White House, July 1, 1863
"	Coleman, A. F.....	9th Louisiana......	"	Bush Valley, La....	Rappahannock, Nov. 7, 1863
"	Cooper, William....	8th "	"	New Orleans, La...	" Nov. 7, 1863
"	Coupland, T. B.....	5th Kentucky Cav..	Tennessee...	Princeton, Ky......	Sugar Creek, October 9, 1863
"	Christian, W. J.....	6th North Carolina.	Northern Va..	Durham, N. C......	Rappahannock, Nov. 7, 1863
"	Cooley, T. L.......	6th "	"	Hillsboro', N. C....	Pine Wood, Nov. 7, 1863
"	Cox, Joseph.......	1st Tennessee Cav..	"	Charlotte, Tenn....	" Oct. 28, 1863
"	Cail, A...........	11th Arkansas.....	Mississippi...	Rockport, Ark.....	Natchez, July 31, 1863
Captain.....	Cockerham, S. D...	54th North Carolina.	Northern Va.	Jonesville, N. C....	Rappahannock, July 7, 1863
"	Chisholm, W. R....	4th Alabama Cav...	Tennessee...	Florence, Ala......	Florence, October 30, 1863
Lieutenant..	Chisholm, B. F.....	4th "	"	"	" October 30, 1863
Captain.. .	Carter, P. T.......	20th Tennessee.....	"	Nashville, Tenn....	Chickamauga, Nov. 25, 1863
Lieutenant..	Candler, Z. M.....	64th North Carolina.	"	Marshall, N. C.....	Cumberl'd Gap, Sept. 9, 1863
"	Cobb, L. G.......	55th Georgia.......	"	Cuthbert, Ga.......	" Sept. 9, 1863
"	Cooley, J. M.......	55th "	"	Grantville, Ga......	" Sept. 9, 1863
"	Cross, H.........	55th "	"	Henderson, Ga.....	" Sept. 9, 1863
Captain.....	Coffin, W. N.......	12th Louisiana.....	"	Cumberla'd, C H.Va	Port Hudson, July 9, 1863
Lieutenant..	Coffin, T. E.......	12th "	"	"	" July 9, 1863
"	Cotton, R. E.......	61st North Carolina.	"	Headley's Mills, N.C.	Morris' Island, Aug. 26, 1863
Captain.....	Clayton, J. P.......	7th S. Carolina Batt.	Northern Va..	Camden, S. C......	Charleston, S.C., July 16, 1863
Lieutenant .	Costin, Matt.......	Forrest Escort......	Tennessee...	Normandy, Tenn...	Chickamauga, Sept. 11, 1863
"	Carr, W. H........	23d Tennessee......	"	Ravena, Ohio......	" Sept. 11, 1863
"	Cooper, G. G......	1st Louisiana......	"	Baton Rouge, La...	" Sept. 11, 1863
"	Cowden, W. N.....	Holman's Batt......	"	Lewisburg, Tenn...	" Sept. 11, 1863
Captain.....	Carson, S. P.......	35th Tennessee.....	"	McMinnville, Tenn..	McMinnville.
Lieutenant..	Cobb, J. E.........	5th Texas.........	Northern Va..	Liberty, Texas.....	Gettysburg, July 2, 1863
"	Coffey, Hiram......	1st Tenn. Leg. Cav..	Tennessee...	Daingerfield, Texas.	Chamberlayne, April 27, 1863
"	Cowling, S. W.....	51st Alabama......	"	Banton, Ala........	Shelbyville, June 29, 1863
"	Cooper, H. M......	3d "	"	Baine Bluff, Ala....	" June 27, 1863
"	Chamberlayne, J H.	Pegram's Batt......	Northern Va..	Richmond, Va......	Chambersburg, June 28, 1863

Rank	Name	Regiment	Army	Residence	Place and Date
Captain	Crowe, G.			N. Point, Miss.	
Lieutenant	Craig, A. P.	21st South Carolina	S. Carolina	Chesterfield, S. C.	Charleston, S. C., July 20, 1863
"	Campbell, J.	Charlotte Batt.	"	Charleston, S. C.	Battery Wagner, July 18, 1863
"	Caldwell, J. H.	23d North Carolina	Northern Va.	Dry Pond, Va.	Gettysburg, July 3, 1863
"	Chilcutt, J. W.	38th Tennessee	Tennessee	Nashville, Tenn.	Dalton, November 25, 1863
Lieut.-Col.	Cantwell, Edward	4th North Carolina	"	Raleigh, N. C.	Middleb'g, Tenn, June 19, 1863
Captain	Caldwell, J. T.	25th "	Northern Va.	Bexar, Ala.	Gettysburg, July 1, 1863
"	Carter, T. M.	5th Tenn. Cavalry	Tennessee	Benton, Tenn.	Paris, Ky., July 29, 1863
Lieutenant	Crawford, James	50th Tennessee	Mississippi	Jonesboro, Tenn.	Vicksburg, May 17, 1863
Major	Carrington, H.	3d Virginia Cavalry	Tennessee	Halifax C. H., Va.	Aldie, Va., June 17, 1863
Lieutenant	Crawford, L.	60th Tennessee	Mississippi	Jonesboro, Tenn.	Vicksburg, May 17, 1863
Captain	Carter, W. B.	Engineer Officer	Trans-Miss.	Searcy, Ark.	Searcy, September 21, 1863
"	Caldwell, G. S.	29th Mississippi	Tennessee	Cofferville, Miss.	Miss'y Ridge, Nov. 24, 1863
"	Crockerville, C. C.	14th Tennessee	Northern Va.	Cumberland, Tenn.	Gettysburg, July 3, 1863
Adjutant	Crocker, J. F.	9th Virginia	"	Norfolk, Va.	" July 4, 1863
Captain	Crocker, E. W.	26th Georgia	"	Marion, Ga.	" July 5, 1863
"	Cloud, A. S.	16th North Carolina	"	Morgantown, N. C.	" July 3, 1863
Lieutenant	Carter, H. S.	53d Virginia	"	Pittsylvania, C. H. Va	" July 3, 1863
"	Campbell, S. C.	5th Missouri	Trans-Miss.	Boonstick, Mo.	Missouri, December 13, 1863
"	Cobb, G. S.	44th North Carolina	Northern Va.	Newbern, N. C.	Hanover Junc., June 25, 1863
"	Carter, G. W.	34th Virginia	"	Clarksville, Va.	Gettysburg, July 5, 1863
"	Crafford, S. J.	6th North Carolina	"	Pleasant Grove, N. C	" July 4, 1863
Captain	Creath, H. D.	Beall's Staff	Mississippi	Jackson, La.	Brooks, Miss., July 20, 1863
Lieutenant	Cassar, C. G.	29th Mississippi	Tennessee	Charleston, Miss.	Miss'y Ridge, Nov. 25, 1863
"	Collier, H.	Faulkner's Cav.	Mississippi	Sarepta, Miss.	Hernando, Miss., April 8, 1863
Captain	Cunningham, W. M.	2d Mississippi	Northern Va.	Tupelo, Miss.	Gettysburg, July 4, 1883
Lieut.-Col.	Campbell, A. W.	33d Tennessee	Tennessee	Jackson, Tenn.	Lexington, July 1, 1863
Lieutenant	Calvert, Thomas	Blythe's Mississippi	"	Palo Alto, Miss.	North Miss., April 21, 1863
Adjutant	Coalter, H. T.	55th Virginia	Northern Va.	King Wm. C H., Va	Gettysburg, July 3, 1863
Lieutenant	Chappell, F. A.	1st Missouri	Trans-Miss.	Petersburg, Ind.	Chock Bluff, May 29, 1863
"	Crile, William	1st Tennessee	Tennessee	Memphis, Tenn.	At Home, June 9, 1863
"	Coleman, C. F.	15th Arkansas	Mississippi	Camden, Ark.	Port Hudson, July 4, 1863
"	Cummings, H. R.	15th "	"	Wiltsburg, Ark.	" July 4, 1863
Captain	Cofer, J. H.	39th Mississippi	"	Brandon, Miss.	" July 4, 1863

Rank.	Name.	Regiment.	Army of	Residence.	Where & When Captured.
Lieutenant..	Colton, James......	1st Florida.........	Tennessee...	Eachanon, Fla.....	Miss'y Ridge, Nov. 25, 1863
"	Cargill, C. W......	10th Arkansas......	Mississippi...	Quitman, Ark......	Port Hudson, July 9, 1863
"	Carter, G. W......	28th Arkansas......	"	Arkadelphia, Ark...	" July 9, 1863
"	Carter, J. P.......	27th Georgia.......	Tennessee...	Augusta, Ga.......	Lookout M't'n, Nov. 24, 1863
Captain.....	Cracroft, G. K.....	23d Arkansas......	Mississippi...	Lake Village, Ark..	Port Hudson, July 9, 1863
Lieutenant..	Clark, J. B........	23d Arkansas......	"	Jonesboro', Ark.....	" July 9, 1863
"	Candle, W. M......	10th Arkansas......	"	Quitman, Ark.....	" July 9, 1863
"	Coon, R. W........	28th Alabama......	Tennessee...	Jonesboro', Ala.....	Miss'y Ridge, Nov. 25, 1863
Captain.....	Carnahan, J. P.....	16th Arkansas......	Mississippi...	Washington, Ark...	Port Hudson, July 9, 1863
"	Campbell, R. F.....	49th Alabama......	"	Blountsville, Ala...	" July 9, 1863
Lieutenant..	Creel, S. G........	39th Mississippi....	"	Morter, Miss.......	" July 9, 1863
"	Chancey, C........	"	"	Decatur, Miss......	" July 9, 1863
"	Clark, L. B........	1st Arkansas Bat...	"	Arkadelphia, Ark..	" July 9, 1863
"	Cook, G. G........	1st Tennessee Art..	"	Columbia, Tenn....	" July 9, 1863
Captain.....	Carter, D. E.......	9th Louisiana Art...	"	Flat Bayou, La.....	" July 9, 1863
Lieutenant..	Cook, W. B........	Miles' Legion......	"	Columbia, Tenn....	" July 9, 1863
"	Collier, T. H.......	18th Arkansas.....	"	Richmond, Va.....	" July 9, 1863
"	Calloway, S. D.....	1st Arkansas.......			" July 9, 1863
"	Cooper, W. C......	39th Mississippi....			" July 9, 1863
"	Cogburn, M. S.....	14th South Carolina,	Northern Va.		Gettysburg, July 5, 1863
Captain.....	Collium, M. V.....	29th Mississippi....	Mississippi...	Crystal Springs, Miss	Port Hudson, July 9, 1863
Lieutenant..	Connelly, J. W.....	16th Texas.........	Trans-Miss...	Dorus Mills, S. C...	Richmond, La., June 15, 1863
"	Coppedge, F. T.....	10th Missouri......	"	Morter, Miss.......	Port Hudson, July 9, 1863
Captain.....	Corbin, J. M.......	1st Louisiana Cav..	Tennessee...	Big Cane, La.......	Winchester, July 30, 1863
"	Coley, J. R........	10th Con. Cavalry..	"	Longstreet, Tenn...	Lancaster, Ky., July 31, 1863
"	Clemons, A. M.....	"	"	Hickory, Ala.......	Jacksboro, Ten., Aug 27, 1863
Lieutenant..	Chrisman, Isaac....	10th Missouri......	Trans-Miss...	Lacon, Mo.........	Helena, Ark., July 11, 1863
"	Coledan, ———.....	3d Alabama........	Tennessee...	Clarksville, Ala....	Chattanooga, Nov. 28, 1863
Captain.....	Chapman, R. D....	55th Georgia.......	"	Colquitt, Ga.......	Cumberl'd Gap, Sep. 9, 1863
"	Canathey, J. S.....	Staff..............	Mississippi...	Memphis, Tenn....	" Sep. 9, 1863
"	Cook, W. B........	Miles' Legion......	"	Covington, La......	Port Gibson, May 1, 1863

Rank	Name	Regiment	Department	Residence	Where Captured	Date
Captain	Cole, S. D.	Bowen's Missouri	Mississippi	California, Mo.	Port Gibson,	May 1, 1863
"	Carson, L. P.	35th Tennessee	Tennessee	McMinnsville, Tenn.	Dunlop,	Aug. 19, 1863
Lieutenant	Cahill, ——	—— North Carolina,				
Major	Cook, ——					
Lieut.-Col.	Carrington, H. A.	18th Virginia	Northern Va.	Charlotte, Va.		
Lieutenant	Casey, W.	9th Tennessee Cav.				
Captain	Cooper, T. F.	52d Georgia		Athens, Ga.		
Lieutenant	Croso, W. J.	15th Arkansas		Magnolia, Ark.		
"	Collier, J. W.	6th Kentucky Cav.		Somerset, Ky.		
"	Cole, W. W.	54th North Carolina,		Carthage, N. C.		
Captain	Cuthbert, ——	54th North Carolina,		Blockersville, N. C.		
Lieutenant	Cole, M. H.	6th North Carolina		Ashebury, N. C.		
Captain	Claiborne, W.	7th South Carolina		Camden, S. C.		
Lieutenant	Camp, R. B.	Gannt's Art.		Augusta, Ark.		
Colonel	Campbell, J. A.	27th Mississippi		Carthage, Miss.		
Captain	Coffer, R. A.	4th Tennessee		"		
Lieutenant	Donnegan, C. A.	2d Kentucky Cav.	Tennessee	Huntsville, Ala.	Kentucky,	May 28, 1863
Captain	Davis, M. J.	A. A. G.	"	Charleston, S. C.	Indiana,	July 12, 1863
Major	Debaren, J. D.	9th Louisiana Cav.	Mississippi	New Orleans, La.	Port Hudson,	July 9, 1863
Lieutenant	Dyes, G. A.	Independent Corps	Trans-Miss.	St. Charles, Mo.	Mississippi,	Sept. 1, 1863
"	Dawson, C. G.	8th Virginia Cav.	Northern Va.	Point of Rocks, Va.	At Home,	July 26, 1863
"	Davis, R. G.	34th Tennessee	Tennessee	Nashville, Tenn.	Miss'y Ridge,	Nov. 25, 1863
"	Daugharts, S. P.	33d Tennessee	"	Troy, Tenn.	"	Nov. 25, 1863
"	Douglas, J. H. T.	3d Virginia Cav.	Northern Va.	Chester C. H., S. C.	Aldie, Va.,	June 17, 1863
Captain	Duncan, J. H.	Wheeler's Scouts	Tennessee	Nashville, Tenn.	Laurgan,	Oct. 10, 1863
"	Dills, J. R.	62d North Carolina	"	Webster, N. C.	Cumberl'd Gap,	Sept. 9, 1863
"	Degrau, W.	Miles' Legion	Mississippi	Opelousas, La.	Port Hudson,	July 9, 1863
Lieutenant	Davidson, J. B.	9th La. Bat. Art.	"	Greensboro, La.	"	July 9, 1863
"	Davis, Bailey.	12th La. Bat. Art.	"	Richmond, Va.	"	July 9, 1863
"	Dismakes, ——	8th Florida	Northern Va.	Quincey, Fla.	Gettysburg,	July 14, 1863
"	Dunn, J. B.	9th Louisiana	Mississippi	Greenville Sp'gs, La.	Port Hudson,	July 9, 1863
Captain	Dew, T. R.	7th Virginia	Northern Va.	Albemarle Co., Va.	Falling Waters,	July 14, 1863
Lieutenant	Dickenson, J. E.	47th Virginia	"	Caroline Co., Va.	"	July 14, 1863
Captain	Donaway, W. F.	40th Virginia	"	Lancaster Co., Va.	"	July 14, 1863

Rank.	Name.	Regiment.	Army of	Residence.	Where & When Captured.
Lieutenant..	Deberry, J. B......	4th Florida........	Mississippi [?].	Caroline Co., Va...	Falling Waters, July 14, 1863
"	Dickenson, M. N...	4th "	Tennessee...	Margaretsville, N. C.	Miss'y Ridge, Nov. 20, 1863
"	Dykes, ——......	4th "	"	"	" Nov. 23, 1863
Captain	Duncan, S. P......	4th Kentucky Cav..	"	Bedford, Ky......	Bogstown, Oct. 11, 1863
"	Doughty, L. G.....	48th Georgia......	Northern Va.	Augusta, Ga......	Gettysburg, July 2, 1863
"	Downing, J. S......	Holman's Regiment.	Mississippi...	Houston, Mo......	Arkansas, March 12, 1863
Lieutenant..	Dodson, J. N......	26th Virginia Bat...	Northern Va.	Slaweville, Va......	Slardidge, July 7, 1863
Captain	Donald, W. P......	12th Arkansas......	Mississippi...	Altonia, Ark......	Port Hudson, July 9, 1863
Lieutenant..	Drake, R. F......	47th North Carolina.	Northern Va.	Hilliardstown, N. C.	Franklin, Ky., Sept. 2, 1863
"	Dean, J...........	28th Tennessee.....	Tennessee...	Bagdad, Tenn......	" Sept. 2, 1863
"	Dugan, J. A......	10th Arkansas......	"	Concraboro. S. C...	Miss'y Ridge, Nov. 25, 1863
"	Dillard, R. G......	16th Arkansas......	Mississippi...	Nashville, Ark......	Port Hudson, July 9, 1863
Captain	Donaldson, W. J...	Bell's Regiment....	Trans-Miss...	Hamburg, Ark......	Helena, July 4, 1863
"	Daniel, J. D......	22d Georgia	Northern Va.	New Orleans. La...	Gettysburg, July 2, 1863
Lieutenant..	Devaughn, J. E....	2d Georgia........	Tennessee...	Jonesboro, Ga......	Sugar Creek, Oct. 9, 1863
Captain	Delto, W. L......	1st Louisiana Cav...	"	Harrisonburg, La...	Hanford, Ky., Aug. 1, 1863
Major......	Douglas, H. K.....	A. A. G...........	Northern Va.	Shepherdstown, Va.	Gettysburg, July 3, 1863
"	Dunn, R. J.......	39th Mississippi....	Mississippi...	Westville, Miss......	Port Hudson, July 9, 1863
Lieutenant..	Dyer, W. S.......	25th Virginia......	Northern Va.	Uppertrack, Va....	Gettysburg, July 2, 1863
"	Dudley, J. R......	Buckner's Escort...	Tennessee...	Pontotoc, Miss......	" July 5, 1863
"	Dillard, J. W....	2d Mississippi......	Northern Va.	Ringgold, Ga......	Caldysville, Nov. 28, 1863
"	Davis, W. B......	30th Mississippi.....	Tennessee...	Grenada, Miss......	Murfreesboro, Jan'y 16, 1863
Captain	Duncan, J. W.....	Arkansas Reg't.....	Trans-Miss ..	Springfield, Ark....	Helena, July 4, 1863
Lieutenant..	Duncan, J. T......	2d Arkansas Cav...	Tennessee...	Elkton, Ky........	Franklin, Tenn., July 4, 1863
"	Dover, W.........	17th Tennessee.....	"	Shelbyville, Tenn...	Stone River, Dec., 1862
Captain	Dickson, E. D.....	55th North Carolina.	Northern Va.	Perryville, N. C.....	Gettysburg, July 1, 1863
"	Davis, R. H.......	34th Mississippi....	Mississippi...	Vicksburg, Miss....	Vicksburg, May, 18, 1863
Lieutenant .	Davis, J. C.......	62d Tennessee.....	"	Middleburg, Tenn..	" July 4, 1663
"	Drewry, S. T......	3d Virginia Cavalry.	Northern Va.	Waverley, Va......	Gettysburg, July 3, 1863
"	Doss, S. P........	5th Alabama......	"	Peconsville, Ala....	" July 1, 1863
Major......	Dye, J. J........	51st Alabama Cav..	Tennessee....	Talladega, Ala......	Shelbyville, June 7, 1863

Rank	Name	Unit	State	Residence	Captured	Date
Lieutenant	Davis, G. W. C.	15th Arkansas	Mississippi	Dover, Ark.	Big Black,	May 17, 1863
Captain	Dabson, J. V.	23d Arkansas	"	Witsburg, Ark.	Port Hudson,	July 9, 1863
Lieutenant	Dorsey, A. L.	43d Georgia	"	Gainesville, Ga.	Champe Hill,	May 16, 1863
Captain	Duncan, J.	6th Missouri	"	Independence, Mo.	"	May 16, 1863
"	Dillingham, W. H.	2d Missouri Cavalry	"	Chewalla, Tenn.	Ripley, Miss.,	July 8, 1863
Lieutenant	Dunavan, J. B.	14th Tennessee Cav.	Tennessee	Covington, Tenn.	"	July 8, 1863
"	Dunigan, J.	4th Tennessee Cav.	"	Eaton, Tenn.	"	July 8, 1863
"	Duncan, H. H.	1st Arkansas	"	Milford, Ky.	Shelbyville,	Oct. 4, 1863
Captain	Dowell, J. J.	2d Tennessee	Northern Va.	Alexandria, Va.	Gettysburg,	July 4, 1863
Lieutenant	Dooley, J. E.	1st Virginia	"	Richmond, Va.	"	July 3, 1863
Captain	Davis, T. H.	1st "	"	"	"	July 3, 1863
Lieutenant	Dyer, S. T.	57th Virginia	"	Pittsylvania, S. C.	"	July 3, 1863
Captain	Dickerson, D. V.	57th "	"	"	"	July 3, 1863
Lieutenant	Dunham, D. L.	2d Florida	"	St. Augustine, Fla.	"	July 3, 1863
"	Dunham, F.	3d "	Tennessee	"	Chickamauga,	Sept. 25, 1863
"	Derricks, J. A.	15th South Carolina	Northern Va.	Centreville, S. C.	Gettysburg,	July 2, 1863
Captain	Davis, J. J.	47th North Carolina	"	Lewisburg, N. C.	"	Sept. 3, 1863
Lieutenant	Dodson, J. M.	10th Tennessee				
"	Dennison, C. E.	5th Florida Bat.			Gettysburg,	July 5, 1863
Captain	Day, J. W.	55th Georgia	Tennessee	Coleman, Ga.	Cumberl'd Gap,	Sept. 9, 1863
Lieutenant	Debase, E. J.	64th North Carolina	"	Greensville, Tenn.	"	Sept. 9, 1863
"	Drois, S. T.	7th Kentucky	"	Blandville, Ky.	Elleston,	Nov. 28, 1863
"	Dickenson, W. J.	2d North Carolina	Northern Va.	Roanoke Co., Va.	Kelley's Ford,	Nov. 7, 1863
"	Dison, H. C.	6th "	"	Tar River, N. C.	Rappahannock,	Nov. 7, 1863
"	Davis, S. B.	60th "	Tennessee	Fingerville, S. C.	Miss'y Ridge,	Nov. 25, 1863
"	Duffill, F.	8th Louisiana	Northern Va.	Donaldsonville, La.	Rappahannock,	Nov. 9, 1863
"	Depriest, C.	23d Virginia	"	Richmond, Va.	Belton,	October 23, 1863
"	Dudley, E. V.	15th Virginia Cav.	"	Pr. Anne C. H., Va.	Culpeper,	Sept. 13, 1863
Major	Davis, J. C.	17th Tennessee	Tennessee	Lewisburg, N. C.	Chickamauga,	Sept. 19, 1863
Lieutenant	Donaldson, A. T.	23d "	"	Wartrucy, N. C.	"	Sept. 19, 1863
"	Dunner, W. C.	— Arkansas	"	Knoxville, Tenn.	Cumberl'd Gap,	Sept. 9, 1863
"	Dadney, F. T.	Engineer Corps	Mississippi	Raymond, Miss.	Port Hudson,	July 9, 1863
Lieut.-Col.	Degourney, T. F.	12th Louisiana Bat.	"	New Orleans, La.	"	July 9, 1863
Lieutenant	Dibble, Samuel	25th South Carolina	So. Carolina	Orangeburg, S. C.	Charleston,	July 7, 1863

Rank.	Name.	Regiment.	Army of	Residence.	Where & When Captured.
Colonel	Davis, J. L	10th Virginia Cav	Northern Va.	Richmond, Va	Hagerstown, Md., July 5, 1863
Lieutenant	Draughn, H. H	20th North Carolina	"	Dranton, N. C	Gettysburg, July 1, 1863
"	Durphey, T. H. B	18th Virginia	"	Pamplin's Depot, Va	" July 3, 1863
"	Durald, A. V	9th Alabama Batt	Mississippi	Benton, Ala	Port Hudson, July 9, 1863
"	Dawson, H. B	17th Georgia			
"	Davis, J. T	7th Kentucky	Tennessee		
"	Duliel, J. D	7th Louisiana Batt	Mississippi	Baton Rouge, La	Port Hudson, July 9, 1863
"	Dixon, W. W	27th North Carolina	Northern Va.	Lawrence, N. C	Gettysburg, July 3, 1863
"	Dick, F. M	44th "	"	Greensboro, N. C	Hanover Junc., June 26, 1863
"	Dillinger, L A	52d "	"	Iva, N. C	Gettysburg, July 3, 1863
"	Davis, W. A	28th Arkansas	Tennessee	Walnut Grove, N. C.	Miss'y Ridge, Nov. 23, 1863
"	Davis, J. M	10th "	"	Quitman, Ark	Port Hudson, July 9, 1863
Captain	Davis, J. C	1st Mississippi	Mississippi	Coffeeville, Miss	" July 9, 1863
Lieutenant	Dewberry, W	13th South Carolina	Northern Va.	Drower, S. C	Gettysburg, July 8, 1863
Captain	Duggett, A. E	12th Arkansas	Mississippi	Centrepond, Ark	Port Hudson, July 9, 1863
Lieutenant	Dunn, B. H	12th "	"	Arkadelphia, Ark	" July 9, 1863
"	Durham, J. H	34th Mississippi	Tennessee	Tyro, Miss	Look-out M't'n, Nov. 24, 1863
Captain	Donaldson, W. J	Bell's Artillery Reg't	Trans-Miss	Hamburg, Ark	Helena, July 4, 1863
Lieutenant	Donahue, A. J	8th Missouri	"	Morristown, Mo	" July 4, 1863
"	Dolan, W	8th "	"	"	" July 4, 1863
"	Decamp, T	10th Kentucky Cav	"	Hempton, Ky	
"	Denton, E. R	1st "	Tennessee	Dresden, Tenn	Tennessee, October 13, 1863
Lieut.-Col	Dawson, W. A	14th Tennessee Cav	"	Dyersburg, Tenn	Tenn. River, May 31, 1863
Lieutenant	Debababan, A. M	8th Alabama	"	——, Ala	
"	Daily, J. A	5th Texas Cavalry		——, Texas	
Captain	Ervin, W. D	18th Virginia Cav	Northern Va.	Warm Springs, Va	McConnellsb'g, June 29, 1863
Lieutenant	Evans, M. D	Louisiana Batt	Mississippi	Parksville, La	Port Hudson, July 9, 1863
Captain	Enate, E	1st Louisiana Cav	Tennessee	Trinity, La	Irving, Ky., July 12, 1863
Lieutenant	Enloe, L. A	62d North Carolina	"	Franklin, N. C	Cumberl'd Gap, Sept. 9, 1863
Captain	Eure, M. S	2d "	Northern Va.	Gatesville, N. C	Hanover, June 30, 1863
Lieut.-Col	Ellis, A	54th "	"	Allisburg, N. C	Rappahannock, May 7, 1863

Rank	Name	Regiment	Army	Home	Place/Date
Lieutenant..	Elley, R. S.........	13th Virginia Cav...	Northern Va.	Suffolk, Va.........	Hagerstown, July 12, 1863
"	Emahart, Wm. P...	50th North Carolina.	"	Marianna, Fla......	Robertsburg, Nov. 7, 1863
"	Everett, T. D......	4th Florida.........	Tennessee ...	Canton, Ark.......	Miss'y Ridge, Nov. 30, 1863
"	Emris, S. V........	16th Arkansas......	Mississippi ...	"	Port Hudson, July 9, 1863
"	Edward, B.........	Miles' Legion.......	"	Covington, La......	" July 9, 1863
"	Ellis, E. J..........	2d Georgia.........	Northern Va.	Griffin, Ga.........	Gettysburg, July 2, 1863
Captain.....	Ellis, W. S.........	2d Louisiana.......	Tennessee ...	Aunt's City, La....	Miss'y Ridge, Nov. 25, 1863
Lieutenant..	Evans, H. M.......	22d Alabama.......	"	Calhoun, Ala......	" Nov. 25, 1863
"	Elkins, J. M........	3d Texas Cav......	Trans-Miss...	Weatherford, Texas.	Benton, June 28, 1863
Captain.....	Earthman, J. H.....	Land Batt.........	Tennessee ...	Nashville, Tenn....	Cumberl'd Gap, Sept. 9, 1863
Colonel.....	Edwards, J.........	49th Alabama......	Mississippi ...	Duck Spring, Ala...	Port Hudson, July 9, 1863
Lieutenant..	Elam, P. R........	55th North Carolina.	Northern Va.	Shelby, N. C.......	Gettysburg, July 3, 1863
Captain.....	Edwards, W. C.....	3d Georgia Cav....	Tennessee ...	Lumpkin, Ga.......	Tennessee, May 17, 1863
Lieutenant..	Edlins, O. F........	1st Mississippi......	Mississippi ...	Byhalin, Miss.......	Port Hudson, July 9, 1863
"	Eller, W...........	1st Missouri Cav....	"	Mexico, Mo........	Big Black River, May 17, 1863
"	Elliott, E. C........	2d Kentucky Cav...	Tennessee ...	Perryville, Ky......	Camden, July 9, 1863
"	Evans, W. E.......	B. "	"	Russellville, Ky....	Ohio, July 26, 1863
Captain.....	Erving, H. T.......		"	Nashville, Tenn....	Giles Co., Tenn., Nov. 3, 1863
"	Ellis, H. M........	13th Arkansas......		Marion, Ark.......	Marion, August 24, 1863
"	Ezell, F. M........	3d Tennessee......	Tennessee ...		Died, October 22, 1863
"	Edward, J.........	48th Alabama......	Northern Va.	Bluntsville, Ala.....	Gettysburg, July 2, 1863
Lieutenant..	Eubanks, J. B......	4th "	"	"	" July 2, 1863
Captain...	Euglist, T. W......	3d N. Carolina Cav.	Tennessee ...	Turkey Cove, Ky...	Kentucky, August 21, 1863
Lieutenant..	Elener, C. E.......	57th North Carolina.	Northern Va.	Lincolnton, N. C....	Gettysburg, July 5, 1863
"	Everett, G. W......	Bell's Ark. Reg't....	Trans-Miss...	Pigeon Hill, Ark...	Helena, July 4, 1863
"	East, W. F.........	50th Virginia.......	Northern Va	Five Oaks, Va......	Gettysburg, July 2, 1863
"	Efland, W. S.......	53d North Carolina.	"	Greensboro, N. C...	Hagerstown, July 5, 1863
"	Evans, S. S........	47th "	"	Lewisburg, N. C....	Gettysburg, July 3, 1863
"	Ellis, W. N........	13th Alabama......	"	Roanoke, Va.......	Green Castle, July 5, 1863
"	Elliott, B. S........	33d Georgia........	"	McDonough, Ga....	Williamsport, July 12, 1863
"	Eastham, A........	5th Virginia Cav....	"	Washington, Va....	
Captain.....	Esoin, W. T........	14th Arkansas......	Mississippi...	West Point, Ark....	Port Hudson, July 9, 1863
Lieutenant .	Easterling, W. G...	39th Mississippi....	"	Port Hudson.......	" July 9, 1863
"	Evans, J. B........	34th "	"	Warford, Miss......	Lookout M't'n, Nov. 4, 1863

Rank.	Name.	Regiment.	Army of	Residence.	Where & When Captured.
Adjutant	Erwin, W. A.	1st Arkansas	Trans-Miss	Napoleon, Ark.	Maron, 1863
Lieutenant	Ellis, J. A.	20th Arkansas	Mississippi	Jonesboro', Ark.	Port Hudson, July 9, 1863
"	Eggers, J W.	16th Arkansas	"	Cane Hill, Ark.	" July 9, 1863
Captain	Edwards, W. H.	49th Virginia	"	Bluntsville, Ala.	" July 9, 1863
"	Furhman, G. P.	1st Alabama Cav.	Tennessee	Montgomery, Ala.	Middletown, May 13, 1863
Lieutenant	Finley, G. W.	56th Virginia	Northern Va.	Clarksville, Va.	Gettysburg, July 3, 1863
Captain	Frazier, S. A.	"	"	Sturgeonville, Va.	" July 3, 1863
"	Fidler, E. W.	C. S. N.			Died July 25, 1862
"	Foster, W. A.	52d North Carolina	Northern Va.	Worksboro', N. C.	Falling Waters, July 14, 1863
Lieutenant	Foster, T. H.	6th Virginia Cav	"	Fauquier co., Va.	Culpeper C H., Sept. 3, 1863
Captain	Foster, J. W.	Mosby's Cav	"	Warrenton, Va.	Warrenton, June 12, 1863
Lieutenant	Fryer, J. H.	5th Alabama	"	Clayton. Ala.	Gettysburg, July 5, 1863
"	Frazier, A. M.	47th Virginia	"	Newtown, Va.	Falling Waters, July 14, 1863
"	Fair, Samuel	13th Missouri Cav.	Trans-Miss	Canton, Miss.	
Captain	Ferring, W. A.	3d C. Cavalry	Tennessee	Oceola, Ark.	
"	Fox, G. R. R.	1st S. C. Cavalry	Northern Va.	Saint George, S. C.	
"	Finley, G.	1st Florida Cavalry	Tennessee	Tallahassee, Fla.	Miss'y Ridge, Dec. 25, 1863
Lieutenant	Footman, J. W.	1st "	"	"	" Dec. 25, 1863
"	Fulks, A. L.	12th Arkansas	Mississippi	Arkadelphia, Ark.	Port Hudson, July 9, 1863
Captain	Furnish, L.	3d Missouri Cavalry	"	Savannah, Missouri	Big Black, May 17, 1863
Colonel	Fry, B D.	13th Alabama	Northern Va.	Tallasse, Ala	Gettysburg, July 3, 1863
Lieutenant	Fain, N.	60th Mississippi	Mississippi	Rogersville, Tenn.	Big Black, May 7, 1863
"	Ford James	2d Tennessee Cav.	Tennessee	War Gap, Tenn.	Shelbyville, Oct. 7, 1863
Major	Foster, French	4th Alabama Cav.	"	Florence, Ala.	" Oct. 20, 1863
Brig.-Gen'l	Frazier, J. W.	C. S. A.	"	Memphis, Tenn.	Cumberland Gap Sep. 9. 1863
Captain	Frazier, C. W.	A. A. G	"	"	" Sep. 9, 1863
Lieutenant	Furgerson, E. K.	62d North Carolina	"	Crab Tree, N. C.	Missouri, May 18, 1863
"	Farr, J. J.	13th Missouri Cav.	Trans-Miss	Canton, Missouri	" May 18, 1863
"	Freeman, A.	2d Georgia Batt	Northern Va.	Macon, Georgia	Gettysburg, July 4, 1863
"	Frencher, B. H.	3d C. Cavalry	Tennessee	Kingston, Georgia	Dalton, Nov. 21, 1863
"	Forrester, J. T.	37th North Carolina	Northern Va.	Burksboro', N. C.	Gettysburg, July 3, 1863

Captain	Frazier, S. J. A.	19th Tennessee	Tennessee	Washington, Tenn.	Lookout M't'n,	Sep. 19, 1863
Lieutenant	Fauman, A. H.	8th Georgia	Northern Va	Lincolnton, N. C.	Gettysburg,	July 5, 1863
"	Finklen, J. C.	10th South Carolina	Tennessee	Conwaysboro', S. C.	Miss'y Ridge,	Nov. 25, 1863
"	Flood, J. W.	2d Kentucky Cav.	"	Owensville, Ky.	Dipplett's,	July 7, 1863
"	Fitzpatrick, J. B.	10th Kentucky	"	Whitesburg, Ky.	Gladesville,	July 7, 1863
"	Furguson, W. W.	8th C. Cav.	"	Picksville, Ala.	Shelbyville,	June 27, 1863
Captain	Fellows, J. K.	Beall's Staff	Mississippi	Camden, Arkansas	Port Hudson,	July 9, 1863
"	Foster, J. D.	22d Georgia	Northern Va	Cummington, Ga.	Gettysburg,	July 2, 1863
Lieutenant	Foster, T. J.	10th Tennessee	"	Franklin, Tenn.	"	July 3, 1863
"	Fulkerson, W. B.		Mississippi	Port Gibson, Miss.	Port Hudson,	July 9, 1863
"	Ford, J. W.	1st Florida Cavalry	Tennessee	Gallaghan, Florida	Chattanooga,	Nov. 25, 1863
"	Fraver, Theophilus,	8th Arkansas	"	Jackson Port, Ark.	Stone River,	Dec. 31, 1862
"	Falls, T. D.	5th North Carolina	Northern Va	Shelby, N. C.	Gettysburg,	July 5, 1863
Captain	Fountain, N.	10th Virginia Inf'y	"	Woodstock, Va.	"	July 3, 1863
Lieutenant	Foot, W. W.	10th Tennessee	Mississippi	Nashville, Tenn.	Raymond, Miss	May 12, 1863
"	Fincher, J. C.	43d Georgia	"	Cumming, Georgia	Champe Hill,	May 16, 1863
"	Furgerson, T. B.	14th Alabama	Northern Va	Milltown, Alabama	Gettysburg,	July 2, 1863
"	Farley, J. B.	3d Tennessee	Tennessee	Campbellsville, Tenn	Raymond,	May 12, 1863
Captain	Frank, T. F.	3d Kentucky Cav.	"	" Miss.	Lebanon,	July —, 1863
Lieutenant	Furager, W. M.	Arkansas Regiment	Trans-Miss.	Augusta, Arkansas	Helena,	July 4, 1863
"	Foster, A. C.	Alabama Batt.	Tennessee	Florence, Ala.	Florence,	Dec. 30, 1863
"	Forrester, J. T.	37th North Carolina	Northern Va	Burksboro', N. C.	Gettysburg,	July 3, 1863
"	Frick, W. T. C.	5th Arkansas	Mississippi	Spring Hill, Ark.	Port Hudson,	July 9, 1863
Major	Furgus, W. C.	42d Alabama	Tennessee	Wilmington, N. C.	Shelbyville,	June 27, 1863
Captain	Force, C. F.	51st Alabama Cav.	"	Jacksonville, Ala.	"	June 27, 1863
Lieutenant	Fain, W. J.	"	"	Rogers' Store, Ala[?]	"	June 27, 1863
"	Ferrell, J. E.	30th North Carolina	Northern Va	" N. C.	Nelson Ford,	Nov. 7, 1863
"	Fitzgerald, P. H.	3d Virginia Cav.	"	Blacks & Whites, Va	Brandy Station,	Oct. 11, 1863
"	Furry, J. J.	54th North Carolina	"	Morgantown, N. C.	Rappahannock,	Oct. 7, 1863
Captain	Foster, J. M.	Cooper's Batt	Tennessee	Santa Fe, Texas	Columbia,	Oct. 13, 1863
Lieutenant	Feriner, R. D.	24th S. C.	"	Chester C. H., S. C.	Chickamauga,	Sep. 20, 1863
"	Farr, S.	3d Missouri	Trans-Miss	Canton, Mo.		
"	Ferguson, J. H.	5th Kentucky Cav.	Tennessee	Stamping Ground Ky	Green River,	July 5, 1863
"	Fenwick, C. C. H.	7th Virginia Cav.	Northern Va	Washington, D. C.	C. Springs,	Aug. 5, 1863

Rank.	Name.	Regiment.	Army of	Residence.	Where & When Captured.
Lieutenant..	Farrington, W. O...	15th Arkansas......	Mississippi...	Magnolia, Ark.....	Port Hudson, July 9, 1863
Captain.....	Franklin, J. H......	15th Arkansas......	"	"	" July 9, 1863
Lieutenant..	Foster, K. B.......	10th Arkansas......	"	Stony Point, Ark...	" July 9, 1863
"	Fletcher, J. B......	49th Alabama......	"	New Hope, Ala....	" July 9, 1863
"	Fanas, R. S........	18th Arkansas......	"	Little Rock, Ark...	" July 9, 1863
Lieut.-Col...	Fowler, P.........	14th Arkansas......	"	St. Joseph, Ark....	" July 9, 1863
Lieutenant..	Farris, Wm........	1st Tennessee......	Northern Va..	Talahoma, Tenn....	Gettysburg, July 5, 1863
"	Ford, L. D........	13th Alabama......	"	Roanoke, Ala.....	" July 1, 1863
"	Franklin, S........	15th Georgia.......	"	Elberton, Ga......	" July 1, 1863
Captain.....	Furst, A.*........	8th Arkansas......	Mississippi...	Pine Bluff, Ark....	Port Hudson, July 9, 1863
Lieutenant..	Faulkner, L. G.....	1st Mississippi.....	"	Chalahoma, Miss...	" July 9, 1863
Lieut.-Col..	Fierson, Wm......	27th Tennessee.....	Tennessee...	Shelbyville, Tenn..	Linden, May 12, 1863
Captain.....	Francis, T. H......	4th Tennessee.....	"	Memphis, Tenn.....	Murfreesboro, Jan. 2, 1863
"	Faulkner, J. W.....	1st Mississippi Cav.	Mississippi...	Wall Hill, Miss....	Holly Springs, May 3, 1863
Lieutenant..	Frierson, J. G.....	30th Mississippi.....	Tennessee....	Oxford, Tenn.......	Lookout M't'n, Nov. 24, 1863
"	Fortson, J. A......	Bell's Regiment....	Trans-Miss...	Augusta, Ark......	Helena, July 4, 1863
"	Fonagan, W. N.....	Artillery Regiment.	"	Warrenburg, Mo...	" July 4, 1863
"	Finley, J. T........	7th Missouri........	"	"	" July 4, 1863
"	Fraime, M. C......	7th Missouri........	"	"	" July 4, 1863
"	Frith, C. N........	Miles' Legion......	Mississippi....	Opelousas.........	Port Hudson, July 9, 1863
Major.......	Furgus, W. P......				
Lieutenant..	Famder, W. R.....	15th Tennessee.....	Tennessee...	Bear's Station, Ten.,	Miss'y Ridge, Nov. 25, 1863
Colonel.....	Fight, John A.....	7th Tennessee......	Northern Va..	Carthage, Tenn.....	Gettysburg, July 3, 1863
Captain.....	Farna, James......	2d Tennessee......			Died, Jan. 4, 1864
Lieutenant..	Ferguson, J. W....	5th Kentucky......		Parrotsville, Ky....	
"	Finley, J. H........	36th Virginia......		Clarksville, Va.....	
Captain.....	Farrenholt, B. L...	53d Virginia........		Buchanan, Va......	
Lieutenant..	Ferguson, R........	18th Virginia.......		Leesburg, Va......	
"	Flannagan, W. C...	19th Arkansas......	Mississippi...	Lisbon, Ark........	Mississippi, May 17, 1863
"	Ferell, W. C.......	4th North Carolina..		Wilson, N. C......	

* "Took the oath of allegiance."

Rank	Name	Regiment	Department	Residence	Captured	Date
Lieutenant..	Ferguson, J. H.....	5th Kentucky Cav...	Tennessee...	Stamping Gr'nd, Ky.	Green River,	July 5, 1863
"	Glass, W. P........	55th Georgia.......	"	Warrenville, Ga....	Cumberl'd Gap,	Sep. 9, 1863
Lieut.-Col..	Garnett, W. N......	64th North Carolina	"	Warren Sp'gs, N. C.	"	Sep. 9, 1863
Lieutenant..	Garrett, T. C.......	6th N. C. Cavalry...	"	"	London, Tenn.,	Oct. 20, 1863
Captain.....	Gunn, W. H........	3d Missouri Cav....	Mississippi..	Knoxville, Tenn....	Big Black,	May 17, 1863
Lieutenant..	Gamble, Robert.....	9th Alabama.......	Northern Va.	Helena, Ala........	Gettysburg,	July 2, 1863
"	Gorrice, M. M......	2d Missouri........	Trans-Miss...	Elk Hill, Mo.......	Helena,	July 4, 1863
Captain.....	Graham, W. L......	43d Georgia........	Mississippi...	Cool Mountain, Ga.	Champe Hill,	May 16, 1863
Lieutenant..	Gibson, T. F.......	15th Arkansas.....	"	Ozark, Ark........	Port Gibson,	May 17, 1863
"	Green, J. W........	19th Arkansas.....	"	Camden, Ark......	Big Black,	May 17, 1863
"	Graham, A.........	1st Kentucky Cav...	Tennessee....	Louisville, Ky......	Alexandria,Ten.,	June 4, 1863
"	Goff, E. H.........	7th Louisiana Bat...	Mississippi...	Pine Ridge, Miss...	Port Hudson,	July 9, 1863
"	Glover, B. F.......	9th Louisiana Bat...	Northern Va.	Harperville, Ala....	Rappahannock,	Nov. 7, 1863
Captain.....	Gubbine, James....	5th Louisiana......	"	New Orleans, La ..	"	Nov. 7, 1863
"	Gusman, A. L......	5th Louisiana......	"	Paton Rouge, La...	"	Nov. 2, 1863
"	Guss, M. G........	6th North Carolina.	"	Durham Sta'n, N. C.	"	Nov. 7, 1863
Lieutenant..	Gray, E. G........	54th North Carolina	"	New Castle, N. C...	"	Nov. 7, 1863
"	Gwynn, W.........	10th Arkansas.....	Mississippi...	Stony Point, Ark...	Port Hudson,	July 9, 1863
"	Gray, C. C.........	10th Arkansas.....	"	Clinton, Ark.......	"	July 9, 1863
Captain.....	Galloway, W.......		Tennessee...	Columbia, Tenn....	At Home,	Oct. 7, 1863
"	Gibb, J G..........	30th Mississippi....	"	Grenada, Miss......	Chickamauga,	Sep. 20, 1863
Lieutenant..	Goldsboro, R. H...	Gen. Stuart's Staff..	Northern Va.	Eastern Md........	Chambersburg,	July 2, 1863
Captain.....	Ginevan, M........	18th Virginia Cav...	"	Hampshire Co., Va.	"	July 2, 1863
Lieutenant..	Gillis, Hugh.......	46th Alabama......	Mississippi...	Troy, Ala..........	Champe Hill,	May 16, 1863
"	Giles, J. R.........	15th Arkansas.....	"	Spring Hill, Ark...	Port Hudson,	July 9, 1863
"	Gibson, E. C.......	8th Virginia........	Northern Va.	Snickersville, Va...	Gettysburg,	July 3, 1863
Captain.....	Glover, S. H.......	4th Tennessee Cav..	Tennessee...	Bridgeport, Ala....	Lookout M't'n,	Nov. 20, 1863
Lieutenant..	Gold, J. E.........	24th Tennessee.....	"	Nashville, Tenn....	Miss'y Ridge,	Nov. 24, 1863
"	Glasgow, W. S.....	13th Alabama......	Northern Va.	Greenville, Ala.....	Gettysburg,	July 3, 1863
Colonel.....	Green, W. J.......	Daniel's Brigade....	"	Warrenton, N. C...	South Mountain,	July 6, 1863
Lieutenant..	Gardiner, N. H.....	3d Alabama........	"	Bridgeville, Ala....	Gettysburg,	July 3, 1863
"	Gregory, W........	Bell's Regiment....	Trans-Miss...	Augusta, Ark......	Helena,	July 4, 1863
"	Gilbert, E. M......	6th Missouri........	Mississippi...	Monroe City, Ill....	Big Black,	July 17, 1863
Captain.....	Green, H. P........	1st Missouri........	Trans-Miss...	Ozark, Mo.........	Arkansas,	Aug. 23, 1863

Rank.	Name.	Regiment.	Army of	Residence	Where & When Captured.
Lieutenant..	Gilmer, M........	2d Maryland......	Northern Va.	Baltimore, Md.....	Martinsburg, July 2, 1863
Captain.....	Gillespie, W. W....	2d Tennessee......	Tennessee...	Maryville, Tenn....	Huntsville, Oct. 12, 1863
Adjutant....	Gaston, G. P......	64th N. C........	"	Abbeyville, N. C...	Cumberl'd Gap, Sep. 9, 1863
Lieutenant..	Grigsby, L........	10th Kentucky.....	"	Hazard, Ky........	Gladesville, Va., July 7, 1863
"	Griggs, L. B	10th Georgia......	Northern Va.	Fayetteville, Ga....	Gettysburg, July 5, 1863
"	Gilbert, J. H......	57th N. C........	"	Newtown, N. C....	" July 5, 1863
"	Gibson, E.........	2d Louisiana......	"	Louisville, Ark.....	" July 5, 1863
"	Gray, A. H........	57th N. C........	"	Salisbury, N. C....	" July 5, 1863
"	Gorrill, R. D......	57th N. C........	"	Winston, N. C.....	Rappahannock, Nov. 7, 1863
Colonel.....	Godwin, A C.....	51st N. C........	"	Richmond, Va.....	" Nov. 7, 1863
Captain.....	Gilham, G. H.....	52d N. C........	"	Edenton, N C.....	Gettysburg, July 3, 1863
"	Grace, W. L.......	1st Tennessee Cav..	"	Pikesville, Tenn....	Greenville, July 3, 1863
"	Gammon, S. R....	60th Tennessee.....	Mississippi...	Rogersville, Tenn..	B. B. River, May 11, 1863
Colonel.....	George, J. L......	— Mississippi Cav...	"	Carrollton, Miss....	At home, Nov. 3, 1863
Major.......	Ghee, J. J........	4th Mississippi.....	"	Carrollton, Miss....	B. B. River, May 17, 1863
Lieutenant..	Guyton, D. S......	40th Mississippi....	"	Bluff Springs, Miss.	" May 17, 1863
"	Gilmer, J W......	1st Bat. Md. Cav...	"	Rienza, Miss.......	Rienza, Miss., April 13, 1863
"	Gaillard, R........	1st Alabama.......	"	Camden, Ala......	Port Hudson, July 9, 1863
Lieut.-Col...	Griggs M.........	60th Tennessee.....	"	Rogersville, Tenn..	Big Black May 17, 1863
Lieutenant..	Gowen, W. B......	30th Alabama......	"	Chalcauga, Ala.....	Champe Hill, May 16, 1863
Captain.....	Griffin, B.........	1st Tennessee......	Tennessee...	Clarksville, Tenn...	Franklin, April 27, 1863
Lieutenant..	Gerry, L. B.......	3d Virginia........	Northern Va.	Deep Creek, Va....	Gettysburg, July 3, 1863
"	Gillock J. W.. ..	27th Virginia......	"	Lexington, Va.....	" July 5, 1863
"	Gwynn, H........	9th Virginia.......	"	Columbia, S. C....	" July 3, 1863
"	Gallon, J. B.......	39th Mississippi....	Mississippi...	Smithville, Miss....	Port Hudson, July 9, 1863
Captain.....	Gardner, R. W.....	5th Florida........	Northern Va.	Tallahassee, Fla....	Gettysburg, July 4, 1863
Lieutenant..	Garig, Wm........	9th La. Bat. Cav....	Mississippi...	Baton Rouge, La...	Port Hudson, July 9, 1863
"	Givins, L. W......	8th Florida........	"	Sansa, Fla.........	" July 9, 1863
"	Guma, John A.....	39th Mississippi....	"	Jackson, Miss......	" July 9, 1863
"	Galloway, J. S.....	62d N. C.........	Tennessee...	High Top, N. C....	Cumberl'd Gap, Sep. 9, 1863
"	Grigsby, M. G.....	5th Kentucky Cav..	"	Ringed Road, Ky...	Green River, Sept. 9, 1863

Captain.....	Gay, J. S............	8th Kentucky Cav..	Tennessee....	Winchester, Ky.....	Salicville, Ohio, July 26, 1863
Lieutenant..	Garrard, A. T......	39th Mississippi....	Mississippi...	Georgetown, Miss..	Port Hudson, July 9, 1863
"	Garrett, George....	1st Tennessee......	Northern Va..	Lincoln Co., Tenn..	Gettysburg, July 5, 1863
"	Googen, M. D. H...	49th Georgia......	"	Crawfordsville, Ga..	" July 2, 1863
"	Gowdlett, D. T......	1st Alabama Art...	Mississippi...	Jacksonville, Ala...	Port Hudson, July 9, 1863
"	Grant, J. C........	1st Tennessee......	Northern Va..	Lincoln Co., Tenn..	Gettysburg, July 1, 1863
"	Griffin, S. H.......	18th Mississippi.....	"	Sulphur Sp'gs, Miss.	Cashtown, Pa., July 5, 1863
"	Goodbread, J. P. B..	4th Florida.........	Tennessee....	White Springs, Fla.	Miss'y Ridge, Nov. 25, 1863
"	Gordon, R. H.......	Wheeler's Scouts...	"	Columbia, Tenn....	R. Springs, Oct. 29, 1863
"	Gentry, L. C.......	20th N. C.........	"	Jefferson, N. C.....	
"	Goldsberry, W. E...	20th N. C.........	"	Haynes' Creek, N. C	
"	Glenn, J. B.........	18th Virginia......	Northern Va..	Prospect, Va.......	Beverley Ford, July 9, 1863
Captain.....	Grabill, J. H.......	35th Va. Bat. Cav...	"	Woodstock, Va.....	" July 9, 1863
Lieutenant..	Grimshaw, H.......	1st Louisiana......	"	New Orleans, La...	Rappahannock, Nov. 7, 1863
"	Garring, G.........	1st Louisiana......	"	Baton Rouge.......	" Nov. 7, 1863
"	Gibson, J. W.......	1st Kentucky Cav..	Tennessee....	Mount Sterling, Ky.	Shelbyville, Oct. 7, 1863
"	Green, R. P.......	Morgan's Cav......	"	Paris, Ky..........	" Oct. 7, 1863
"	Green, C...........	1st Louisiana......	Northern Va..	New Orleans, La...	Rappahannock, Nov. 7, 1863
"	Gale, D. D.........	3d Virginia Cav....	"	Virginia...........	Gettysburg, July 3, 1863
"	Guerrant, S. P.....	14th Virginia......	"	Meadsville, Va.....	" July 3, 1863
"	Gunnells, W. M....	3d S. C. Batt.......	"	Laurens C. H., S. C..	" July 5, 1863
"	Godwin, A. L.....	32d Alabama......	Tennessee....	Tallahassee, Fla ...	Miss'y Ridge, Nov. 25, 1863
"	Grason, H. C......	1st Kentucky Cav...	"	Mount Sterling, Ky.	Shelbyville, Oct. 7, 1863
Lieut.-Col...	George, M. J.......	1st Tenn...........	Northern Va..	George's Store, Ten	Gettysburg, July 3, 1863
Lieutenant..	Griffin, J. R.......	1st Louisiana Cav..	Tennessee....	Simsport, La.......	Lincolnton, Aug. 1, 1863
"	Gleeson, T. H......	3d Virginia........	Northern Va..	Portsmouth, Va....	Gettysburg, July 3, 1863
"	Gill, S P...........	41st N. C..........	"	Franklinton, N. C...	" July 3, 1863
"	Gibson, J. R.......	8th Missouri........	Trans-Miss..	Warsaw, Mo.......	Helena, July 4, 1863
"	Girard, E..........	38th Alabama......	Tennessee....	Mobile, Ala........	Miss'y Ridge, Nov. 25, 1863
"	Gibbon, W. R.....	38th Alabama......	"	Coperlaw, Ala......	" Nov. 25, 1863
"	Gurley, T. P.......	4th Alabama Cav..	"	Maskville, Ala......	Huntsville, Oct. 20, 1863
Captain.....	Griffith, J. R.......	10th Arkansas.....	Mississippi...	Goodhope, Ark....	Port Hudson, July 9, 1863
Lieutenant..	Grayson, W. C.....	49th Alabama......	"	New Hope, Ark....	" July 9, 1863
"	Green, H. H.......	28th Alabama......	Tennessee....	Blount Co., Ark....	Lookout M't'n, Nov. 24, 1863

Rank.	Name.	Regiment.	Army of	Residence.	Where & When Captured.
Captain	Griffin, H. B.	21st Mississippi	Tennessee	Pargegola, Miss.	Miss'y Ridge, Nov. 25, 1863
Lieutenant	Gilbert, A. S.	28th Alabama	"	Eutaw, Ala.	Lookout M't'n, Nov. 25, 1863
Captain	Gilbert, L. E.	28th "	"	"	" Nov. 25, 1863
Lieutenant	Grayson, J. W.	21st Mississippi	"	Ellesville, Miss.	" Nov. 25, 1863
"	Green, Thomas	5th Texas	"	Port Lafaco, Texas	" Nov. 25, 1863
"	Garrard, A. S.	39th Mississippi	Mississippi	Bearder, Miss.	Port Hudson, July 9, 1863
"	Gwin, J. T.	24th Mississippi	Tennessee	Dekalb, Miss.	Lookout M't'n, Nov. 24, 1863
"	Green, W. A.	1st Miss. Artillery	Mississippi	Port Gibson, Miss.	Port Hudson, July 9, 1863
"	Gibbon, J. W.	22d Mississippi	"	Rodney, Miss.	Vicksburg, June 1, 1863
Colonel	Granberry, J. G.	N C. Militia	Northern Va.	Edenton, N. C.	Gettysburg, July 3, 1863
Lieutenant	Graham, S. R.	3d Texas Cavalry	Tennessee		
"	Gash, J. B.	62d North Carolina	"		
"	Gentry, L C.	20th S. C. C.	Northern Va.	South Carolina	Gettysburg, July 4, 1863
"	Goldsby, W. E.	21st North Carolina	"	Harris Creek, N. C.	Williamsport, July 14, 1863
Captain	Gregory, J. M.	9th Virginia	"	Portsmouth, Va.	1863
Lieutenant	Garrison, A.	9th "	"	Norfolk, Va.	Lookout M't'n, Nov. 25, 1863
Captain	Graves, J.	22d North Carolina	"	Yanceyville, N. C.	
"	Goff, J. B.	2d Va. Sharpshoot'rs	"	Louisa, Ky.	
"	Griggard, W. B.	Green's Battalion		Fountainton, Tenn.	
Lieut.-Col.	Graves, J. A.	47th North Carolina		Yanceyville, N. C.	
Major	Gholston, J. O.	16th Georgia		Danielsville, Ga.?	
Lieutenant	Gammond, W. M.	60th Tennessee		Jonesboro, Tenn.	
Captain	Glenn, W. H.	3d Missouri Cav		Harrison's, Mo.	
"	Gathright, J. R.	Candy Rear (?)		Davisville, Ky.	
Lieutenant	Heuson, L.	16th Georgia	Tennessee	St. Cloud, Ga.	Blountsville, Sept. 20, 1863
"	Hartsell, J. J.	64th North Carolina	"	Jonesboro, Tenn.	Cumberl'd Gap, Sept. 9, 1863
"	Howard, R.	64th "	"	Henders'nville, N.C.	" Sept 9, 1863
Captain	Hardman, W. H.	55th Georgia	"	Lawrenceville, Ga.	" Sept. 9, 1863
Lieutenant	Heard, C.	8th Georgia	Northern Va.	Greensburg, Ga.	Gettysburg, July 5, 1863
"	Hourshan, W.	Miles' Legion	Mississippi	Natchez, Miss.	Port Hudson, July 9, 1863
"	Hogan, Alex.	7th Tennessee	Northern Va.	Nashville, Tenn.	Gettysburg, July 4, 1863

Lieutenant..	Hendricks, J. D....	48th Mississippi.....	Northern Va.	Big Creek, Miss.....	Fredericksb'g, June 5, 1863
"	Hicks, J. R..........	A. D. C............	Tennessee....	Paris, Tenn........	Cleveland, Sept. 12, 1863
"	Holton, E. H.......	8th Arkansas.......	"	Covington, Ky.....	Chickamauga, Sept. 19, 1863
"	Houston, H. W.....	4th Con. Cavalry...	"	Natural Bridge, Ky.	" Sept. 19, 1863
Captain.....	Hatchcraft, J. L.....	A. D. C............	"	North Middlet'n, Ky	Harrison, March 20, 1863
Lieutenant..	Haley, Frank	26th Alabama.....	Northern Va.	Fayette C. H., Va...	Gettysburg, July 1, 1863
"	Hutchinson, J. L....	8th Virginia Cav....	"	Aldie, Va..........	" July 3, 1863
"	Harper, G. W......	5th Tenn. Cavalry..	Tennessee ...	Newport, Tenn.....	Willisburg, August 2, 1863
"	Holt, E. A.........	38th Alabama......	Northern Va.	Mobile, Ala........	Miss'y Ridge, Nov. 25, 1863
Major......	Hall, W. C.........	A. A. G...........	"	Baltimore, Md......	Gettysburg, July 3, 1863
Adjutant....	Hollingsworth, T...	5th Virginia Cav....	"	"	Maryland, July 8, 1863
Lieutenant..	Hudgins, L. M.....	C. S. N............		Mathews C. H., Va..	Hanover co.Va. June 28, 1863
Lieut.-Col...	Humphries, J. C....	7th Mississippi.....	Mississippi...	Port Gibson, Miss..	Port Gibson, July 1, 1863
Adjutant....	Haywood, F. J.....	5th North Carolina.	Northern Va.	Raleigh, N. C......	Gettysburg, July 4 1863
Lieutenant..	Have, Peter.......	6th Louisiana......	"	New Orleans, La...	Rappahannock, Nov. 7, 1863
"	Harring, J. A......	9th "	"	Vicksburg, Miss....	" Nov. 7, 1863
"	Holmes, P. S......	9th "	"	Mansfield, La.....	" Nov. 7, 1863
"	Harris, J. M.......	26th North Carolina.	"	Poplar Bridge, N. C.	Bristoe Station, Oct. 14, 1863
"	Hinchey, G. H.....	8th Louisiana......	"	New Orleans, La...	Rappahannock, Nov. 7, 1863
Adjutant....	Heath, E. M.......	20th Texas.........	Mississippi...	Buckman, Texas...	Holly Springs, July 17, 1863
Captain.....	Heath, B..........	10th Missouri......	Trans-Miss...	Hickory Sp'gs., Mo.	Helena, July 4, 1863
Lieutenant..	Hartsville, A. M....	4th Georgia........	Tennessee....	Unionville, Ga.....	Miss'y Ridge, Nov. 25, 1863
Captain.....	Harper, R. L......	5th Texas..........	Northern Va.	Mortington, Texas..	Gettysburg, July 2, 1863
"	Hubert, R. R	5th "	"	Mayorsville, Texas.	" July 2, 1863
Lieutenant..	Hicks, F. Y........	49th North Carolina.	"	Camp Call, N. C...	Sandridge, April 20, 1863
"	Hanner, C. H.......	26th "	"	Goldston, N. C.....	Gettysburg, July 5, 1863
"	Hart, G. W........	46th Tennessee.....	Mississippi...	Paris, Tenn........	Waraly, May 1, 1863
"	Horn, H...........	28th Florida.......	Tennessee....	Sparta, Tenn.......	Hillsboro, July 28, 1863
"	Hanford, A. W.....	16th Louisiana......	"	Springfield, La.....	Middle Tenn.. May 6, 1863
"	Hearod, B.........	9th Arkansas......	Mississippi...	Laurel Gap, Ark...	Big Black, May 17, 1863
"	Howard, R. J......	1st Missouri.......	"	Bihala, Miss.......	Port Hudson, July 9, 1863
"	Harris, G. L.......	56th Georgia......	"	Carlton, Ga........	Champe Hill, May 17, 1863
Captain....	Hall, J. J..........	56th Georgia......	"	Augusta, Ark......	Helena, July 4, 1863
Lieutenant..	Hart, G. M........	16th South Carolina.	Tennessee....	Greenville, S. C....	Griggsville, Nov. 25, 1863

Rank.	Name.	Regiment.	Army of	Residence.	Where & When Captured.
Captain	Hogg, George	10th Kentucky	Tennessee	Whitesburg, Ky.	Glendale, July 7, 1863
"	Hord, J. C.	11th Virginia	Northern Va.	Lynchburg, Va.	Gettysburg, July 5, 1863
"	Hayes, A.	10th Kentucky	Tennessee	Whitesburg, Ky.	Glendale, July 7, 1863
Lieutenant	Hall, R. M.	4th Florida	"	Applepie, Fla.	Miss'y Ridge, Nov. 25, 1863
Captain	Herley, J. D.	18th Arkansas			
"	Hodge, J. R.	51st Tennessee			
Lieutenant	Hunsacker, J.				
"	Holston, T. A.	2d Virginia Cav.	Northern Va.		
"	Hackworth, N. N.	3d Kentucky	Tennessee		
"	Hudson, N. J.	2d N. Carolina Batt.	"		
"	Hanes, W. A.	51st Georgia	"		
"	Harden, W. P.	5th North Carolina	Northern Va.		
"	Harry, S. W.	9th Tennessee Cav.	Tennessee		
"	Howard, J. C.	2d " "	"	Morgan, Tenn.	Shelbyville, October 8, 1863
"	Holt, W. S.	15th Tennessee	"	Nashville, Tenn.	" October 26, 1863
Captain	Hannant, J. A.	12th South Carolina	Northern Va.	Waynesboro, S. C.	Gettysburg, July 5, 1863
"	Hayner, A. S.	11th North Carolina	"	Lincolnton, N. C.	" July 5, 1863
Lieutenant	Hampton, J. N.	16th Arkansas	Mississippi	Pekin, Ark.	Port Hudson, July 9, 1863
"	Hickson, M.	"	"	Shell Creek, Ark.	" July 9, 1863
Captain	Hamilton, J. E.	2d Choctaw Reg't	Trans-Miss.	Eagleton, Choctaw N	Perryville, August 26, 1863
Lieutenant	Haliburton, W.	Freeman's Batt.	"	Lint County, Mo.	Evening Shade, Oct. 7, 1863
Captain	Howard, R. G.	21st South Carolina	S. Carolina	Florence, S. C.	Morris Island, July 10, 1863
Lieutenant	Hundley, J. W.	13th Arkansas	Mississippi	Blancerville, Ark.	Port Hudson, July 9, 1863
"	Hinch, T. H.	2d Tennessee Cav.	Tennessee	Armstore, Ark.	Huntsville, August 12, 1863
"	Houre, J. M.	C. S. A.	"	Kuskville, Tenn.	Miss'y Ridge, Nov. 25, 1863
Captain	Howard, C. A.	14th Tennessee Cav.	"	Newberne, Tenn.(?)	Duck River, May 30, 1863
Lieutenant	Heslip, J. A.	4th Alabama Batt.	"	Harrison's St'e, Tenn	Fort Pillow, June 8, 1863
Captain	Hallard, J. A.	18th Virginia	Northern Va.	Danville, Va.	Gettysburg, July 1, 1863
Lieutenant	High, W. S.	Bell's Ark. Reg't	Trans-Miss.	Boorisville, Ark.	Helena, July 4, 1863
"	Hamilton, R. A.	64th North Carolina	Tennessee	Columbia, N. C.	Fishing Creek, June 26, 1863
Adjutant	Howard, J. A.	7th Tennessee	Northern Va.	Lebanon, Tenn.	Gettysburg, July 3, 1863

Adjutant....	Houston, T. D.....	11th Virginia.......	Northern Va.	Natural Bridge, Va..	Gettysburg,	July 3, 1863
"	Hale, M. C........	Alabama Batt......	Tennessee...	Montgomery, Ala..	Tennessee,	May 2, 1863
Lieut.-Col..	Hoffman, J. M.....	2d Kentucky Cav...	"	Plains, Texas......	Ohio,	July 19, 1863
Lieutenant..	Henson, W. R.....	2d Missouri Cav....	Mississippi...	Patton, Missouri....	Salem,	April 4, 1863
"	Hail, T. B.........	1st Arkansas Batt...	"	Powhatan, Ark.....	Port Hudson,	July 9, 1863
"	Holt, A. B.........	1st C. Cavalry.....	Tennessee...	Columbus, Ga.....	Linden,	May 17, 1863
"	Haggard, R........	7th Kentucky Cav..	"	Winchester, Ky....	Ohio,	July 26, 1863
"	Hays, J. G........	15th Tennessee Cav.	"	Nashville, Tenn....	Sugar Creek,	Oct. 19, 1863
"	Haycroft. J........	4th Kentucky Cav..	"	Elizabethtown, Ky.	Lexington,	June 15, 1863
"	Hanel, J. F........	48th Georgia......	Northern Va.	Augusta, Ga......	Millertown,	July 6, 1863
"	Hack, J. W........	9th Virginia.......	"	Pungoteague, Va...	Gettysburg,	July 3, 1863
Captain.....	Haley, W.........	24th Tennessee.....	Tennessee...	Lafayette, Tenn....	Cumberl'd River,	Mar. 14 1863
Lieutenant..	Herbert, A. M.....	5th Alabama......	Northern Va.	Waynesville, Ala...	Gettysburg,	July 1, 1863
"	Hester H. T.......	11th Mississippi....	"	Herbilt, Miss......	"	July 3, 1863
"	Holland, H........	28th Virginia......	"	Liberty, Tenn......	"	July 2, 1863
"	Howe, J. T........	4th "	"	Blacksburg, Va.....	"	July 3, 1863
"	Hutchinson, H. R..	4th Arkansas......	Mississippi...	Gellinck, Ark......	Port Hudson,	July 9, 1863
"	Hardy, James......	12th Arkansas.....	"	Oakland, Ark......	"	July 9, 1863
"	Hughes, R. J......	12th Louisiana....	"	New Orleans, La...	"	July 9, 1863
Colonel.....	Holman, J. H.....	12th "	"	Fayetteville, Tenn..	Winchester,	Sept. 28, 1863
"	Harris, E. B......	1st Alabama.......	"	Cockport, Ala......	Port Hudson,	July 9, 1863
Lieut.-Col..	Hargrove, J. L.....	44th North Carolina.	Northern Va.	Oxford, N. C......	South Arm Ridge,	June 6, 1863
Captain.....	Hartsfield, W. W...	13th Georgia......	"	Thompson, Ga.....	Gettysburg,	July 4, 1863
"	Hawkins, H. J.....	1st Tennessee......	"	Cowan, Tenn......	"	July 3, 1863
Lieutenant..	Harwood, J.......	53d Virginia.......	"	Charles City Co., Va.	"	July 5, 1863
"	Haskin, C. H......	C. S. N..........	S. Carolina...	Petersburg, Va.....	Charles'n Harbor,	July 7, 1863
Lieut.-Col...	Hansburg, S. Z.....	15th Georgia......	Northern Va.	Lincoln County, Ga.	Gettysburg,	July 1, 1863
Lieutenant..	Hill, S. P.........	6th North Carolina..	"	Yanceyville, N. C...	Rappahannock,	Nov. 7, 1863
Captain.....	Heron, A. J.......	1st Mississippi Art..	Mississippi...	Yazoo City, Miss...	Port Hudson,	July 9, 1863
Lieutenant..	Hughes, J. T......	26th Georgia......	Northern Va.	Milledgeville, Ga...	Pennsylvania,	July 5, 1863
"	Hughes, J. T......	49th "	"	Wilkinson Co., Ga..	Gettysburg,	July 2, 1863
"	Holder, W.........	9th Louisiana.....	Mississippi...	St. Helena, La.....	Port Hudson,	July 9, 1863
"	Hurt, B. H. N......	5th Texas.........	Northern Va.	Cistern, Texas.....	Gettysburg,	July 2, 1863
"	Hoye, M. J. L......	39th Mississippi....	Mississippi...	Decatur, Miss......	Port Hudson,	July 9, 1863

Rank.	Name.	Regiment.	Army of	Residence.	Where & When Captured.
Captain	Huzzard, J. B.	24th Alabama	Tennessee	Mobile, Ala	Miss'y Ridge, Nov. 25, 1863
Lieutenant	Hutchinson, E. L.	1st Florida Cavalry	"	Maneta co., Florida	" Nov. 25, 1863
"	Harris, A. A.	2d Kentucky Cav.	"	Franklin, Kentucky	At Home, Nov. 25, 1863
Captain	Helms, W. T.	1st Tennessee	"	Winchester, Tenn.	" July 17, 1863
Lieutenant	Hurt, J. H.	12th Virginia Cav.	Northern Va.	Charlestown, Va.	Brandy Station, July 9, 1863
Captain	Hardy, W. B.	Fitts' Batt.	"	Saluda, Va.	Middlesex co, Va. May 22, 1863
Lieutenant	Hegward, D. G.	Beauregard's (?)	So'th Carolina	Charleston, S. C.	Morris' Island, July 22, 1863
"	Harmon, A. W.	1st Florida	Mississippi	Daydesville, Ala.	Port Hudson, July 9, 1863
"	Harris, O. C.	18th Alabama	Tennessee	Bridgetown, Ala.	Miss'y Ridge, Nov. 25, 1863
"	Hollowman, J. F.	58th Alabama	"	Fayetteville C.H., Va	" Nov. 25, 1863
Major	Henegard, C. S.	36th Alabama	"	Gainesville, Ala.	" Nov. 25, 1863
Lieutenant	Holley, J. E.	3d Mississippi Cav.	"	Hermont, Miss.	" Nov. 25, 1863
Captain	Harding, J.	1st Kentucky Cav.	"	Kentonton, Ky.	Shelbyville, Oct. 2, 1863
Lieutenant	Harrison, Thos. R.	A. D. C.	Northern Va.	Richmond, Va.	Gettysburg, July 4, 1863
Captain	Harris, J. M.	3d S. C. Batt.	"	Abbeyville Dis., S.C.	Hagerstown, July 14, 1863
"	Harper, W. P.	7th La.	"	New Orleans, La.	Rappahannock, Nov. 7, 1863
Lieutenant	Henry, A. W.	14th Tennessee	Tennessee	Perryville, Tenn.	" Nov. 7, 1863
"	Howell, W. G.	6th Mississippi	Mississippi	Westerville, Miss.	Port Gibson, May 1, 1863
Captain	Hainess, A. F.	22d Virginia	Northern Va.	King Wm co., Va.	Falling Water, July 14, 1863
Lieutenant	Harber, T. B.	9th Louisiana	Mississippi	New Orleans, La.	Port Hudson, July 9, 1863
Captain	Hunter, F. C. S.	30th Virginia	Northern Va.	King George C.H, Va	King George co. Aug. 24, 1863
"	Herd, J. W.	1st Maryland Cav.	"	Frederick City, Md.	Frederick City.
Lieutenant	Hall, J. B.	15th Virginia Cav.	"	Westmoreland co. Va	Culpeper C. H., Sep. 13, 1863
Captain	Hooper, R. S.	54th North Carolina	"	Giffonsville, N. C.	Rappahannock, June 7, 1863
Lieutenant	Hickman, A. H.	"	'	Giffin, N. C.	Pennsylvania, Oct. 20, 1863
"	Henderson, F.	3d Tennessee	Tennessee	Lawrenceburg, N.C.	Mississippi, Oct. 16, 1863
"	Horton, N.	37th North Carolina	Northern Va.	Boone, N. C.	Gettysburg, July 3, 1863
"	Hailey, —	— Tennessee	Tennessee	Springfield, Georgia	Miss'y Ridge, Nov. 25, 1863
"	Hall, W. J.	22d Georgia	Northern Va.	Kinston, N. C.	Gettysburg, July 2, 1863
"	Hickman, J. A.	Arkansas Cavalry	Mississippi	Rockhill, Ark.	Big Black, May 17, 1863
Major	Hanley, J. M.	46th Alabama	"	Lafayette, Alabama	Champe Hill, May 16, 1863

Rank	Name	Regiment	Army	Residence	Place	Date
Lieut.-Col.	Herbert, J. R.	1st Maryland Batt.	Northern Va.	Baltimore, Md.	Gettysburg,	July 4, 1863
Captain	Hodge, J. C.	60th Tennessee	Mississippi	Morristown, Tenn.	Vicksburg,	May 17, 1863
Lieutenant	Huffstuttler, ——	1st Arkansas				
Captain	Henry, S. W.	9th Tennessee	Mississippi			
Lieutenant	Hammond, ——	4th Tennessee	Tennessee			Nov. 26, 1863
"	Handley, A. M. J.	10th Missouri	Trans-Miss.	Ridgely, Missouri	Helena, Ark.,	July 4, 1863
Adjutant	Hope, R. A.	10th "	Tennessee	Rockport, Missouri	Gladesville,	July 10, 1863
Lieutenant	Hurlbert, H. A.	10th "	Trans-Miss.	Cleavesville, "	Helena,	July 4, 1863
"	Hicks, J. D.	10th "	"	Roanoke, Missouri	"	July 4, 1863
"	Harper, J. B.	27th Tennessee	Tennessee	Union City, Tenn.	Harsby, Tenn.,	July 4, 1863
"	Herren, J. W.	1st Arkansas	Mississippi	Hamburg, Arkansas	Port Hudson,	July 9, 1863
"	Henton, W.	12th "	"	Richmond, Arkansas	"	July 9, 1863
"	Horton, W. H.	14th "	"	Big Flat, Arkansas	"	July 9, 1863
"	Hatch, G.	8th Alabama	Northern Va.	Greenville, Alabama	Gettysburg.	July 3, 1863
"	Hughes, A. J.	1st Batt. Arkansas	Mississippi	Nashville, Tenn.	Port Hudson,	July 9, 1863
"	Hoffman, J.	14th "	"	Rock Fish, Ark.	"	July 9, 1863
"	Hoye, M. J. L.	39th Mississippi	"	Decatur, Mississippi	"	July 9, 1863
"	Hudspeth, J. B.	24th "	Tennessee	Woodlong, Miss.	Lookout M't'n,	Nov. 24, 1863
"	Hannah, T. L.	27th "	"	Whitfield, Miss.	"	Nov. 24, 1863
"	Hall, J. W.	2d Florida	Northern Va.	Jasper, Florida	Gettysburg,	July 4, 1863
Captain	Hogges, J. F.	2d North Carolina	"	Ayresville, N. C.	"	July 5, 1863
Lieutenant	Hill, J. T.	2d Georgia	"	Florence, Georgia	Green Castle, Pa,	July 5, 1863
"	Hudgins, J. J.	20th North Carolina	"	Fairson, N. C.	Gettysburg, Pa.,	July 1, 1863
"	Hyde, W. A.	26th Alabama	"	Sheffield, Alabama	"	July 1, 1863
"	Hayes, J. W.	2d Kentucky	Tennessee	Clinton, Kentucky	Murfreesboro',	July 4, 1863
"	Herndon, A. S.	14th Tennessee	Northern Va.	Clarksville, Tenn.	Gettysburg,	July 4, 1863
Captain	Hicks, L. T.	20th North Carolina	"	Fairson, N. C.	"	July 1, 1863
Lieutenant	Hagler, W. J.	14th Tennessee	"	Fort Donelson, Tenn	"	July 1, 1863
"	Harris, S. J.	38th Virginia	"	Pittsylvania C. H., Va	"	July 3, 1863
"	Hayes, C. W.	2d Missouri	Mississippi	Jackson, Mississippi	Clinton,	July 16, 1863
Major	Hancock, J. W.	2d N. C. Batt.	Northern Va.	Ashborough, N. C.	Gettysburg,	July 4, 1863
Captain	Haggard, W. B.	44th Georgia	"	Walkersville, Ga.	Hagerstown,	July 12, 1863
Colonel	Harman, A. W.	12th Virginia Cav.	"	Staunton, Va.	Harper's Ferry,	July 4, 1863
Lieutenant	Harry, L. E.	Robertson's Staff	"	Powhatan, Va.	Gettysburg,	July 4, 1863

Rank.	Name.	Regiment.	Army of	Residence.	Where & When Captured.
Lieutenant.	Horner, J. K.	8th Tennessee	Tennessee	Florenceburg, Ala.	Lexington, May 27, 1863
"	Houston, R. M.	22d Missouri	"	Moss Spring, Miss.	Vicksburg, June 1, 1863
Adjutant.	Hickman, W. D.	10th Arkansas	"	Perryville, Ark.	Port Hudson, July 9, 1863
Lieutenant.	Hooker, T. B.	25th Arkansas	Mississippi	Clarendon, Ark.	" July 9, 1863
Captain.	Henry, P.	49th Alabama	"	Henryville, Ala.	" July 9, 1863
Lieutenant.	Howty, J. H.	32d Alabama	Tennessee	McKinley, Ala.	Miss'y Ridge, Nov. 25, 1863
Captain.	Hopkins, F. M.	28th Alabama	"	Summerfield, Ala.	" " 1863
"	Hayer, S. C.	16th Arkansas	Mississippi	Indian Nation, Ark.	Port Hudson, July 9, 1863
Lieutenant.	Heath, H. N.	Glen's Regiment.	Trans-Miss.	Searcey, Ark.	Helena, July 4, 1863
"	Harrison, W. J.	Glen's Regiment.	"	Springfield, Ark.	" July 4, 1863
Captain.	Holt, B.	10th Missouri.	"	Mountain Store, Mo	" July 4, 1863
Lieutenant.	Hudson, G. W.	Haye's Regiment.	"	Gordonsville, Ark.	" July 4, 1863
"	Hudson, J.	Haye's Regiment.	"	Jacksonport, Ark.	" July 4, 1863
"	Harwood, J. S.	10th C. Cav.	Tennessee	Lawrence Hill, Ga.	Lancaster, Ky., July 30, 1863
"	Hale, M. B.	Bell's Ark. Reg't.	Trans-Miss.	Searcey, Ark.	Helena, July 4, 1863
"	Howard, J. L.				
"	Haley, J. W.	45th Tennessee	Tennessee	Lawrence, Tenn.	Miss'y Ridge, Nov. 25, 1863
"	Hall, Jacob.	45th Tennessee	"	Murfreesboro', Tenn	" Nov. 25, 1863
"	Hill, J. T.	37th Alabama	"	Milton, Ala.	" Nov. 25, 1863
"	Hamilton, J. W.				
Captain	Henson, J. R.	12th Missouri.	Trans-Miss.	Paton, Mo.	Summerville, Nov. 2, 1863
Lieutenant.	Harding, R. A.	Faulkner's Ky. Cav.	"	Mayfield, Ky.	Bridgeville, Dec. 15, 1863
"	Hendricks, J. L.	10th C. Cav.	Tennessee	Silver Run, Ala.	Somerset, Ky., Aug 30, 1863
"	Heard, Columbus.	—— Georgia Reg't.			
"	Hall, J. W.	22d Georgia.			
Colonel.	Hamilton, A. S.	1st Mississippi	Mississippi	Monerville, Miss.	Port Hudson, July 9, 1863
Lieutenant.	High, J. Q.				
Captain.	Heamstead, Beall.	A. A. G.	Mississippi	Little Rock, Ark.	Port Hudson, July 9, 1863
"	Hale, J. A.	Bell's Ark. Reg't.	Tennessee	Augusta, Ark.	Helena, July 4, 1863
Lieutenant.	Heggie, J. T.	—— Tenn. Reg't.		Camden, Tenn.	
Captain.	Hare, F. M.	5th Arkansas		Whitesburg, Ark.	

Lieutenant..	Hall, C. W	34th Mississippi.....	....	Rockford, Miss.....	
"	Houston, John......	1st Arkansas.......	Mississippi...	Powhatan, Ark.....	Ripley's Creek, Dec. 25, 1863
Major.......	Hill, W. J.........	5th North Carolina.	Northern Va.	Gatesville, N. C....	Gatesville, June 5, 1863
Lieutenant..	Irwin, J. R........	5th Tennessee......	"	Morgansville, Tenn.	Gettysburg, July 2, 1863
Captain.....	Isbell, R. H.......	1st Alabama.......	Mississippi...	Talladega, Ala.....	Port Hudson, July 9, 1863
"	Ingram, James.....	Staff.............	Tennessee...	Henderson, Ky.....	Kentucky, June 1, 1863
Lieut.-Col..	Inzen, J. M........	32d Alabama......	"	Asheville, Ala.....	Miss'y Ridge, Nov. 25, 1863
Captain.....	Inge, J. E.........	12th Arkansas.....	Mississippi...	St. Clair, Mo.......	Port Hudson, July 9, 1863
Lieutenant..	Inge, J. A.........	31st Tennessee.....	Tennessee...	....	Ellis' Mill, Nov 26, 1863
"	Ivey, D. L.........	55th Georgia......	"	Byumville, Ga......	Cumberl'd Gap, Sept 9, 1863
"	Icard, H A........	49th Alabama.....	Mississippi...	New Hope, Ala....	Port Hudson, July 9, 1863
"	Ingram, J. C.......	7th Tennessee.....	Northern Va.	Lebanon, Tenn.....	Gettysburg, July 5, 1863
Captain.....	Imboden, James....	1st Arkansas Batt...	Mississippi...	Lake Village, Ark..	Port Hudson, July 9 1863
Lieutenant..	Inman, A. A.......	18th North Carolina.	"	Leesville, N. C....	
"	Jones, W. B........	64th North Carolina.	Tennessee...	Greenville, Tenn...	Cumberl'd Gap, Sept. 9, 1863
Captain.....	Jones, T. F........	16th Georgia Cav...	"	Cartersville, Ga....	Brownsville, Sept. 27, 1863
Colonel.....	Johnson, B. W.....	15th Arkansas......	Mississippi...	Magnolia, Ark......	Port Hudson, July 9, 1863
Lieutenant..	Jordan, W. C. S ...	10th Virginia Cav...	Northern Va.	Milboro' Springs, Va	McConnelsb'g, June 23, 1863
Captain. ...	Jones, A J........	11th Virginia......	"	Moonsville, Va.....	Gettysburg July 3, 1863
Adjutant....	Jordan, H. F.......	55th North Carolina	"	Rocksboro', N. C...	" July 1, 1863
Captain.....	Jordan, C. L.......	5th Texas Cavalry..	Trans-Miss...	Weatherford, Texas	Fort Butler, June 28, 1863
Lieutenant..	Joyner, J. S........	47th North Carolina.	Northern Va.	Frankterton, N. C..	Gettysburg, July 3, 1863
Captain.....	Johnson, R. G......	8th Missouri........	Trans-Miss...	Harrisonville, Mo...	Helena, July 4, 1863
Lieutenant..	Jones, F. M........	23d Alabama.......	"	Mt. Pleasant, Ala...	Champe Hill, May 17, 1863
"	Johnson, J. G......	62d Tennessee......	"	London, Tenn......	Big Black, May 17, 1863
"	Johnson, W. B......	62d Tennessee......	"	London, Tenn.....	" May 19, 1863
Captain.....	Jones, C. H........	12th Arkansas......	"	New Orleans, La...	Port Hudson, July 9, 1863
Lieut.-Col..	Johnson, J. C......	Bell's Regiment.,..	"	Searcy, Arkansas...	Helena, July 4, 1863
Captain.....	Johnson, W. J......	61st Tennessee.....	"	Midway, Tenn......	Midway, Oct. 8, 1863
"	Jackson, Phil......	61st Tennessee.....	"	Morristown, Tenn..	Big Black, May 17, 1863
Lieutenant..	Jones, J. M........	61st Tennessee.....	"	Blountsville, Tenn..	" May 17, 1863
Captain.....	Jones, J. P.........	C. S. A............	"	Little Rock, Ark...	Port Hudson, July 9, 1863
Lieutenant..	Julian, T. J........	18th Arkansas......	"	Pine Bluff, Ark.....	" July 9, 1863
Captain.....	Jones, J. P.........	56th Virginia.......	Northern Va.	Well Water, Va....	Gettysburg, July 3, 1863

Rank.	Name.	Regiment.	Army of	Residence.	Where & When Captured.
Captain	Johnson, W. H.	23d North Carolina	Northern Va.	Kittrell's Sp'gs, N. C	Gettysburg, July 5, 1863
Lieutenant	Jarvis, S. A.	54th North Carolina	"	Farmington, N. C.	Rappahannock, Nov. 7, 1863
"	Jenkins, T. M.	6th North Carolina	"	Williams' Mill, N. C.	" Nov. 7, 1863
"	Jemison, J. B.	15th Louisiana	"	Red River L'd'g, La	Kelley's Ford July 8, 1863
"	Jones, R. C.	9th Alabama	"	Memphis, Tenn.	Gettysburg, July 3, 1863
Captain	Johnson, N. D.	15th Alabama	Tennessee	Talladega, Ala.	Shelbyville, June 27, 1863
Lieutenant	Justice, F.	3d Kentucky Cav.	"	Ryeburg, Ky.	Blunt Cave, Nov. 5, 1863
Captain	Jones, J. K.	3d Virginia Cav.	Northern Va.	Nottoway C. H., Va	Aldie, Va., June 7, 1863
Lieutenant	Jarrard, C. L.	52d Georgia	Mississippi	Nachoocha, Ga.	Champion Hill, May 17, 1863
"	Jackson, J. M.	11th Georgia	Northern Va.	Lafayette, Ga.	Gettysburg, July 4, 1863
"	Jones, G. W.	18th Virginia	"	Ridgeville, Ala.	" July 4, 1863
"	Jackson, T.	16th Virginia	"	Sorrett's, Va.	Wayne C. H., May 12, 1863
Captain	Johnson, J. W.	11th Georgia	"	Pierceville, Ga.	Gettysburg, July 2, 1863
Lieutenant	Jemison, W. M.	12th Georgia	"	Alexandria, Va.	Manassas, July 21, 1863
Colonel	Jones, Buehring H.	60th Va. Infantry	"	Lewisburg, W. Va.	New Hope Ch., June 5, 1864
Lieut.-Col	Jones, B.	14th Arkansas Bat.	Mississippi	Lakeville, Ark.	Port Hudson, July 9, 1863
Lieutenant	Johnson, J. E.	22d Va. Battery	Northern Va.	King Wm. C. H., Va	Falling Waters, July 14, 1863
Captain	Jackson, J. A.	38th Alabama	Tennessee	Camden, Ala.	Miss'y Ridge, Nov. 25, 1863
Lieutenant	Jackson, T. B.	3d Virginia	Northern Va.	Petersburg, Va.	Gettysburg, July 3, 1863
"	Jones, T. B.	35th Georgia	"	Hog Mountain, Ga.	" July 2, 1863
"	Jordan, J. B.	26th North Carolina	"	Raleigh, N. C.	" July 2, 1863
"	Jenkins, B. P.	7th Cavalry C. S. A.	Tennessee	Tarboro', N. C.	" July 2, 1863
Major	Jenkins, T. F.	53d Alabama	"	Alton, Ala.	Florence, May 28, 1863
Lieutenant	Johnson, M. F.	33d North Carolina	Northern Va.	Trap Hill, N. C.	Gettysburg, July 3, 1863
"	Jett, T. C.	22d Va. Battery	"	Jettinsville, Va.	Falling Waters, July 14, 1863
"	Jones, Calvin	43d Tennessee	Tennessee	War Gap, Tenn.	Hookinsville, Oct. 4, 1863
Lieut.-Col	Jones, H. C.	57th North Carolina	Northern Va.	Salisbury, N. C.	Rappahannock, Nov. 7, 1863
Captain	Jones, G. H.	22d Georgia	"	Wilson, Ga.	Gettysburg, July 4, 1863
Brig.-Gen.	Jones, J. R.		"	Harrisonburg, Va.	July 4, 1863
Captain	Johnson, B. F.	Porter's Cav.	Trans-Miss	Alexandria, Miss.	Kirksville, Aug. 4, 1863
"	Jones, G. S.	2d Georgia Bat.	Northern Va.	Macon, Ga.	Gettysburg, July 4, 1863

Rank	Name	Regiment	Department	Residence	Battle/Date
Colonel	Jones, E. P.	109th Virginia	Northern Va.	Free Shade, Va.	Rappahannock, June 5, 1863
Lieutenant	Jones, O S.	8th Arkansas	Tennessee	Batesville, Ark.	Chickamauga, Sep. 8, 1863
Major	Jones, T. P.	64th North Carolina	"	Honey Creek, N. C.	Cumberl'd Gap, Sep. 9, 1863
Lieutenant	Joiner, W. F.	20th Arkansas	Mississippi	Camden, Ark.	Big Black, May 17, 1863
"	Justice, Geo. F.	62d North Carolina	Tennessee	Dunn's Rock, N. C.	Cumberl'd Gap, May 17, 1863
Captain	Jones, W. J. F.	Hawthorne's Reg't	Trans-Miss.	Clarendon, Ark.	Helena, July 4, 1863
Lieutenant	Jones, J. A.	Bell's Ark Reg't	"	"	July 4, 1863
"	Johnston, W. S.	1st Louisiana Cav.	Tennessee	Baton Rouge, La.	Kentucky, Aug. 9, 1863
"	Johnston, J. W.	37th Virginia	Northern Va.	Abingdon, Va.	Gettysburg, July 5, 1863
"	Johnston, J. S.	P. A. C. S.	"	Church Hill, Miss.	Natchez, Aug. 24, 1863
Captain	Johns, St. Clair	5th Louisiana	"	New Orleans, La.	Rappahannock, Nov. 7, 1863
"	Jones, J. J.	33d Alabama	Tennessee	Bellefonte, Ala.	Jackson, Ala., Oct. 20, 1863
Lieutenant	Jones, G. B.	3d Mississippi	Mississippi	Bluntsville, Ala.	Port Hudson, July 9, 1863
Captain	Jones, J. W.	C. S. A. Cavalry	Tennessee	Maysville, Ala.(?)	Madison City, Oct. 20, 1863
"	Johnson, A. J.	3d Mississippi	"	Carrolton, Miss.	Nov. 27, 1863
Major	Johnston, Thos. H.	1st Mississippi	Mississippi	Hernando, Miss.	Port Hudson, July 9, 1863
Lieutenant	Johnson, J. W.	1st Mississippi	"	"	July 9, 1863
"	Jones, H. S.	2d Arkansas	Tennessee	Gravel Hill, Ark.	Murfreesboro', Dec. 31, 1862
"	Jones, J. S.	38th Virginia	Northern Va.	Mt. Joy, Va.	Gettysburg, July 3, 1863
"	Julian, R. M	38th Virginia	"	Republican Grove	" July 3, 1863
"	Jones, J. W.	1st Mississippi	Mississippi	Smithville, Miss.	Port Hudson, July 9, 1863
"	Jordan, A. F.	14th South Carolina	Northern Va.	Aiken, S. C.	Gettysburg, July 5, 1863
"	Jenning, T. L.	7th Tennessee	"	Statesville, Tenn.	" July 5, 1863
"	Jennings, W. W.	24th Mississippi	Tennessee	Hohenlinden, Miss.	Lookout M't'n, Nov. 24, 1863
"	Jones, H. E.	34th Mississippi	"	Waterford, Miss.	" Nov. 24, 1863
"	Johnson, D. L.	48th Tennessee			1863
Captain	Jackson, T. M.	61st Tennessee	Trans-Miss.		1863
Lieutenant	Jones, S. D.	1st Louisiana Cav.	Tennessee	New Orleans, La.	1863
"	Joyce, J. J.	Burns' Battery		Louisville, Ky.	1863
"	Jordan, L. B.	38th Alabama	Northern Va.	Chocktaw, Ala.	1863
Captain	Jackson, W. G.	22d Virginia	"	Union Level, Va.	1863
Lieutenant	Jaques, J. W.	24th Tennessee	Tennessee	Nashville, Tenn.	1863
Captain	Jett, E. D.	17th Arkansas		Washington, Ark.	1863
Lieutenant	Jarvas, J. A.			Columbia, Ark.	1863

RANK.	NAME.	REGIMENT.	ARMY OF	RESIDENCE.	WHERE & WHEN CAPTURED.
Lieutenant..	Kilby, J. E.	13th Virginia Cav..	Northern Va..	Suffolk, Va.	Hagerstown, July 12, 1863
"	Klugh, W. B.	57th North Carolina.	"	Gold Hill, N. C.	Rappahannock, Nov. 7, 1863
"	Kelley, F. M.	48th Georgia	"	Gibson, Ga.	Gettysburg, July 3, 1863
Captain.....	Kohnley, A.	8th Alabama	"	Mobile, Ala.	" July 4, 1863
"	Knowles, C. C.	1st Alabama	Mississippi	Tuskegee, Ala.	Port Hudson, July 9, 1863
Lieutenant..	Kent, J F.	16th Louisiana	Tennessee	Osyka, La.	Miss'y Ridge, Nov. 25, 1863
"	Kent, W. C.	16th "	"	Clinton, La.	" Nov. 25, 1863
"	Kelley, B. W.	60th Tennessee	"	Jonesboro', Tenn	Big Black, May 17, 1863
"	Kempton, J. C.	21st Mississippi	Northern Va.	Yazoo City, Miss	Gettysburg, July 5, 1863
Captain.....	Kennedy, R. C.	1st Louisiana	Tennessee	Horner, La.	Trenton, Ga., Oct. 16, 1863
"	Kenan, T. S.	43d North Carolina	Northern Va..	Kenansville, N. C.	Gettysburg, July 4, 1863
"	Kenars, J. G.	43d "	"	"	" July 4, 1863
Lieutenant..	Knittle, H.	Batte's(?) Tex. Leg..		Wine Grove, Texas.	1863
"	King, A. A.	3d South Carolina..		Pittsville, Tenn.	1863
"	Knox, A. E.	7th Louisiana	Northern Va .	New Orleans, La.	1863
"	Kingcaid, N J	11th North Carolina.	"	Morgantown. N. C.	1863
"	Kidd, E. M.	2d Louisiana	Tennessee	Vernon, La.	1863
"	Kinzer, C. S.	4th Virginia	Northern Va..	Blackburn, Va.	Gettysburg, July 3, 1863
"	Kirby, B. B.	10th Kentucky Cav.	Tennessee....	Cashville, Tenn.	Ohio, July 10, 1863
Lieut.-Col..	Kyle, O.	46th Alabama	Mississippi	Wetumpka, Ala.	Champion Hill, May 16, 1863
Lieutenant..	Kemps, M. W.	13th "	Northern Va .	Westover, Ala.	Gettysburg, July 14, 1863
"	Keller, J. W.	9th Louisiana Cav.	Mississippi....	Baton Rouge, La.	Port Hudson, July 9, 1863
Captain.....	Kiroff, S. E.	37th Tennessee	Tennessee	Cageville, Tenn.	Lexington, July 27, 1863
Lieutenant..	King, W. I.	51st Georgia	Northern Va.	Macon, Ga.	Gettysburg, July 4, 1863
"	Kitzmatter, L.	60th Tennessee	Mississippi....	Ford Town, Tenn.	Big Black, May 17, 1863
"	Kelley, M. L.	62d North Carolina.	Tennessee	Franklin, N. C.	Cumberland, Sept. 9, 1863
"	Keys, J H. O.	1st Mississippi	Mississippi....	Wood Lawn, Miss..	Port Hudson, July 9, 1863
Captain.....	King J. M. D.				
Lieutenant.	Knight, T. B.	2d Kentucky Cav..	Tennessee	Lexington, Ky.	Nicholasville, July 16, 1863
"	Kendrick, J. M.	23d North Carolina.	Northern Va.	Chapel Hill, N. C.	Gettysburg, July 1, 1863
Colonel.....	King, H. C.	1st C. S. A. Cav.	Tennessee	Memphis, Tenn.	Shelbyville, June 27, 1863

Rank	Name	Regiment	Army	Residence	Place/Date
Lieutenant	Keans, E. D.	7th Alabama Cav	Tennessee	Rollinsville, Ala	Shelbyville, June 27, 1863
"	Keans, W. C.	7th "	"	"	" June 27, 1863
Captain	Kubler, G. B.	54th Alabama	Northern Va.	Morgantown, N. C.	Rappahannock, Nov. 7, 1863
Lieutenant	Keesee, J	61st North Carolina	Beauregard	Pink Hill, N. C.	Battery Wagner, Aug. 26, 1863
"	Kelly, S. A.	55th Georgia	Tennessee	Gainesville, Ga.	Cumberland, Sept. 9, 1863
Captain	Kay, R.	Staff	Trans-Miss.	St. Joseph, Mo.	Pocahontas, August 22, 1863
Lieutenant	Kelly, J. G.	1st Missouri Cav	"	"	Big Black, May 17, 1863
"	Kennerly, H C	2d Kentucky Cav.	Tennessee	Russellville, Ky.	Barge Town, Ky., July 5, 1863
"	Keiningham, Wm. H	1st Virginia	Northern Va.	Richmond, Va.	Gettysburg, July 3, 1863
Captain	Kirkman, H.	Rodgers' Staff	"	Florence, Ala.	Huntsville, October 12, 1863
Lieutenant	Kerr, J.	H. B. Cavalry	Tennessee	Nashville, Tenn.	Middle Tenn., Sept. 9, 1863
"	Kniceley, H. C.	18th Virginia Cav.	N. W. B.(?)	Seven Fountains, Va	Hancock, June 23, 1863
"	Keys, J. B.	9th Louisiana Batt.	Mississippi	Springfield, La.	Port Hudson, July 9, 1863
"	Kimbrough, Frank	3d Alabama Cav	Tennessee	Pine Hill, Ala.	Shelbyville, June 27, 1863
"	Kelland, W. W.	10th North Carolina	Northern Va.		Falling Waters, July 14, 1863
Captain	Kean, J. M.	12th Louisiana Batt.		Beunavista, Ga.	Green Castle, July 5, 1863
"	Killen, W. E.	45th Georgia	Northern Va.	"	" July 5, 1863
Lieutenant	Kennelly, W. W.	2d "	"	Henderson, Ga.	Gettysburg, July 5, 1863
"	Kiernan, J.	Miles' Legion	Mississippi	Natchez, Miss.	Port Hudson, July 9, 1863
"	Kent, B. F.	30th Mississippi	Tennessee	Kilimichael, Miss.	Lookout M't'n, Nov. 24, 1863
"	King, T. B.	4th Alabama Cav	"	Mayesville, Ala.	Madison City, Oct. 20, 1863
"	King, T. J.	49th Alabama	Mississippi	Guntersville, Ala.	Port Hudson, July 9, 1863
"	Kelsey, J. R.	10th Arkansas	"	Good Hope, Ark.	" July 9, 1863
"	Kiken, E. R.	28th Alabama	Tennessee	Bluntsville, Ala.	Miss'y Ridge, Nov. 25, 1863
Captain	Kyle, T. J.	3d Mississippi Cav.	Mississippi	West Depot, Miss.	Hudsonville, Oct. 7, 1863
Lieutenant	King, A. A.	3d S. Carolina Batt	Northern Va.	Batesville, Ark.	
"	Kelly, A.	10th Arkansas	"	Jacksonville, N. C.	
"	Kinsey, Joseph	61st North Carolina	"	Pink Hill, N. C.	
"	Kinney, B. F.			New Orleans, La	
Captain	Kear, John M.	12th Louisiana Batt		Washburn Prai'e, Mo	
Lieutenant	Keely, W. J.	8th Missouri			
Captain	Latimer, M S.	40th Mississippi	Mississippi	Plattsburg, Miss.	Big Black River, May 17, 1863
Lieutenant	Latham, L. J.	1st Missouri Cav.	"	Orizato, Miss.	Ripley, Miss., April 3, 1863
Captain	Lacke, S. E.	33d Alabama Cav.	Tennessee	Camden, Ala.	Florence, Ala., May 28, 1863

Rank.	Name.	Regiment.	Army of	Residence.	Where & When Captured.
Lieutenant	Lamar, E. F.	A. D. C. Longstreet	Northern Va.	Ashton, La.	Gettysburg, July 3, 1863
"	Lassiter, C.	8th Florida	"	Houston, Fla.	" July 4, 1863
"	Lum, Q. A.	15th Georgia	"	Goshen, Ga.	" July 2, 1863
"	Laffoon, N. S.	2d N. C. Battalion	"	Dabson, N. C.	" July 4, 1863
"	Lemon, George	Gen. Archer's Staff	"	Baltimore, Md.	Cashtown, July 5, 1863
Lieut.-Col	Luce, W. H.	18th Mississippi	"	Benton, Miss.	Gettysburg, July 2, 1863
Captain	Lee, W. E.	58th Alabama	"	Uniontown, Ala	Miss'y Ridge, Nov. 24, 1863
"	Lynn, David	18th Virginia Cav.	"	Cumberland, Md.	Hampson, March 11, 1863
Lieutenant	Lebalance, A.	30th Louisiana	Mississippi	Plaque Mine, La.	Port Hudson, July 9, 1863
"	Lovell, H. P.	54th North Carolina,	Northern Va.	Siloam, N. C.	Rappahannock, Nov. 7, 1863
Colonel	Lee, R. H.		"	Orange C. H., Va.	Orange C. H., Sept. 22, 1863
Lieutenant	Litaker, J. F.	56th North Carolina,	"	Concord, N. C.	Rappahannock, Nov. 7, 1863
"	Lentz, J. C.	56th "	"	South River, N. C.	" Nov. 7, 1863
"	Long, M. C.	7th Louisiana	"	New Orleans, La.	" Nov. 7, 1863
"	Lampkin, E. O.	C. S. Cavalry	Tennessee	———, Miss.	Archula, Nov 3, 1863
"	Lockett, B. H.	38th Alabama	"	Pine Hill, Ala.	Miss'y Ridge, Nov. 25, 1863
"	Lacklin, J.	30th North Carolina.	"	Washington, N C.	
"	Lee, B C.	38th Alabama	"	Burnsville, Ala.	Miss'y Ridge, Nov. 25, 1863
Adjutant	Lindsay, T. P.	12th Arkansas	Mississippi	Bloomington, Ark.	Port Hudson, July 9, 1863
Lieutenant	Lovejoy, W. H.	19th Tennessee	Tennessee	Baltimore, Md.	Chickamauga, Sept. 24, 1863
"	Lear, F. F.	Ordnance officer		Hillsboro, Mo.	
"	Lawrence, M N	8th North Carolina.	Northern Va.	Tarboro, N. C.	
"	Lawrence, W. F.	1st Texas		St. Augustine, Tex(?)	1863
"	Lenhart, M.	7th Louisiana	Northern Va.	New Orleans, La.	Rappahannock, Nov. 7, 1863
"	Lenderbuck, F. M.	7th Kentucky Cav.	Tennessee	Canton, Ky.	Chickamauga, Nov. 24, 1863
Captain	Lee, W. T. F.	4th Virginia	Northern Va.	Blacksburg, Va.	July 3, 1863
Lieutenant	Lee, J. A. J.	28th Virginia	"	New Castle, Va.	Gettysburg, July 3, 1863
"	Lewis, J. H.	9th Virginia	"	Portsmouth, Va.	" July 3, 1863
"	Logan, G. W.	8th Kentucky	Tennessee		
Adjutant	Lewis, C. W.	23d Arkansas	Mississippi	West Point, Ark.	Port Hudson, July 9, 1863
Lieut.-Col	Lockhart, J. W.	14th Tennessee	Tennessee	Clarksville, Tenn.	Gettysburg, July 3, 1863

Rank	Name	Regiment	Army	Residence	Place and Date
Lieutenant..	Locke, B. T........	——— Ark.........	Trans-Miss...	Augusta, Ark......	Little Rock, Nov. 7, 1863
Lieut.-Col..	Locke, M. B........	1st Alabama.......	"	Detroit, Ala.......	Port Hudson, July 9, 1863
Lieutenant..	London, A.........	16th Mississippi....	Northern Va..	Somerset, Miss....	Gettysburg, July 4, 1863
"	Lockett, O. W......	1st Alabama.......	Mississippi...	Dadesville, Ala ...	Port Hudson, July 9, 1863
Captain.....	Lawey, W. L.......	62d Tennessee......	Tennessee ...	Cleveland, Tenn....	P. R. River (?), May 17, 1863
Lieutenant..	Lowdermilk, D. W.	30th Georgia.......	Mississippi...	Woodland, Ga.....	Baker's Creek, May 16, 1863
"	Lard, J. J.........	24th "	"	Waterford, Ga.....	Champion Hill, May 16, 1863
"	Leatherwood, M. H.	62d North Carolina..	Tennessee ...	Johnson, N. C.....	Cumberl'd Gap, Sept. 9, 1863
Captain.....	Liggin, John........	24th Georgia......			
"	Lewis, G. W.......	9th Louisiana......			
"	Lunsford, Richard...	White's Battalion...	Northern Va..	Brownsville, Va....	Brownsville, Aug. 21, 1863
Lieutenant..	Lang, R. C.........	1st Mississippi......	Mississippi...	Brandon, Miss.....	Port Hudson, July 9, 1863
"	Long, S. P.........	62d North Carolina.	Tennessee ...		Cumberl'd Gap, Sept. 9, 1863
"	Logan, M..........	12th Arkansas......	Mississippi...	Holly Springs, Miss	Port Hudson, July 9, 1863
"	Lyles, A. M........	2d Tenn. Cavalry...	Trans-Miss...	Plains, Texas......	Fort Butler, June 28, 1863
"	Lysey, P...........	1st Kentucky Cav..	Tennessee....	Hawesville, Ky....	Buck Grove, June 24, 1863
Captain.....	Love, J. S.........	64th North Carolina.	"	Greensville, N. C...	Cumberl'd Gap, June 24, 1863
"	Lusk, D. G........	5th "	"	Asheville, N. C.....	Richmond, Ky., Aug. 2, 1863
Lieutenant..	Lytton, E.........	64th Virginia.......	"	"	" Aug. 2, 1863
Captain.....	Lee, J. A..........	6th North Carolina.	"	Yanceyville, N. C...	Rappahannock, Nov. 7, 1863
Lieutenant..	Langton, F. B......	5th Kentucky Cav..	"	Eddysville, Ky.....	Sugar Creek, Oct. 9, 1863
"	Lawrence H. C....	60th North Carolina.	"	Leicester, N. C.....	Miss'y Ridge, Nov. 25, 1863
Lieut.-Col..	Lebreton, E. S. M..	4th Louisiana......	Mississippi...	New Orleans, La...	Port Hudson, July 9, 1863
Lieutenant..	Latimore, J. T......	55th Georgia.......	"	Grantsville, Ga.....	" July 9, 1863
"	Lahey, J...........	1st Tenn. Artillery..	"	Nashville, Tenn....	" July 9, 1863
"	Lane, H. N.........	A. D. C...........	Tennessee....	St. Louis, Mo......	Chickamauga, Sept. 20, 1863
"	Lee, J. T...........	15th Arkansas.....	Mississippi...	Bentonville, Ark...	Big Black, May 17, 1863
Captain.....	Law, J. T..........	43d Georgia,......	"	Grantsville, Ga.....	Champion Hill, May 16, 1863
Lieutenant..	Latspuck, W. C....	60th Tennessee.....	"	Newport, Tenn....	Big Black, May 17, 1863
"	Lee, W............	22d Georgia.......	Northern Va..	Huntsville, Ga.....	Gettysburg, July 2, 1863
"	Larkins, J. R.......	38th Alabama......	Tennessee....	Coatopa, ———.....	Miss'y Ridge, Nov. 25, 1863
"	Lawrence, R. S.....	24th Mississippi....	"	Greensboro, Miss..	Lookout M't'n, Nov. 24, 1863
"	Lodgerwood, Wm..	1st Missouri Cav...	Mississippi...	Grant's Hill Mo...	Big Black, May 17, 1863
"	Lewis, J. T.........	14th Virginia Cav..	Northern Va..	Clarksville, Va.....	Gettysburg, July 2, 1863

Rank.	Name.	Regiment.	Army of	Residence.	Where & When Captured.
Lieutenant..	Logan, J. A.........	14th Virginia Cav...	Northern Va.	Halifax co., Va.....	Gettysburg, July 4, 1863
Captain.....	Livingston, T B....	8th Florida.........	"	Fernandina, Fla....	" July 4, 1863
Lieutenant..	Leemar, A. W......	14th Virginia......	"	Richmond, Hill.....	" July 3, 1863
Colonel.....	Lewis, L. M........	7th Missouri........	Trans-Miss...	Liberty, Missouri...	Helena, July 4, 1863
Major......	Lloyd, W. D.C.....	Jackson's Staff......	Tennessee...	Macon, Mississippi..	Chickamauga, Sept. 9, 1863
Lieut.-Col..	Lee, T. L..........	15th Arkansas......	Mississippi...	Camden, Arkansas.	Port Hudson, July 9, 1863
Lieutenant..	Locke, A. J........	30th Mississippi.....	Tennessee...	Canton, Tennessee..	Murfreesboro, Dec. 31, 1862
Colonel.....	Lyles, O. P........	23d Arkansas......	Mississippi...	Marion, Arkanas...	Port Hudson, July 9, 1863
Lieutenant .	Leonard, J. R.......	5th Virginia Cav....	Northern Va.	Salem, Virginia.....	Aldie, June 7, 1863
"	Lewis, A. F........	38th Georgia......	"	Hamptonville, N.C.	Falling Waters, July 14, 1863
Captain.....	Leaschler, George..	1st Tennessee Cav..	Tennessee...	Nashville, Tenn....	Columbia, July 13, 1863
Lieutenant..	Langley, S. S......	Bell's Ark. Reg't....	Trans-Miss...	Arkadelphia, Ark..	Helena, July 4, 1863
Captain.....	Leophart, S. L.....	2d South Carolina..	Northern Va.	Columbia, S. C.....	Gettysburg, July 2, 1863
Lieutenant..	Lapsley, James L...	51st Alabama......	Tennessee..	Selma, Alabama....	Kingston, Oct. 25, 1863
"	Lawrence, E. D....	Byrne's Battery.....	"	Louisville, Ky......	Ohio, July 26, 1863
Major......	Long. L. W........	Staff.............	"	Morgansville, Ky...	Kentucky, May 3, 1863
Lieutenant.	Lee, J. V..........	1st Arkansas Cav...	Trans-Miss...	Bentonville, Ark....	Benton City, Ark. June 17, 1863
"	Leslie, S D........	8th Virginia........	Northern Va.	Union, Virginia.....	Upperville, May 27, 1863
Captain	Laird, J. S........	1st Mississippi.....	Mississippi...	Orezaba, Mississippi	Ripley, Miss., Nov. 29, 1863
"	Love, J. A........	10th Missouri......	Trans-Miss...	Lane's Prairie, Mo..	Helena, July 4, 1863
Lieutenant..	Littwich, J. E......	9th Tennessee Cav.	Tennessee...	Columbia. Tenn....	Columbia, Aug. 10, 1863
Captain.....	Long, J. W........	20th Arkansas.....	Mississippi...	Jacinto, Mississippi.	Champion Hill, May 16, 1863
Lieutenant..	Lane, J. M........	55th Georgia......	Tennessee....	Colquitt, Georgia...	Cumberl'd Gap, Sept. 9, 1863
"	Lofton, W. G......	42d Alabama......	"	Olney, Alabama....	Lookout M't'n, Nov. 24, 1863
"	Ligon, J. S........	23d Arkansas.	Mississippi...	Marion, Arkansas..	Port Hudson, July 9, 1863
"	Livingston, A. R....	10th Arkansas.....	"	Springfield, Ark....	" July 9, 1863
"	Lane, P. W........	23d Arkansas......	"	Helena, Arkansas ..	" July 9, 1863
"	Little, R. J........	12th Georgia......	Northern Va.	Eatonville, Georgia.	Chambersburg, July 4, 1863
"	Lawson, W. T.....	49th Alabama.....	Mississippi...	Stevensonville, Ala.	Port Hudson, July 9, 1863
"	Lawrence, E. H....	30th Mississippi.....	Tennessee...	Kosciusko, Miss....	Lookout M't'n, Nov. 24, 1863
"	Lunsdale, J. V......	23d Arkansas.......	Mississippi...	Marion, Arkansas...	Port Hudson, July 9, 1863

Rank	Name	Regiment	Army	Origin	Captured / Date
Captain	Lewis, L. H.	23d Arkansas	Mississippi	Arkadelphia, Ark.	Port Hudson, July 9, 1863
Lieutenant	Lumpkin, E. H.	2d Tennessee Cav.	Tennessee	Holly Springs, Miss.	Mississippi, 1863
"	Lawrence, J. M.	23d North Carolina	Northern Va.	Cedar Falls, N. C.	Gettysburg, July 5, 1863
Captain	Lewis, W. P.	53d Tennessee	Mississippi	Connersville, Tenn.	Giles co., Tenn., Dec. 3, 1863
Lieutenant	Ludlow, William	39th Mississippi	"	Morton Mississippi	Port Hudson, July 9, 1863
"	Lusher, G. W.	11th Mississippi	Northern Va.	Memphis, Tenn.	Gettysburg, July 3, 1863
"	Lanier, A. M.	38th Virginia	"	Whiteman, Virginia	" July 3, 1863
"	Largen, J.	16th Tennessee	"	Fort Donelson, Tenn	" July 5, 1863
"	Lindsay, J. A.	26th Alabama	"	Fayette C. H., Ala.	" July 5, 1863
"	Lucas, S. M.	6th Louisiana	"	St. Louis, Missouri	" July 4, 1863
"	Long, B. A.	39th Tennessee	Tennessee	Morristown, Tenn.	Tallahoma, July 2, 1863
"	Lanier, B. W.	Miles' Legion	Mississippi	Tickfall, Louisiana	Miles' Leg., P.H.[?] " 9, 1863
"	Leach, C. E.	26th Alabama	"	Columbus, Miss.	Gettysburg, July 5, 1863
"	Landrum, J. M.	15th Arkansas	"	Taylor's Creek, Ark	Port Hudson, July 9, 1863
"	Love, R. C.	1st Mississippi Art.	"	Burtonton, Miss.	" July 9, 1863
"	Lee, W C.	18th Arkansas	"	Princeton, Arkansas	" July 9, 1863
"	Lee, S. M.	14th Arkansas	"	Dover, Arkansas	" July 9, 1863
"	Lyles, S. T.	39th Mississippi	"	Morton, Mississippi	" July 9, 1863
"	Logan, M.	12th Arkansas	"	Holly Springs, Miss.	" July 9, 1863
"	Lillard, W. R.	52d Tennessee	Tennessee	Dresden, Tennessee	Dresden, Tenn., May 17, 1863
"	Lanier, J. L.	Staff	Mississippi	Columbus, Miss.	Port Hudson, July 9, 1863
"	Laughlin, J. J.	30th North Carolina	"	Warrenton, N. C.	Gettysburg, July 4, 1863
Captain	Laswell, R. M.	2d Mississippi	"	Cherry Creek, Miss.	" July 4, 1863
"	Latané, J. L.	53d Virginia	Northern Va.	Aylett's, Va.	" July 4, 1863
"	Lister, J G	55th Georgia	Tennessee	Cummings, Georgia	
"	Lewis, W. R.	8th Kentucky	"	Lexington, Ky.	
"	Landrum, W. L.	10th Kentucky	"	Lost Creek, Ky.	Kentucky, 1863
Lieutenant	Lockhart, W. G.	56th North Carolina	Northern Va.	Red Creek, N. C.	Gettysburg, July 3, 1863
"	Lane, T. O.	20th North Carolina	"	Red Creek, N. C.	" July 3, 1863
Major	Lewis, H. G.	32d North Carolina	"	Tarboro', N. C.	" July 3, 1863
Lieutenant	Moore, P.	64th Alabama	Tennessee	Anderson Mills, Ten.	Cumberland Gap Sep. 19, 1863
"	Martin, P. C.	55th Louisiana	"	Bedford, Georgia	" Sep. 19, 1863
"	Morris, W. L.	64th Georgia	"	Hendersonville, N.C.	" Sep. 19, 1863
"	Miller, John	64th Virginia	"	Jonesville, Va.	" Sep. 19, 1863

Rank.	Name.	Regiment.	Army of	Residence.	Where & When Captured.
Captain	Mosely, Alexander	2d Florida	Northern Va.	Palatka, Fla	Gettysburg, July 2, 1863
Lieutenant	Monly, W. F.	13th Mississippi	Mississippi	Merasiur, Miss	" July 2, 1863
"	Moore, A. P.	64th Georgia	Northern Va.	Reidsville, Ga	" July 4, 1863
Major	Moore, W. R.	2d Florida	"	Lake City, Fla	" July 4, 1863
Lieutenant	Matthew, W. E.	38th Georgia	"	Landrensville, Ga	South Mountain, July 4, 1863
"	Mobley, J. P.	61st "	"	Perry Mills, Ga	" July 4, 1863
"	McBee, J. W.	6th "	"	Mt. Vernon, Ga	Gettysburg, July 4, 1863
"	McBride, J. R.	9th Alabama	"	Moulton, Ala.	" July, 3, 1863
"	Mitchell, W. H.	3d Texas	Tennessee	El Paso, Texas	Fort Butler, June 28, 1863
Captain	Martin, C. P.	11th Tennessee	"	Charlotte, N. C.	Cumberl'd Gap, Sept. 9, 1863
"	Moffett, A. A.	18th North Carolina	Northern Va.	Salisbury, N. C.	Gettysburg, July 3, 1863
"	Moore, John	18th "	"	Calvin Creek, N. C.	Falling Waters, July 12, 1863
Major	Morgan, P.	Martin's Staff	Tennessee	Talladega, Ala	" July 12, 1863
Captain	Malone, T. H.	17th Alabama Cav.	"	Nashville, Tenn	Shelbyville, June 27, 1863
"	Momfort, J. P.	1st Louisiana	"	Bayou Sara, La	Hill's Gap, Ky.
Lieutenant	Miner, William	Martin's Staff	"	Natchez, Miss	Shelbyville, June 27, 1863
"	Myers, L. M.	— Georgia Cavalry	"	Rossville, Ga	Manchester, June 26, 1863
"	Moseley, E. B.	1st Mississippi	Mississippi	Smithville, Miss	Ripley, Miss., May 5, 1863
Captain	Millam, J. J.	1st "	"	Wall Hill, Miss	Port Hudson, July 9, 1863
Lieutenant	Mumph, W.	1st Missouri	"	Athens, Miss	Ripley, Miss., May 5, 1863
Captain	Murs, A. J.	21st Arkansas	"	Clarksville, Ark	Big Black, May 17, 1863
Lieutenant	Martin, J. J.	21st "	"	Wild Haws, Ark	" May 17, 1863
"	McDonald, D. M.	56th North Carolina	N. Carolina	Fayetteville, N. C.	Green Swamp, May 22, 1863
Captain	McKibben, R.	31st Alabama	Mississippi	Silver Run, Ala	Champion Hill, May 16, 1863
"	McB——, J. B.	1st S. C. Artillery	S. Carolina	Charleston, S. C.	Morris Island, July 10, 1863
Lieutenant	Moore, J. L.	13th Alabama	N. Carolina	Camden, Ala	Gettysburg, July 1, 1863
Captain	Monly, A. S.	7th Florida	Tennessee	Gadsden Depot, S C	Miss'y Ridge, Nov. 25, 1863
Lieutenant	Masez, L. L.	10th C. S.	"	Vutina, Ala	Jacksboro', August 27, 1863
Major	McDaniel, H. D.	11th Georgia	Northern Va.	Menicia, Ga	Hagerstown, July 12, 1863
Captain	McAfee, T.	22d "	"	Duncanville, Ga	Gettysburg, July 4, 1863
Lieutenant	McDonald, H. A.	38th North Carolina	"	Fayetteville, N. C.	Falling Waters, July 14, 1863

Rank	Name	Regiment	Army	Residence	Killed/Battle
Colonel	Morris, W. J.	37th North Carolina	Northern Va.	Fayetteville, N. C.	Gettysburg, July 3, 1863
Captain	Magee, W. G.	39th Mississippi	Mississippi	Old Hickory	Port Hudson, July 9, 1863
Lieutenant	Marlan, W. A.	20th North Carolina	N. Carolina	East Bend, N. C.	Gettysburg, July 3, 1863
"	McCrary, M. S.	9th Georgia	"	Genero, Ga.	" July 3, 1863
Captain	McGenesy, W.	1st Louisiana	Tennessee	Fort Jefferson	Sanford, Ky., August 1, 1863
"	McGrensey, W.	8th Louisiana	Northern Va.	Baton Rouge, La.	Gettysburg, July 2, 1863
"	Muse, W. B.	1st Tennessee	"	Shelbyville Tenn.	" July 3, 1863
"	McLester, J. D.	4th Missouri	"	Big Lick	South Mountain, July 5, 1863
"	Miles, W. A.	1st South Carolina	"	Wathello, S. C.	Falling Waters, July 14, 1863
"	McCarty, C. F.	1st "	Tennessee	New Orleans, La.	Miss'y Ridge, Nov. 25, 1863
"	Markham, G. S.	58th Alabama	"	Bernopolis, Ala.	" Nov. 25, 1863
Lieutenant	Mitchell, J. B.	34th "	"	Glenville, Ala.	" Nov. 25, 1863
"	Moody, W. C.	2d "	Northern Va.	Ripley, Miss.	Gettysburg, July 3, 1863
"	Mull, F. P.	55th North Carolina	"	Knob Creek, N. C.	" July 3, 1863
Captain	Manis, D. B.	38th "	"	Camp Call	" July 3, 1863
Lieutenant	Moore, H. C	38th "	"	Wilson	" July 3, 1863
"	McNeeley, J. R.	8th Virginia	"	Lewisburg, Va.	" July 3, 1863
Captain	McRed, J.	2d Georgia	"	High Shoals, Ga.	Green Castle, Pa., July 8, 1863
Lieutenant	McAlphine, R. M.	3d "	"	Athens, Ga.	Falling Waters, July 5, 1863
"	Metts, J. J.	2d North Carolina	"	Wilmington, N. C.	Gettysburg, July 4, 1863
"	Mican, A. R.	55th Georgia	"	Lege, Va.	Falling Waters, July 14, 1863
"	McMulley, John	— Arkansas Batt.	"	Laurel Factory Md.	Culpeper C. H., July 14, 1863
"	McKnew, M. E.	1st Maryland Cav.	"	Bellerun, Md.	Potomac River, June 2, 1863
"	McNeeley, C. R.	24th North Carolina	"	Cape Hatteras, N. C	Gettysburg, July 4, 1863
"	Maher, P. E.	4th Alabama	Tennessee	Montgomery, Ala.	" July 4, 1863
"	McCampbell, J. H.	37th Georgia	"	Paris, Tenn.	West Tenn., June 9, 1863
Gov.'s Aid	Methrow, W. R.	57th "	Mississippi	Irvington, Ga.	Champion Hill, May 16, 1863
Lieutenant	Moore, W. F.		Trans-Miss	Brunswick, Mo.	
Captain	Martin, O. P.	66th Tennessee	Mississippi	Jonesboro', Tenn.	Big Black, May 17, 1863
Lieutenant	Mullins, B. B.	1st Kentucky Cav.	Tennessee	Dover, Ky.	Shelbyville, Oct. 7, 1863
"	Moore, J. P.	55th Georgia	"	Jones Mills, Ga.	Cumberl'd Gap, Sept. 19, 1863
Captain	Miller, J. H.	Ord. Officer	Trans-Miss	St Louis, Mo.	Pocahontas, August 2, 1863
"	Miller, John J.	M. S. G.	"	"	St. Louis, May 3, 1863
Major	McKnight, George	A. A. G.	Mississippi	New Orleans, La.	Jackson, Miss., July 19, 1863

Rank.	Name.	Regiment.	Army of	Residence.	Where & When Captured.
Lieut.-Col...	Matheny, W. G....	21st Arkansas......	Mississippi...	Evening Shade, Ark	Big Black, May 17, 1863
Lieutenant..	Mornin, J. N....	7th Texas.......	"	Coffeeville, Texas..	Raymond, Miss., May 12, 1863
"	Morrison, G. S.....	30th Alabama......	"	Syllaconga, Ala....	Champion Hill, May 16, 1863
"	Middleton, J. A....	8th Kentucky Cav..	Tennessee...	Shelbyville, Ky.....	Buffington, O, July 19, 1863
"	Morgan, H. W......	8th " ..	"	Louisville, Ky.....	Wilson co., Ten , Sept. 9, 1863
"	Melvin, G. W.....	9th Louisiana......	Northern, Va.	Liberner, Ky......	Rappahannock, Nov. 7, 1863
"	Mosely, J. W......	2d Tennessee......	Tennessee....	Murfreesboro, Tenn.	Miss'y Ridge, Nov. 25, 1863
Captain.....	McGurk, J........	6th Louisiana......	Northern Va..	Salisbury, N. C.....	Rappahannock, Nov. 7, 1863
Lieutenant..	Miller, A. H.......	6th North Carolina.	"	New Orleans, La...	" Nov. 7, 1863
"	Moore, J. B........	Mosby Battalion...	"	Richmond, Va.....	Madison, Va., Sept. 22, 1863
"	Murphy, J. R......	8th Louisiana......	"	Chaunceyville, La..	Rappahannock, Nov. 7, 1863
"	Manly Matthew....	2d North Carolina..	"	Hillsboro, N. C.....	Chancellorsville, May 3, 1863
"	Mitchell, J. C......	35th Tennessee.....	"	McMinnville, Tenn..	Cleveland, Nov. 25, 1863
Captain.....	Moore, M. W......	62d North Carolina.	Tennessee ...	Fort Embue, N. C..	Cumberl'd Gap, Sept. 9, 1863
Lieutenant..	McClare, J. J......	62d "	"	Honnissa, Ga......	" Sept. 9, 1863
Captain.....	Morris, W. G. B....	64th "	"	Hendersonville, N.C	" Sept. 9, 1863
"	Mason, J. P........	Commis'y Dept....	"	Greenville, Tenn...	" Sept. 9, 1863
"	Marett, E. J........	45th Mississippi....	"	New Albany, Miss..	Murfreesboro, Jan'y 4, 1863
"	Montgomery, J. N..	16th Georgia.......	Northern Va .	Fort Lamar, Ga....	Gettysburg, July 2, 1863
"	Middlebrook, J.....	40th "	Mississippi...	Brownsville, La....	Champion Hill, May 15, 1863
Lieutenant..	Matthews, J.......	40th "	"	"	" May 16, 1863
"	McMurray, W. F...	46th Alabama......	"	Lonina, Ala........	" May 16, 1863
"	McGill, W. R......	46th "	"	"	" May 20, 1863
"	Murphy, J. B......	3d Tennessee......	"	Bigbeeville, Tenn..	Bayou Nine, May 12, 1863
"	Moody, B. D......	18th Arkansas......	"	Ozark, Ark........	Big Black, May 17, 1863
"	Mitchell, A........	15th Arkansas......	"	Cane Hill Ark.....	" May 17, 1863
Captain.....	Makely, W........	18th Virginia Cav...	Northern Va	Alexandria, Va....	Clear Spring, July 8, 1863
"	Myers, J. W.......	31st Virginia.......	"	Monterey, Va......	Monterey, Aug. 20, 1863
Colonel.....	Mybs, W. B.......	Miles' Legion......	Mississippi...	New Orleans, La...	July 9, 1863
Captain	Meadows, J. D.....	1st Alabama.......	"	Dadeville, Ala.....	July 9, 1863
Lieutenant..	McKay, D. H......	46th Alabama......	"	Leachapikeala, ——	Champion Hill, May 16, 1863

Adjutant....	McCrane, S. N.....	5th Alabama Cav...	Tennessee...	Selma, Ala..........	Shelbyville, May 16, 1863
Lieutenant..	Mahan, J. T........	1st Missouri.......	Mississippi...	St. Joseph, Mo......	Big Black, May 17, 1863
"	McLain, H.........	1st Missouri.......	"	Mexico, Mo.........	" May 17, 1863
"	Miles, W. A........	1st South Carolina..	Northern Va..	South Carolina....	Falling Waters, July 14, 1863
Captain.....	Murphy, E. D......	37th Alabama......	Mississippi...	Troy, Ala..........	Vicksburg, May 22, 1863
"	Morgan, J. H.......	12th Arkansas Batt..	"	Larisville, Ark.....	Port Hudson, May 1, 1863
Lieutenant..	Matthew, E W.....	19th Arkansas......	"	Hot Springs, Ark...	Big Black, May 17, 1863
"	McLean, W. L......	12th Arkansas......	"	Memphis, Tenn....	" May 17, 1863
"	Morris, L..........	3d Missouri........	"	Salina, Mo.........	" May 17, 1863
"	Martin, S. J........	19th Virginia.......	Northern Va..	Troy, Va..........	Gettysburg, July 3, 1863
Captain	Moore, W. J........	14th Tennessee.....	"	Clarksville, Tenn...	" July 3, 1863
Lieutenant..	Moore, J. H........	14th Tennessee.....	"	"	" July 3, 1863
"	Moore, C. W.......	7th Virginia........	"	Rapid Anne	" July 3, 1863
Adjutant...	Matchell, T. F......	10th C. S. Cavalry..	Tennessee ...	Liberty, Va.......	Richmond, Ky.. May 17, 1863
Major......	Moore, H..........	2d Arkansas.......	Mississippi...	Duval Bluff, Ark...	Big Black, May, 17, 1863
Adjutant ...	McAllister, W. A...	39th Georgia......	"	La Fayette, Ga.....	Champion Hill, May 16, 1863
Major......	McCreary, A. T....	2d Missouri.......	Trans-Miss...	St. Louis, Mo......	" July 29, 1863
Lieutenant..	Maury, E. P. G.....	12th North Carolina.	Tennessee....	Forks of Pegram...	Cumberl'd Gap, Sept. 9, 1863
"	McMiller, W. A.....	27th Mississippi.....	"	Macon, Miss.......	Chickamauga, Sept. 20, 1863
"	Marberry, M. P.....	27th Mississippi.....	"	Winchester, Tenn..	" Sept. 20, 1863
Captain.....	McDonald, G. W...	17th Tennessee.....	"	Granville, Tenn....	" Sept. 20, 1863
Lieutenant..	Malloy, D. W......	20th Tennessee.....	"	Spencer, Tenn......	" Sept. 20, 1863
Captain	Murphy, J. J.......	Morgan's Regiment.	"	Lexington, Ky.....	Powell Co.,Ky., Sept. 20, 1863
Lieutenant..	Montgall, G. R.....	1st Kentucky Cav..	"	Simptonville, Ky...	Chickamauga, Sept. 22, 1863
Major......	McCann, Dick......	15th Tennessee Cav.	"	Nashville, Ky......	Middle Tenn., Aug. 19, 1863
Lieutenant..	Musselman, J. N...	14th Louisiana.....	"		
Captain.....	McWhister, J. W...	3d Mississippi......	"		
"	Mayes, R. E........	30th Tennessee	"		
"	Mizell, Joshua......	18th Florida.......	Northern Va..	....	Gettysburg, July 2, 1863
Lieutenant..	McFadgen, A. M...	5th North Carolina.	"	Fayetteville, N. C...	Hagerstown, July 12, 1863
"	Moore, James......	5th N. C. Cavalry..	"	Clinton, N. C......	" July 12, 1863
"	Murdock, A. G.....	38th North Carolina.	"	Hill's Store, N. C...	Falling Waters, July 14, 1863
"	Musgrove, J. T.....	10th Missouri.......	Trans-Miss...	Eaton, Mo.........	Helena, Ark., July 4, 1863
Captain	Morris, J...........	A. Q. M............	Tennessee ...	Sharpsburg, Ky....	Hadensville, Ky., July 7, 1863

Rank.	Name.	Regiment.	Army of	Residence.	Where & When Captured.
Captain	Monroe, A. J.	16th South Carolina.	Tennessee	Honey-path, S. C.	Graysville, Ga., Nov. 26, 1863
"	Miller, Alex.	2d North Carolina.	Northern Va.	Newberne, N. C.	Kelly's Ford, Nov. 7, 1863
Lieutenant	McGhee, C. A.	53d "	"	Madison, N. C.	Green Castle, July 5, 1863
"	Morris, J. F.	8th C. S. Cavalry.	Tennessee	Pickensville, Ala.	Shelbyville, June 27, 1863
"	Murrick, G. A.	10th Arkansas.	Mississippi	Little Rock, Ark.	Port Hudson, July 8, 1863
"	Manning, J. A.	Bell's Regiment.	Trans-Miss.	Hamburg, Ark.	Helena, Ark., July 4, 1863
Adjutant	Minnis, J. A.	4th Tennessee Cav.	Tennessee	Gallatin, Tenn.	Bluff Co., Tenn., May 20, 1863
Major	Michell, J. A.	C. S. A.	Northern Va.	Charleston, S. C.	South Mountain, July 6, 1863
Captain	McMurray, James.	A. Q. M. 2d Ark.	Mississippi	Chicot Co., Ark.	Port Hudson, July 9, 1863
Adjutant	McDaniel, H. C.	54th North Carolina.	Northern Va.	Fayetteville, N. C.	Rappahannock, Nov. 7, 1863
Lieutenant	Moore, R. L.	— Louisiana Art.	"	Canton, Miss.	" Nov. 7, 1863
Captain	Miller, J. H.	57th North Carolina.	"	Salisbury, N. C.	" Nov 7, 1863
Major	Mayo, J. M.	4th "	"	Ashland, N. C.	Upperville, June 25, 1863
Lieutenant	Mason, H.	3d Tennessee.	Tennessee	Strawb'y Plain, Tenn	Hull Co., Tenn., Oct. 27, 1863
Captain	Murray, T. M.	1st Tennessee Cav.	"	Bernardville, Tenn.	Roane Co., Tenn., Oct. 27, 1863
"	Milliken, J. D.	3d Tennessee.	"	Mossy Creek, Tenn.	Jeffer'n co., Tenn., Oct. 25, 1863
Lieutenant	Mayo, R E.	44th North Carolina.	Northern Va.	Sparta, N. C.	Boyton Station, Oct. 14, 1863
"	Mebane, W. A.	27th North Carolina.	"	Woodville, N. C.	Bristow Station, Oct. 14, 1863
"	McMurray, M.	7th Louisiana.	"	New Orleans, La.	Rappahannock, Nov. 7, 1863
"	Murrell, S. F.	McLean's Cav. Batt.	Tennessee	Tall Branch, Tenn.	Sullivan co., Tenn., Oct. 27, 1863
"	Mills, J. P.	47th Virginia.	Northern Va.	Camden, Miss.	Fredericksburg, May 5, 1863
"	Moncure, W. P.	47th "	"	Richmond, Va.	Falling Waters, July 14, 1863
"	Maurras, A.	30th Louisiana.	Mississippi	New Orleans, La.	Port Hudson, July 9, 1863
"	Matthews, W. W.	4th Florida.	Tennessee	Providence, Fla.	Miss'y Ridge, Nov. 25, 1863
Colonel	Murchison, K. M.	54th North Carolina.	Northern Va.	Lexington, Va.	Rappahannock, Nov. 7, 1863
Lieutenant	McDonald, R. A.	11th Mississippi.	"	Houston, Miss.	Gettysburg, July 3, 1863
"	Michie, H. C.	56th Virginia.	"	Charlottesville, Va.	" July 2, 1863
"	Morris, T. C.	14th "	"	Union Mills, Va.	" July 2, 1863
"	Miller, J. A.	56th "	"	Waynesboro', Va.	" July 3, 1863
"	Merrill, W. C.	8th Kentucky Cav.	Tennessee	Lexington, Ky.	Saylesville, Ohio, July 26, 1863
"	McGraw, T. J.	10th " "	"	Caseyville, Ky.	Corydon, Ind., July 9, 1863

Rank	Name	Regiment	Army	Residence	Place & Date
Lieutenant..	Moore, J. B.......	11th Mississippi....	Northern Va	Landeneth, Miss....	Gettysburg, July 3, 1863
Captain....	McArtney, T. B.....	28th Virginia.......	"	Portsmouth, Va....	" July 3, 1863
"	McCorkle, G. B....	4th Virginia........	"	Lexington, Va......	" July 3, 1863
"	Mullins, B. B......	1st Kentucky.......	Tennessee...	Demasville, Ky....	Shelbyville, Oct. 2, 1863
"	Mathers, A........	Wall's Legion......	"	Bellesville, Texas...	
"	Mullins, H. H......	King's Regiment...	Trans-Miss...	Huntsville, Ark....	Helena, July 4, 1863
"	Morgan, T. G......	1st Louisiana......	Northern Va.	New Orleans, La...	Rappahannock, Nov. 7, 1863
Lieutenant..	McClelland, J. T....	58th Alabama......	Tennessee....	Asheville, Ala......	Miss'y Ridge, Nov. 25, 1863
"	Mouly, B. F........	36th Alabama......	"	Carthage, Ala.....	" Nov. 25, 1863
Colonel.....	Maxwell, G. T.....	1st Florida........	"	Tallahassee, Fla....	" Nov. 25, 1863
Lieutenant..	McChesney, W. L..	63d Virginia.......	"	Allington, (?) Va....	" Nov. 25, 1863
"	Morris, J. R.......	39th Mississippi....	"	Westville, Miss....	Port Hudson, July 9, 1863
"	Murray, T. J......	39th Mississippi....	"	Westville, Miss.....	" July 9, 1863
Captain....	Matthews, L......	1st Louisiana Cav..	"	Plagremense, La...	Stanford, Ky., Aug. 1, 1863
Lieutenant..	Malone, J. W......	8th Florida........	Northern Va.	Quincy, Fla.......	Gettysburg, July 3, 1863
"	Matthew, C. A.....	Wall's Legion......	Mississippi...	Belleville, Texas....	Yazoo City, July 4, 1863
"	McCoy, W.........	Wall's Legion......	"	Alabama, Texas....	" July 1, 1863
"	McLucan, M. M...	9th Louisiana Cav..	"	Jackson, La........	Port Hudson, July 9, 1863
"	Murphy, J. D......	3d Missouri Cav...	"	Alexandria, Mo.....	Vicksburg, July 4, 1863
Major......	Messick, E. H......	14th Arkansas.....	"	Yellville, Ark.	Port Hudson, July 9, 1863
Captain....	McBee, S..........	30th Mississippi....	Tennessee...	Yazoo City, Miss...	Lookout M't'n, Nov. 24, 1863
Lieutenant.	Murdett, F. H......	12th Kentucky Cav.	"	Springfield, Ky.....	—— Ohio, July 26, 1863
Captain....	McCaunn, T. W....	8th Kentucky Cav..	"	Lexington, Ky.....	Soulsville, Ohio, July 26, 1863
"	McChristy, G. W...	10th Missouri......	Trans-Miss...	Palmyra, Mo......	Helena, July 4, 1863
"	McKill, James......	8th Missouri.......	"	Nevada City, Mo...	Miss'y Ridge, Aug. 18, 1863
"	McKee, S. F......	2d Kentucky Cav...	Tennessee....	New Orleans, La...	—— Ohio, July 26, 1863
Lieutenant..	McDowell, E. C....	1st Tennessee Art..	Mississippi...	Memphis, Tenn....	Port Hudson, July 9, 1863
"	McLaughlin, H. B..	35th Alabama......	"	Florence, Ala......	Big Black River, May 17, 1863
Captain....	McLean, F. J.......	9th Tennessee Cav.	Tennessee...	Columbia, Tenn....	Port Hudson, July 9, 1863
Major......	Merchant, A.......	C. S. Cavalry......	Mississippi...	Mobile, Ala........	" July 9, 1863
Lieutenant..	McDonald, M. R....	52d North Carolina.	Northern Va.	Rockingham, N. C.	Gettysburg, July 6, 1863
"	McEacher, J. C.....	1st Alabama.......	Mississippi...	Clayton, Ala........	Port Hudson, July 9, 1863
Lieut.-Col..	McCarty, M.......	23d Mississippi.....	"	Ripley, Miss.......	Grenada, June 9, 1863
Lieutenant.	McIntire, W. R.....	9th Georgia Art....	Tennessee....	Atlanta, Ga........	Cumberl'd Gap, Sept. 9, 1863

Rank.	Name.	Regiment.	Army of	Residence.	Where & When Captured.
Lieutenant..	Morphis, W. J......	....	Tennessee...		
Captain.....	McDonald, J. C.....	1st Missouri Cav....	Trans-Miss...	Hannibal, Mo......	Little Rock, Sep. 10, 1863
Lieutenant..	Marshall, J. T......	29th Mississippi....	Tennessee...	Charleston, Miss...	Miss'y Ridge, Nov. 24, 1863
Captain.....	McKenzie, A. D....	44th Georgia.......	Northern Va.	Bear Creek, Ga.....	Gettysburg, July 4, 1863
"	McKenzie, A. A....	16th North Carolina.	"	Rutherford, N. C...	" July 3, 1863
Lieutenant..	McInturf, J. T	16th North Carolina.	"	"	" July 3, 1863
"	McIntire, R. M.....	4th North Carolina..	"	Wilmington, N. C..	" July 5, 1863
"	McLauren, S. H....	13th Alabama......	"	Gold Ridge, Ala....	" July 5, 1863
"	Martin, J. T........	21st North Carolina.	"	Ayresville, N. C....	" July 4, 1863
"	Monday, T. N.....	11th Alabama......	"	Greensboro', Ala...	" July 3, 1863
"	Minter, B. W.......	53d North Carolina.	"	Mt. Airy, N. C.....	" July 4, 1863
"	Martin, B. F.......	25th Texas.........	Trans-Miss...	Goliad, Texas......	Arkansas Post, June 11, 1863
"	Morris, W. S......	15th Louisiana.....	Northern Va.	Trinity, La.........	Gettysburg, July 4, 1863
"	Matthew, W. M....	53d North Carolina.	"	Charlotte, N. C.....	South Mountain, July 4, 1863
"	Miller, J. C........	53d North Carolina.	"	Elkville, N. C......	Gettysburg, July 4, 1863
Captain.....	McLaughlin, L. W..	1st Louisiana.......	"	New Orleans, La...	" July 4, 1863
Lieutenant..	Martin, B. Y.......	34th North Carolina.	"	Laurel Springs, N. C	" July 5, 1863
"	Maxwell, P........	33d Virginia........	"	Mt. Jackson, Va....	Chambersburg, July 5, 1863
Captain.....	Malone, H. E......	8th Georgia........	"	Greenville, Ga.....	Gettysburg, July 4, 1863
Lieutenant..	Malone, C. B.......	9th Louisiana......	"	Franklinton, La....	Rappahannock, Nov. 7, 1863
"	Morris, C. B.......	9th Louisiana......	"	"	" Nov. 7, 1863
"	McCann, D.........	9th Louisiana Cav..	Mississippi...	"	Port Hudson, July 9, 1863
Captain.....	McGreen, T........	18th Arkansas......	"	Pine Bluff, Ark.....	" July 9, 1863
Lieutenant..	Mann, J. S.........	12th Arkansas......	"	Henderson, Ark....	" July 9, 1863
"	McCaw, W. M......	7th Tennessee......	Northern Va.	Gallatin, Tenn......	Gettysburg, July 5, 1863
"	McGahee, W. W. J..	39th Mississippi....	Mississippi...	Port Hudson, La...	Port Hudson, July 9, 1863
"	Miles, L............	39th Mississippi....	"	Stearns' Creek, Miss	" July 9, 1863
"	Mallory, W. S......	49th Tennessee.....	"	Clarksville, Ark....	" July 9, 1863
Captain.....	Moore, J. W........	18th Arkansas......	"	Caton Plant, Ark...	" July 9, 1863
Lieutenant .	McGarrah, S.......	39th Mississippi....	"	Pela Hatchie, Miss.	" July 9, 1863
Adjutant....	Melvin, J. S........	39th Mississippi.....	"	Brandon, Miss......	" July 9, 1863

Rank	Name	Regiment	Department	Residence	Place and Date
Lieutenant..	Morris, B. T.	27th Mississippi	Mississippi...	Dunnsville, Miss....	Lookout M't'n, Nov. 24, 1863
Captain.....	Morgan, J. E.	13th Arkansas	Tennessee...	Marion, Ark.	Ohio, July 24, 1863
Lieutenant..	Marshall, J. M.	15th Arkansas	Mississippi...	Columbia, Ark.	Port Hudson, July 9, 1863
Captain.....	McClung, R. L.	15th Arkansas	"	Bright Star, Ark.	" July 9, 1863
Lieutenant..	McBoon, B. F.	23d Arkansas	"	Harrisonburg, Ark.	" July 9 1863
"	McLean, T.	1st Mississippi	"	Shannon, Miss.	" July 9, 1863
"	Miller, E. W.	28th Alabama	Tennessee...	Holly Grove, Ala.	Miss'y Ridge, Nov. 25, 1863
"	McKenan, A. S.	16th Arkansas	Mississippi...	Carrollsville, Ark.	Port Hudson, July 9, 1863
"	McClung, W. B.	49th Alabama	"	Huntsville, Ala.	Madison co, Ala., Sep. 10, 1863
"	McClary, L. W.	4th Alabama Cav.	"	"	" Oct. 20, 1863
"	Myers, P. S.	30th Mississippi	Tennessee...	Oxford, Miss.	Lookout M't'n, Nov. 24, 1863
"	Moore, H. F.	30th Mississippi	"	Grenada, Miss.	" Nov. 24, 1863
"	Meek, J. J.	30th Mississippi	"	Atlanta, Miss.	" Nov. 24, 1863
"	McGinnis, J. M.	37th Mississippi	"	Pasgagrata, Miss.	" Nov. 24, 1863
"	McCloskey, A. P.	48th Alabama	"	Guntersville, Ala.	" Nov. 24, 1863
"	Murphy, J.	4th Alabama Cav.	"	Huntsville, Ala.	Madison co, Ala., Oct. 20 1863
"	Miller, F. M.	8th Alabama	"	Mobile, Ala.	Gettysburg, July 3, 1863
Captain....	Morris, J. R.	—— Arkansas Reg.	Trans-Miss...	Pleasant Plains, Ark	Helena, July 4, 1863
Lieutenant..	McLaney, L.	Hart's Regiment	"	Gainesville, Ark.	" July 1, 1863
"	McGill, C. R.	8th Missouri	"	Morristown, Ark.	" July 4, 1863
Captain.....	McDaniel, John	10th Missouri	"	Trenton, Mo.	" July 4, 1863
Lieutenant..	McKenney, R. T.	Gaw's Regiment	"	Pleasant Plains, Ark	" July 4, 1863
"	Merrill, Robert	10th C. S. Cavalry	Tennessee...	Lamar, Ala.	Lancaster, Ky., July 31, 1863
Major......	Malone, J. W.	1st Kentucky Cav.	Mississippi...	Columbus, Ky.	Swallow Bluff, July 30, 1863
Lieutenant..	McMullin, L.	12th Tennessee Cav.	"	Memphis, Tenn.	Wyatt's, Oct. 13, 1863
"	Malone, C. B.	C. S. Cavalry	Tennessee...	Hillabie, Ala.	Lancaster, Ky., July 31, 1863
"	Moses, L. L.	10th C. S. Cavalry	"	Victoria, Ala.	Jacksboro', Aug. 27, 1863
Captain.....	McDonald, Robert.	—— Artillery	"	St. Louis, Mo.	
"	McConnell, J. H.	14th Georgia	Northern Va.	Ackworth, Ga.	Gettysburg, July 4, 1863
Lieutenant..	Moore, S. T.	King's Regiment	Trans-Miss...	Pea Ridge, Ark.	Helena, July 4, 1863
Captain.. ..	Morose, P. J.	10th Kentucky Cav.	Tennessee...	Henderson, Ky.	
"	Miller, R. T.	10th Kentucky Cav.	"		
Lieutenant..	McFarland, James.	Miles' Legion	Mississippi...	New Orleans, La.	Port Hudson, July 9, 1863
Captain.....	Meriwether, S. O.	23d Alabama	"	Haynesville, Ala.	Port Gibson, May 1, 1863

Rank.	Name.	Regiment.	Army of	Residence	Where & When Captured.
Lieutenant..	Murray, J............	Hampton's Staff....	Mississippi....	Port Gibson, Miss..	Willow Springs, May 3, 1863
Captain.....	Monroe, J. A.......	9th Mississippi......	Tennessee...	Hernando, Miss....	At Home, May 24, 1863
Major.......	McBrooks, J........	Q. M. Stuart's Brig..	Mississippi...	Memphis, Tenn.....	Bolivar, Tenn., Aug. 1, 1863
Lieutenant..	Morrison, J. F.....	....	"	Port Gibson........	Vicksburg, July 1, 1863
Captain.....	Monley, W. W......	15th Arkansas......	"	Madison, Arkansas..	Port Hudson, July 9, 1863
Lieutenant..	Moody, B. D.......	15th Arkansas......	"	Ozark, Arkansas....	Big Black, May 17, 1863
Major	McDonald, —— ...	15th Georgia.......	Northern Va.		
Colonel.....	Mattock, C. H.....	Enrolling Officer....	....	Augusta, Ark......	
Lieutenant..	Munson, S. A......				
"	McCurley, J. H.....	2d Mississippi......	....	Pontetoc, Miss......	
Captain	McGeehee, W. G....	A Q. M. 30th Miss..			
"	Morgan, E. S.......	9th La. Cav.........		Baton Rouge, La...	
Lieutenant..	Morris, C. B.......	9th La. Cav.........		Washington, La....	
"	Mattocks, J. W.....	55th Georgia.......		Culbert, Georgia...	
Captain....	McCulloch, R......	18th Virginia.......		Oceola, Mississippi..	
"	McLean, N. C.....	Buckner's Escort...		Covington, Ky.....	
Lieutenant..	Northfield, M. W...	77th North Carolina	Northern Va.	Yanceyville, N. C...	Gettysburg, July 5, 1863
"	Nash, D. W......	1st Florida Cavalry.	Tennessee...	Tallahassee Fla....	Miss'y Ridge, Nov. 25, 1863
"	Nitchell, H. P.....	5th Kentucky	"	West Liberty, Ky...	Morgan co., May 16, 1863
Captain.....	Nicholas, W. S.....	8th Kentucky Cav..	"	Winchester, Ky.....	Soulsville, Ohio, July 26, 1863
Lieutenant..	Newman, A. M.....	7th Virginia........	Northern Va.	Harrisonburg, Va..	Gettysburg, July 3, 1863
Captain.....	Norman, W. M.....	2d North Carolina..	"	Rockford, N. C.....	Kelly's Ford, Nov. 7, 1863
Lieutenant..	Norman, M. H.....	28th North Carolina	"	Indisville, N. C.. ..	Liberty Mills, Sept. 22, 1863
"	Nance, ——	7th Tennessee......	Tennessee...	Shelbyville, Tenn...	Ringgold, Nov. 27, 1863
"	Nash, C. C.........	6th Louisiana......	Northern Va.	Chaunceyville, La..	Rappahannock, Nov. 7, 1863
"	Nuckols, W. L.....	1st Missouri Cav...	Mississippi...	Millsville, Missouri..	Big Black, May 17, 1863
"	Norvell, Charles....	14th Virginia......	Northern Va.	Lynchburg, Va.....	Winchester, June 12, 1863
Adjutant....	Newman, C. S......	60th Tennessee.....	Mississippi...	Gordonsville, Va...	Big Black, May 10, 1863
Lieutenant..	Noliner, James.....	44th Tennessee.....	Tennessee...	Carthage, Tenn.....	Murfreesboro', Jan. 4, 1863
"	Norris, J. E.........	Watson's Batt......	Mississippi...	New Orleans, La....	Port Hudson, July 9, 1863
Captain.....	Neill, L. C.........	62d North Carolina.	Tennessee...	Franklin, N. C......	Cumberl'd Gap, Sep. 9, 1863

Rank	Name	Regiment	Army	Residence	Where/When
Lieutenant..	Neill, W. B......	Bragg's Scout......	Tennessee...	Danville, Virginia..	
"	Newsom, J. D......	41st N. C...........	Northern Va.	Raleigh, N. C......	Gettysburg, July 3, 1863
Captain.....	Nelson, P. D......	A. A. G...........	"	Brandon, Virginia...	Millwood, Va., Oct. 25, 1863
Lieutenant..	Norwood, W. T....	6th North Carolina.	Tennessee...	Huntsville, Ala......	Lookout M't'n, Oct. 28, 1863
"	Naburs, C.........	14th Louisiana......	Northern Va.	Blockbook.........	Gettysburg, July 4, 1863
Colonel....	Nixon, J. O.......	1st Louisiana Cav...	Tennessee...	New Orleans, La...	Lancaster, Ky., July 31, 1863
Lieutenant..	Nicholson, H. P....	....	"	Columbia	Columbia, July 13, 1863
"	Norwood, J. W.....	3d Alabama Cav....	"	Mt. Sterling, Ala...	Sequatchen, August 2, 1863
"	Nicholson, E. G....	9th Alabama.......	"	Guntersville, Ala...	Gettysburg, July 2, 1863
Captain.....	Nicholas, P........	11th North Carolina.	Northern Va.	Castalin, N. C......	Rocky Mount, July 20, 1863
Lieutenant..	Newman, A. N....	Kune Artillery......	Tennessee...	Greenville, Tenn...	Cumberl'd Gap, Sept. 9, 1863
"	Norton, W. P.......	62d North Carolina.	"	Franklin, N. C......	Cumberl'd Gap, Sept. 9, 1863
"	Newsom, L. J......	Hart's Regiment....	Trans-Miss...	Kenyon, Ark.......	Helena, July 4, 1863
"	Newton, A. E......	4th Louisiana Batt..	Mississippi...	Church Hill, Miss...	Nollkey, August 22, 1863
"	Nesmith, A........	5th Alabama Cav...	Tennessee...	Danville, Tenn.....	Brown's Ferry, Oct. 2, 1863
"	Nash, C. B........	30th Mississippi.....	"	Wenona, Mississippi	Lookout M't'n, Nov. 24, 1863
"	Nelms, A. M.......	28th Tennessee.....	"	Tazewell, Tenn.....	Miss'y Ridge, Nov. 24, 1863
"	Nolley, W. F.......	10th Arkansas......	Mississippi...	Muddy Bayou, Ark.	Port Hudson, July 9, 1863
"	Noland, P. J.......	Eng'r Batt........	"	Natchez, Mississippi	Port Hudson, July 9, 1863
Captain.....	Nelson, C. A.......	49th Virginia	Northern Va.	Dumfries, Virginia..	South Mountain, July 5, 1863
Lieutenant..	Nelson, E.........	15th Virginia Cav...	"	Dumfries, Virginia..	South Mountain, July 5, 1863
"	Nelson, J. H.......	32d North Carolina.	"	Germantown, N. C.	Dumfries, Va., June 21, 1863
Adjutant....	Noman, J. S.......	23d Alabama......	"	Union Springs, Ala.	Gettysburg, July 3, 1863
Lieutenant..	Nolan, W. M......	16th North Carolina	"	Dallas, N. C.	
Captain.....	Orea, A. J.........	53d Georgia........	Tennessee...	Owensville, Georgia	Cumberl'd Gap, Sept. 9, 1863
"	Osborn, J. M......	16th Georgia Cav...	"	ChinquapinGro'e,Ga	Cumberl'd Gap, Sep. 22, 1863
"	Orr, J. P..........	64th North Carolina	"	Jonesville, Va......	Cumberl'd Gap, Sept. 9, 1863
"	Oliver, J. B........	20th North Carolina	Northern Va..	Mt. Olive, N. C....	Gettysburg, July 1, 1863
"	Owens, L. S........	4th Florida.........	Tennessee...	Tallahassee, Florida	Miss'y Ridge, Nov. 25 1863
"	Oliver, Victor......	13th Louisiana......	"	New Orleans, La....	Miss'y Ridge, Nov. 25, 1863
"	Owens, J. J........	1st Alabama.......	Mississippi...	Brandage, Alabama	Port Hudson, July 9, 1863
"	Odorn, J. G.......	12th North Carolina	Beauregard..	Jackson, S. C......	Northampton, July 28, 1863
"	O'Connor, T.......	D. C. Artillery......	Tennessee...	Knoxville, Tenn....	Cumberl'd Gap, Sept. 9, 1863
"	Oliver, E. D........	18th Virginia.......	Northern Va..	Pittsylvania C.H.,Va	Gettysburg, July 3, 1863

Rank.	Name.	Regiment.	Army of	Residence.	Where & When Captured.
Lieutenant..	Owens, J. A........	57th North Carolina.	Northern Va..	Salisbury, N. C....	Rappahannock, Nov. 7, 1863
"	Owen, V. J........	34th Mississippi.....	Tennessee...	Salem, Miss........	Lookout M't'n, Nov. 24, 1863
Captain.....	O'Connor, M......	6th Louisiana......	Northern Va..	New Orleans, La...	Rappahannock, Nov. 7, 1863
Lieutenant..	Oliver, P. D......	8th Louisiana......	"	St. Martinsville, La.	" Nov. 7, 1863
Adjutant....	Orr, John.........	8th Louisiana......	"	New Orleans, La...	" Nov. 7, 1863
Lieutenant..	Osborn, E. W.....	54th North Carolina.	"	Jonesville, N. C.....	" Nov. 7, 1863
Adjutant ...	Otis, N. G.........	46th Alabama......	Mississippi...	Georgetown, Ga....	Champion Hill, May 16, 1863
Lieutenant..	Owens, R. L.......	62d North Carolina.	Tennessee...	Maysville, N. C.....	Cumberl'd Gap, Sept. 9, 1863
Captain.....	Owens, W. V.....	2d Tennessee Cav..	"	Bluntville, Tenn....	July 30, 1863
"	Owens, E.........	9th Louisiana......	Northern Va..	Milwaka Bend, La..	Gettysburg, July 3, 1863
Lieutenant..	Owen, F. A........	10th Kentucky.....	Tennessee...	Madisonville, Ky...	Salesville, Ohio, July 22, 1863
"	Owen, G. W......	44th Kentucky Cav.	"	Shelbyville, Ky....	Spargford, Ky., July 6, 1863
"	Orilan F..........	1st Louisiana.......	"	Eggsville, La......	Mill Spring, May 30, 1863
"	Orr, E. H. M.......	62d North Carolina.			
Captain.....	Ohlsom, P M......	McNair's Staff......	Tennessee....	Washington, Ark...	Chickamauga, Sept. 18, 1863
Lieutenant..	Owen, B. N......	60th North Carolina.	"	East Port, N. C....	Cumberl'd Gap, Sept. 9, 1863
"	Oglesby, G. S......	3d Georgia.........	Northern Va..	Augusta, Ga.......	Gettysburg, July 4, 1863
"	O'Bannon, B. C....	Mosby's Cav.......	"	Skipwith, Miss.....	Washington City Aug. 2, 1863
Captain.....	Ogden, W. F......	7th Louisiana......	Mississippi....	New Orleans, La...	Rappahannock, Nov. 6, 1863
Lieutenant..	O'Brien, J. E......	1st Kentucky Cav..	Tennessee...	Knoxville, Tenn....	Shannonville, Aug. 24, 1863
"	Oglesby, J.........	Kick's Battalion....	Northern Va.	Gainesville, Ga....	Cash Town, July 5, 1863
Captain	Owen. W. F.......	18th Arkansas......	Mississippi ...	Pine Bluff, Ark.....	Port Hudson, July 9, 1863
Lieutenant..	O'Neal, E. T.......	Rhett's Battalion...	Northern Va.	Charlotte, N. C....	Gettysburg, July 4, 1863
"	Offett N. S........	5th Kentucky Cav..	Tennessee....	New Town, Ky...	Salemville, July 26, 1863
Captain	O'Neil, J..........	Miles' Legion......	Mississippi ...	Natchez, Miss......	Port Hudson, July 9, 1863
"	O'Brien, John......	30th Arkansas.....	Tennessee....	Little Rock, Ark...	Murfreesboro, Jan. 5, 1863
"	O'Brien J	5th Louisiana	Mississippi....	L'ke Providence, La	Port Hudson, July 9, 1863
"	Owens, J. A.......	57th North Carolina.	Northern Va..	Salisbury, N C....	Rappahannock, Nov. 7, 1863
Colonel.....	Parks, M. A.......	52d North Carolina.	"	Wilkes, Co., N. C...	Gettysburg, July 3, 1863
Lieutenant..	Pittman, J J.......	10th Kentucky Cav.	Tennessee...	Mt Sterling, Ky....	" June 10, 1863
Captain	Preist, Wm	2d Missouri........	Trans-Miss...	Georgetown, Mo...	" July 1, 1863

Rank	Name	Regiment	Theater	Home	Place & Date
Lieutenant..	Proctor, Wm.......	2d Kentucky Cav...	Tennessee....	Elyarsville, Ky.....	Shelbyville, Oct. 7, 1863
"	Price, T. W.......	16th Mississippi.....	"	Utica, Miss.........	Utica, Miss., Oct. 7, 1863
Captain.....	Pendergrast, ——...	7th Georgia........	Northern Va..	New Orleans, La...	Rappahannock, Nov. 7, 1863
Lieutenant..	Petty, J. W........	Young's Regiment..	Trans-Miss...	Carthage, Mo......	Feb. 22, 1863
Captain	Petticon, C. H......	—— Cavalry.......	Tennessee....	Fountain Head, Ten	May, 5, 1863
Ex-Capt ...	Pitts, J. H.........				Gallatin, May 9, 1863
Lieutenant..	Phillips, H. R......	10th Virginia Cav...	Northern Va..	Glade Hill, Va.....	Pennsylvania, July 5, 1863
"	Philpot, B. W......	57th Virginia......	"	Wanville, Va.......	Gettysburg, July 3, 1863
"	Pigman W. P......	8th Florida........	"	Cedar Ridge, Fla...	" July 3, 1863
"	Peels, W...........	11th Mississippi....	"	Oakland, Miss......	" July 3, 1863
"	Palmer, N. H......	7th South Carolina..	"	Beuxdeux, S. C.....	" July 3, 1863
"	Perkins, A.........	14th Virginia......	"	Palmyra, Va.......	" July 3, 1863
"	Prow, J. W........	10th Kentucky.....	Tennessee ...	Claysville, Tenn....	Tullahama.
Captain	Perkins, C. A......	16th South Carolina.		Grainwell, S. C.....	Gainesville, Nov. 26, 1863
Lieutenant..	Pierson, L.........	14th Arkansas......	Mississippi...	Yellville, Ark......	Port Hudson, July 9, 1863
"	Parker, P. M......	60th North Carolina.	Tennessee...	East Port, N. C.....	Cumberland Gap Sep. 9. 1863
"	Peeler, A. J.......	5th Florida........	Northern Va.	Tallahassee, Fla....	Gettysburg, July 4, 1863
"	Powell, J. W......	46th Alabama......	Mississippi...	Montgomery	Champion Hill,
"	Pratt, M. E........	7th Alabama... ...	"	Prattsville, Ala.....	Port Hudson,
"	Pelham, W........	51st Alabama......	Tennessee....	Alexander, Ala....	Shelbyville, June, 10, 1863
Lieut.-Col...	Payne, Wm. H.....	4th Virginia.......	Northern Va..	Warrenton, Va.....	Gettysburg. July 3, 1863
Captain.....	Perry, Wm. E......	16th Virginia.......	"	Payrell. Va........	Boonesboro,
Colonel.....	Pean, D. B........	7th Louisiana......	"	New Orleans, La...	Rappahannock, Nov. 7, 1863
Lieutenant..	Price, S. R........	1st Missouri........	Mississippi...	St. Joseph, Mo. ...	Big Black, May 17, 1863
Captain	Parker, J. P.......	20th Arkansas......	"	Albany, Ark.......	" May 17, 1863
"	Parham, S. J.......	54th North Carolina.	Northern Va.	Henderson, N. C...	Rappahannock, Nov. 7, 1863
"	Parish, W. R......	6th North Carolina.	"	Flat River, N. C....	" Nov. 7, 1863
Lieutenant..	Price, T. A	6th North Carolina.	"	Salisbury, N. C.....	" Nov. 7, 1863
"	Poole, J. P........	27th North Carolina.	"	Taylorsville, N C...	Gettysburg, July 3, 1863
"	Paul, G. W........	1st Arkansas.......	Mississippi...	Greenfield, Mo......	Port Gibson, May 1, 1863
"	Petty, J...........	1st Arkansas.......	"	Dover, Ark........	Big Black, May 17, 1863
Major.......	Printub, D. S......	56th Louisiana.....	Tennessee....	Rome, Geo.......	Cumberl'd Gap, Sept. 9, 1863
Lieutenant..	Porter, J. N.......	4th Kentucky......	"	Hadley, Ky.......	Bardstown, June, 17, 1863
"	Perry, Thomas.....	17th Virginia.......	Northern Va..	Alexandria, Va.....	Manassas Gap, July 21, 1863

Rank.	Name.	Regiment.	Army of	Residence.	Where & When Captured.
Lieutenant..	Power, Thomas....	17th Virginia......	Northern Va..	Alexandria, Va.....	Manassas Gap, July 21, 1863
"	Pierce, Charles H..	7th Louisiana.......	"	New Orleans, La...	Rappahannock, Nov. 7, 1863
"	Pearce, B. F........	54th North Carolina.	"	Fayetteville, N. C..	" Nov. 7, 1863
"	Pharr, J. E. W......	51st North Carolina.	"	Harris' Depot......	" Nov. 7, 1863
"	Peele, A. E........	51st North Carolina.	"	Jackson, N. C......	" Nov. 7, 1863
Lieut.-Col...	Parker, J. P........	Acting Chief of Art.	Mississippi...	Jackson, Miss......	Port Hudson, July 9, 1863
Lieutenant..	Phillips, D. D......	1st Penn Bat.......	"	Nashville, Tenn....	" July 9, 1863
"	Porter, D..........	26th North Carolina.	Northern Va..	Hagersville, N. C ..	Gettysburg, July 3, 1863
"	Phillips, J. M......	2d Mississippi......	"	Holly Springs, Miss.	" July 3, 1863
"	Philpot, G. B......	7th Virginia Cav...	"	Warrenton, Va.....	Boonesboro, July 24, 1863
"	Pritchard, C.......	32d North Carolina.	"	Windsor, N. C.....	Gettysburg, July 4, 1863
"	Propst, W.........	57th North Carolina.	"	Concord, N. C.....	" July 5, 1863
Colonel.....	Province, D........	16th Arkansas......	Mississippi....	Strother, S. C.....	Port Hudson, July 9, 1863
Adjutant....	Perry, R. T........	8th Louisiana.......	Northern Va..	Vermillion, La.....	Rappahannock, Nov. 1, 1863
Lieutenant..	Patterson, E. D.....	9th Alabama.......	"	Hatterford, Ala....	Gettysburg, July 2, 1863
"	Pond, W. W........	13th Alabama......	"	Rockford, Ala......	Gettysburg, July 5, 1863
"	Patton, M..........	9th Alabama.......	"	Greenville, Ala.....	" July 5, 1863
"	Phillips, J. L.......	64th North Carolina.	Tennessee ...	Fauquier, Va......	Cumberl'd Gap, Sept. 9, 1863
"	Proffit, Ira........	16th North Carolina.	Northern Va..	Marshall, N. C.....	Gettysburg, July 3, 1863
"	Proffit, W. A......	62d North Carolina	Tennessee ...	"	Williamsburg, Aug. 2, 1863
"	Prevalt, L.........	3d Alabama........	"	Mobile, Ala........	Shelbyville, June 27, 1863
"	Price, J. E.........	7th Alabama.......	"	Nashville, Tenn....	" June 27, 1863
"	Powell, C H.......	6th Kentucky......	"	Carroten, Ky......	Camp Den, July 14, 1863
"	Parks, B. F........	1st Tennessee......	Northern Va..	Pettham, Tenn.....	Gettysburg, July 5, 1863
"	Pickett, G. W......	1st Tennessee......	"	Gustave, Tenn.....	" July 5, 1863
"	Purvis, J. A.......	1st Mississippi......	Mississippi....	Yazoo City, Miss...	Port Hudson, July 9, 1863
"	Prator, J. H.......	25th Louisiana......	Tennessee ...	Monterey, La.......	Miss'y Ridge, Nov. 25, 1863
"	Piper, G. A........	60th Louisiana......	Mississippi...	Jonesboro, Tenn....	Big Black, May 17, 1863
"	Portman, S........	60th Louisiana......	"	Russellville, Tenn..	" May 17, 1863
Captain.....	Plunkett, W. A....	—— Ark. Reg't.....	Trans-Miss...	Brownsville, Ark...	Helena, Ark., July 4, 1863
Lieutenant..	Puburn, W. H. H..	"	"	"	" July 4, 1863

Rank	Name	Regiment	Army	Residence	Where/When Killed	
Lieutenant..	Puckett, E. N......	21st Arkansas Reg't	Mississippi...	Wild Haws.........	Big Black,	May 17, 1863
"	Pruett, R. B........	31st Alabama.......	"	Mount Olive.......	Champion Hill,	May 16, 1863
"	Pierce, W. N.......	8th Missouri.......	Trans-Miss...	Newton, Mo..	Helena,	July 4, 1863
"	Purcell, A. M	40th Virginia.......	Northern Va.	Farnham Church...	Gettysburg,	July 5, 1863
"	Purcell, W. A......	86th Georgia.......	Mississippi...	Orange, Ga.......	Champion Hill,	May 16, 1863
"	Purvis, J...........	1st Arkansas.......	"	Benton, Miss......	Port Hudson,	July 9, 1863
"	Powell, T. C........	47th North Carolina	Northern Va.	Raleigh, N. C......	Gettysburg,	July 1, 1863
"	Pegress, E. D......	38th Florida........	Tennessee...	Liberty Hill, Ala...	Miss'y Ridge,	Nov. 25, 1863
"	Park, J. S..........	16th Florida........	Trans-Miss...			
Captain.....	Patton, John........	1st Missouri Cav....	"	Gannt's Hill, Mo...	Big Black,	May 17, 1863
Colonel.....	Phillips, C. D......	52d Georgia........	"	Minata, Ga........	"	May 17, 1863
Lieutenant..	Perry, Jock.........	17th Tennessee.....	Tennessee...	Beck Grove, Tenn..	Coffee Town,	June 24, 1863
"	Pearson, J. M......	30th Alabama......	Mississippi...	Dadesville, Ala.....	Vicksburg,	May 22, 1863
Colonel.....	Powell, R. M.......	5th Texas..........	Northern Va.	Danville, Texas....	Gettysburg,	July 2, 1863
"	Pumley, W. C......	C. S A............	....	Mossy Creek, Tenn.		
Lieutenant..	Person, S. A........	30th Tennessee.....				
"	Passmore, M	62d North Carolina.	Tennessee...	Fort Henry, N. C...	Cumberl'd Gap,	Sep. 9, 1863
"	Pacetty, Lewis.....	2d Florida..........	Northern Va.	St. Margos, Ga.....	Fredericksburg,	June 5, 1863
"	Phelps, C. V.......	10th Virginia Cav..	"	Parkersburg, Va....	Barrsville, Md.,	June 25, 1863
"	Praker, H. C.......	Prof. Cav..........	Tennessee....	Hickory Flat, Ala..	Lancaster, Ky.,	Aug. 30, 1863
"	Putnam, A. W......	18th Georgia.......	Northern Va..	Wandstuck, Ga....	Gettysburg,	July 4, 1863
Captain.....	Palmer, B..........	—— Artillery......	....	Memphis, Tenn....		Oct. 13, 1863
Lieutenant..	Pruitte, P. N.......	10th Arkansas......	Mississippi...	Kentucky Valley...	Port Hudson,	July 9, 1863
Lieut.-Col ..	Pitman, J. N........	16th Arkansas......	"	Fayetteville, Ark...	"	July 9, 1863
Lieutenant..	Pitman, W. E.......	16th Arkansas......	"	Fayetteville, Ark...	"	July 9, 1863
"	Parker, G. W.......	49th Alabama......	"	Mayesville, Ala....	"	July 9, 1863
"	Penvis, H..........	49th Alabama......	"	Guntersville, Ala...	"	July 9, 1863
"	Pankey, S H	49th Alabama......	"	Stephenson, Ala...	"	July 9, 1863
"	Pope, T. A..........	29th Mississippi.....	Tennessee...	Goodson, Miss.....	Lookout M t'n,	Nov. 24, 1863
Captain.....	Pratt, R. H.........	20th Alabama......	Mississippi...	Centreville........	Port Gibson,	May 17, 1863
Adjutant....	Price, F. L.........	—— Texas Reg't...	Northern Va..	Austin, Texas......	Gettysburg,	July 1, 1863
Lieut.-Col ..	Parish, W. N.......	18th Arkansas......	Mississippi...	Little Rock, Ark....	Port Hudson,	July 9, 1863
Captain.....	Perle, M. C.........	2d Mississippi......	"	Ripley, Arkansas [?]	"	July 9, 1863
Lieutenant..	Perry, J. A.........	53d Tennessee......	Tennessee...	Camersville, Tenn..	"	July 9, 1863

Rank.	Name.	Regiment.	Army of	Residence.	Where & When Captured.
Captain....	Powers, H. N......	2d Mississippi.......	Northern Va.	Ripley, Miss....[?]..	Williamsport, July 5, 1863
Lieutenant..	Pate, W. R.........	24th "	Tennessee ...	Brunswick, Miss....	Lookout M't'n, Nov. 2 1863
Captain.....	Powell, W. W......	13th North Carolina.	....	Troy, Mo.........	
"	Pulliam, A. J......	17th Mississippi.....	Northern Va.	Buena Vista, Miss..	Williamsport, July 5, 1863
Lieutenant..	Porter, J. W.......	1st "	Mississippi...	Shannon, Miss......	Port Hudson, July 9, 1863
Captain....	Poindexter, J. E....	30th Virginia........	Northern Va.	Pittsylvania C. H, Va	Gettysburg July 3, 1863
Lieutenant..	Pagler, W.........	45th North Carolina.	"	Salisbury, N. C.....	" July 4, 1863
"	Peyton, J. H.......	45th Tennessee.....	Tennessee....	Lavergne, Tenn.....	Millahoma July 2, 1863
"	Province, R. N.....	49th Mississippi.....	"	Coles' Creek, Miss..	Miss'y Ridge, Nov. 24, 1863
"	Preble, Joseph.....	C. S. Navy.........	....	New Orleans, La...	Arkansas Post, July 9, 1863
"	Phillips, D.........	7th Tennessee......	Northern Va.	Lebanon, Tenn.....	Gettysburg, July 3, 1863
"	Polk, L............	C. S. Mil. Ct. Ml....		St. Louis, Mo.......	
"	Patton, W. H......	17th Mississippi.....	Northern Va.	Rienza, Miss........	Gettysburg, July 5, 1863
"	Purcelle, W N.....	56th Georgia........	....	Orange, Ga........	
"	Parker, David......	52d North Carolina.			
"	Quinn, J. P........	1st Maryland.......	Northern Va.	Baltimore, Md......	Winchester, Va., June 4, 1863
"	Queen, A. A.......	18th North Carolina.	"	East Port, N. C.....	Gettysburg, N. C. July 5, 1863
Captain.....	Quinn, W. A......	10th "	Tennessee....	Henderson, Ky. ...	
"	Roane, W. L.......	16th Alabama:......	Northern Va.	Dadeville, Ala......	Gettysburg, July 4, 1863
Lieutenant..	Rasseam. W. J.....	48th Mississippi.....	"	Double Spring, Miss	Fredericksburg, July 5, 1863
Lieut.-Col..	Rankin, W. P......	21st North Carolina.	"	Greensboro', N. C..	Gettysburg, July 4, 1863
Captain.....	Ramsey, D. W.....	1st Alabama........	Mississippi...	Allenton, Ala.......	Port Hudson, July 9, 1863
Major.......	Ramseur, O. A.....	1st Arkansas........	Tennessee....	Augusta, Ark......	Murfreesboro'. Dec. 31, 1863
Lieutenant..	Ramseur, L. M.....	11th North Carolina.	Northern Va.	Lincoln Co , N. C...	Gettysburg, July 30, 1863
"	Reed, L............	1st Mississippi Batt.	Mississippi...	Ringgold, Miss.....	Ringgold, April 19, 1863
"	Russell, W. R. C....	55th Georgia........	Tennessee....	Lawrenceville, Ga..	Cumberl'd Gap, Sept. 9, 1863
"	Reasor, D. S.......	64th Virginia.......	"	Lucky Cove, Va....	" Sept. 9, 1863
"	Reese, D. G........	64th "	"	Jonesville, Va......	" Sept. 9, 1863
"	Roberts, J. A.......	55th Georgia........	"	Byronsville, Ga.....	" Sept. 9, 1863
Captain	Randall, S. D......	55th North Carolina.	Northern Va.	Shelby, N. C.......	Gettysburg, July 1, 1863
Lieutenant..	Randall, J. H.......	55th "	"	"	" July 1, 1863

Rank	Name	Unit	Department	Residence	Captured/Killed
Lieutenant..	Rountree, S. J......	5th North Carolina..	Northern Va..	Gatesville, N. C....	Gettysburg, July 1, 1863
Captain	Roberts, M. P......	Vance's Staff.......	Tennessee...	Asheville, N. C.....	Falling Water, July 14, 1863
Lieutenant..	Roberts, A. W......	4th Louisiana.......	Mississippi...	Lake Providence, La	Port Hudson, July 9, 1863
"	Richardson, J......	52d Georgia........	"	Nachooche, Ga.....	Champion Hill, May 16, 1863
"	Reegus, J. M.......	36th "	Tennessee....	Tunnel Hill........	" May 16, 1863
"	Rowe, E. D.......	1st Mississippi Art..	Mississippi...	Yazoo City, Miss...	Port Hudson, July 9, 1863
"	Rogers, J. C........	60th Tennessee.....	"	Laurel Gap........	Big Black, May 16, 1863
"	Rice, C. R.........	8th Alabama.......	Northern Va	Mobile, Ala........	Gettysburg, July 5, 1863
"	Robertson, W. G...	18th "	Tennessee ...		Miss'y Ridge, Nov. 25, 1863
"	Ricker, Winston....	3d Kentucky.......	Mississippi ...	Princeton, Ky.....	Mechanicsville, June 27, 1863
Major......	Richardson, W. J...	9th Virginia........	Northern Va.	Portsmouth, Va....	Gettysburg, July 3, 1863
Captain	Reed, Isaac........	A. Q. M. 6th La....	"	St. Joseph, Mo.....	" July 4, 1863
"	Richardson, H. B ..	Engineer Corps....	Mississippi...	"	" July 5, 1863
"	Richardson, W. N..	15th Alabama.....	Tennessee...	Glenville, Ala......	Wills' Valley, Nov. 29, 1863
Lieutenant..	Richardson, J. J....	25th "	"	Providence, Ala....	Miss'y Ridge, Nov. 25, 1863
"	Richardson, M. C...	White's Batt........	Northern Va.	Strasburg, Va......	Warren Co., Oct. 27, 1863
Captain	Reed, W. J.........	Enrolling Officer....		Columbia, Tenn....	At Home, August 22, 1863
Lieutenant..	Reed, R. L.........	44th North Carolina.		Tunnellville, N C...	South Bridge, June 26, 1863
"	Randolph, T. E.....	ADC.Gen.Pendleton	Northern Va.	Millwood, Va......	Millwood, October 23, 1863
Captain	Richards, D. W.....	25th Alabama......	Tennessee...	Prentiss, Ala.......	Miss'y Ridge, Nov. 25, 1863
Major......	Reed, D. G........	Wheeler's Staff.....	"	Woodville, Ky.....	Sequatchie Vall'y, Oct 2, 1863
Lieutenant..	Ratican, D. P.	1st Kentucky Cav ..	"	Lebanon, Ky......	Winchester, Tenn. June 27, '63
Captain	Ralston, George....	White's Art........	Trans-Miss...	Natchez, Miss.....	Natchez, Miss., June 13, 1863
Lieut.-Col...	Robinson, C. S.....	1st C. S. Cavalry ...	Tennessee...	Bolivar, Tenn......	Shelbyville, Tenn., June 27, '63
Major	Ridley, A	3d Texas Cavalry...	Trans-Miss...	El Paso, Texas.....	Fort Battery, June 28, 1863
Lieutenant..	Reed, W. H........	12th Arkansas......	Mississippi...	Tulip, Ark........	Port Hudson, July 9, 1863
"	Ruffin, Thomas.....	4th N. C. Cavalry..	Northern Va.	Scotland Neck.....	Gettysburg, July 4, 1863
"	Reed, J. B.........	8th Kentucky Cav ..	Tennessee...	Rogersville, Ky.....	Ohio, Nov. 25, 1863
"	Rawlings, T. R.....	35th Tennessee.....	"	Fillmore, Tenn.....	Nov. 25, 1863
Captain	Roberdean, J. D....	5th Texas.........	Northern Va.	Columbus, Tex....	Gettysburg, July 2, 1863
Lieutenant..	Robinson, James....	4th Tenn Cavalry..	Tennessee...	Pickensville, Tenn..	Cropville, August 27, 1863
"	Robertson, C.......	23d Virginia........	Northern Va.	Rehobeth, Va......	Gettysburg, July 4, 1863
Captain.....	Russell, L..........	22d North Carolina.	"	Wine Hill, N. C....	Falling Waters, July 14, 1863
Lieutenant..	Rhodes, D. V......	54th "	"	Mariettaville, S. C..	Rappahannock, Nov. 7, 1863

Rank.	Name.	Regiment.	Army of	Residence.	Where & When Captured.
Lieutenant..	Rudland, J. N......	57th North Carolina	Tennessee...	Mossy Creek, Tenn.	Jefferson co., Oct. 28, 1863
"	Reese, Joseph......	3d Tennessee......	"		
"	Riddle, A. N.......	La. G. Artillery....	Northern Va..	New Orleans, La...	Rappahannock, Nov. 7, 1863
"	Ryan, E............	7th Louisiana......	"	New Orleans, La...	Rappahannock, Nov. 7, 1863
Lieut.-Col...	Rice, E............	55th Virginia......	"	Middlesex co., Va..	Falling Waters, July 14 1863
Lieutenant..	Robertson, E. D....	53d Georgia........	"	Elliott, Virginia.....	Gettysburg, July 3, 1863
"	Rucker, Robert.....	3d Kentucky.......	Mississippi...	Princeton, Ky......	Jackson, Miss., June 16, 1863
"	Richardson, T. E...	47th Tennessee.....	Tennessee...	Dyersburg, Tenn...	Dyersburg, Tenn.," 3, 1863
"	Riggs, Frank.......	Morgan's Cavalry...	"	Covington, Ky.....	Ohio, July 26, 1863
"	Roberts, F. A......	7th Alabama.......	"	Dawsville, Alabama	Shelbyville, June 7, 1863
Captain.....	Russell, W. G......	14th Tennessee....	"	Palmyra, Tennessee	Clarksville, Feb. 4, 1863
"	Rabenau, P. J......	5th Louisiana......	Northern Va.	New Orleans, La...	Rappahannock, Nov. 7, 1863
"	Reddman, Thomas.	6th Louisiana......	"	New Orleans, La...	Rappahannock, Nov. 7, 1863
Lieutenant..	Rerson, S. N.......	52d North Carolina.	"	Dunbury, N. C.....	Bristow Station, Oct. 14, 1863
Captain.....	Rich, J. E..........	Cobbs' Georgia Leg.	"	Athens, Georgia....	Brandy Station, June 9, 1863
Lieutenant..	Rutledge, W. W....	3d Tennessee......	Mississippi...	Nashville, Tenn....	Raymond, Miss., May 12, 1863
Captain.....	Rowan, J. C.......	62d Tennessee.....	"	Sweet Water, Tenn.	Big Black, May 17, 1863
Lieutenant..	Riley, E. H........	Bell's Art. Reg....	Trans-Miss...	Hawsburg, Ark....	Helena, July 4, 1863
"	Rader, L. F........	61st Tennessee.....	"	Midway, Tenn.....	Big Black, May 17, 1863
Captain....	Raishler, C. W.....	54th Alabama.....	"	Athens, Alabama..	Champion Hill, May 16, 1863
Lieutenant..	Reeves, E. W......	13th Alabama......	Northern Va.	Wedence, Alabama.	Gettysville, July 1, 1863
Captain.....	Ray H.............	30th Mississippi.....	Tennessee...	Carrollton, Miss....	Lookout M't'n, May 24, 1863
"	Riddle, F. C.......	Morgan's D. R.....	"	Parisville, Ky.	Ohio, July 4, 1863
"	Robinson, W. J.....	10th Tennessee.....	"	Nashville, Tenn....	Williams co., Sept. 17, 1863
Lieutenant..	Ratliff, N. J........	62d North Carolina.	"	Wagersville, N. C..	Cumberl'd Gap, Sept. 9, 1863
"	Rivis, H...........	8th Louisiana......	Northern Va.	New Orleans, La...	Rappahannock, Nov. 7, 1863
"	Robison, J. W......	15th North Carolina	"	Salisbury, N. C.....	Bristow Station, Oct. 4, 1863
"	Rothrock, L. H.....	6th North Carolina.	"	Salisbury, N. C.....	Rappahannock, Nov. 7, 1863
"	Rucker, W.........	3d Kentucky.......	Mississippi...	Princeton, Ky......	Jackson, Miss., May 15, 1863
"	Roberts, E.........	2d Florida.........	Northern Va.	Green Cave, Fla....	Fredericksburg, June 5, 1863
Captain.....	Rass, A............	14th Arkansas......	Mississippi...	Jasper, Arkanas....	Port Hudson, July 9, 1863

Rank	Name	Regiment	Army	Residence	Place/Date
Captain	Rawland, R.	8th Kentucky	Tennessee	Hopkinsville, Ky.	Tallow Creek, Sept. 20, 1863
"	Riddick, ——	53d Virginia	Northern Va.	Suffolk, Virginia	Gettysburg, July 3, 1863
"	Robison, E. G.	57th Virginia	"	Pittsylvania C. H.	" July 3, 1863
"	Robinson, C. C.	9th Virginia Cav.	"	Oak Grove, Virginia	Upperville, June 23, 1863
"	Robison, E. M.	1st Alabama	Tennessee	Arkadelphia, Ark.	Middleton, May 22, 1863
"	Riley, C.	8th Kentucky	"	Allensville, Ky.	Tulahoma, July 24, 1863
"	Rager, J.	15th Georgia Cav.	"	South River, Ky.	Lebanon, Ky., July 4, 1863
"	Richardson, S. H.	52d Virginia	Northern Va.	Brownsville, Va.	Gettysburg, July 2, 1863
"	Reynolds, W. G.	8th South Carolina	"	Lawrenceville, S. C.	" July 5, 1863
"	Royster, R. M.	55th N. C.	"	Buchanan, N. C.	" July 5, 1863
"	Rudisille, J. R.	56th Virginia	"	Aaron, Virginia	" July 3, 1863
Captain	Rankin, S. C.	45th North Carolina	"	Greensboro', N. C.	" July 5, 1863
Lieutenant	Ringstaff, H.	45th North Carolina	"	Monroe, N. C.	" July 3, 1863
Captain	Ratliff, J. E.	10th Kentucky Cav.	Tennessee	Piketon, Kentucky	Pike co., Ky,, Sept. 30, 1863
Lieutenant	Ross, J. B.	9th Missouri	Trans-Miss.	Cledonia, Missouri	Little Rock, Sept. 8, 1863
"	Root, G. J.	Shaw's Cavalry	"	St. Louis, Missouri	Hook Run, Mo., Oct. 8, 1863
"	Ryan, R. E.	Davis's Batt.	Tennessee	Bardstown, Ky.	Blunt co., Tenn., Sep. 24 1863
"	Robertson, B. F.	9th Tennessee Cav.	"		Blunt co., Tenn., Nov. 5, 1863
"	Repass, S. A.	28th Virginia	Northern Va.	Wytheville, Virginia	Gettysburg, July 3, 1863
"	Rowland, J. K.	3d Missouri Cavalry	Tennessee	Connersville, Miss.	
"	Rush, John	12th Virginia Cav.	Northern Va.	Charleston, Va.	Bristow Station, June 9, 1863
Captain	Randolph, H. J.	Ewell's Guard	"	Plains, Virginia	
Lieutenant	Rankin, J.	7th Louisiana	"	New Orleans, La.	Rappahannock, Nov. 7, 1863
Captain	Ross, J. A.	—— Artillery	Mississippi	Port Gibson, Miss.	Port Hudson, July 9, 1863
"	Rowan, W. H.	3d Kentucky Cav.	Tennessee	Bardstown, Ky.	Farmington, Oct. 8, 1863
"	Roy, R. N.	18th Tennessee			Died, May 25, 1862
"	Rogers, A. T.	62d North Carolina	Tennessee	Crab Tree, N. C.	Cumberl'd Gap, Sept. 9, 1863
"	Randolph, W. W.	9th Tennessee	"	Campbellton, Tenn.	Bullock, July 8, 1863
Lieutenant	Rosenberger, J. B.	18th Virginia Cav.	Northern Va.	Shenandoah, Va.	Clear Spring, Md., " 8, 1863
Captain	Ridden, J. C.				Died, Nov. 11, 1863
Lieutenant	Redbout, W. B.	38th Tennessee	Tennessee		Died, Nov. 26, 1863
"	Roberts, J. C.	12th Arkansas	Mississippi	Clear Spring, Ark.	Port Hudson, July 9, 1863
Captain	Riley, R. H.	1st Alabama	"	Perote, Alabama	Port Hudson, July 9, 1863
Lieutenant	Russell, A. S.	Bell's Arkansas Reg.	Trans-Miss.	Princeton, Arkansas	Helena, July 4, 1863

RANK.	NAME.	REGIMENT.	ARMY OF	RESIDENCE.	WHERE & WHEN CAPTURED.
Lieutenant..	Robins, W. E......	52d Tennessee.....	Tennessee...	Sparta, Tenn......	Helena, Sep. 28, 1863
"	Roger, W. J.......	13th Tennessee.....	"	Moscow, Tenn.....	Holly Springs, Oct. 5, 1863
"	Richardson, A.....	5th Louisiana.....	Northern Va.	New Orleans, La...	Rappahannock, Nov. 7, 1863
"	Rollins, T. R......	35th Tennessee.....	"	Shell Mound.......	" Nov. 7, 1863
"	Randolph, W......	52d North Carolina.	"	Catersville, N. C....	Gettysburg, July 3, 1863
"	Ryan, W. A.......	8th Alabama......	"	Mobile, Ala........	" July 3, 1863
"	Rodgedale, W. A..	10th Arkansas.....	Mississippi...	Springfield, Ark....	Port Hudson, July 9, 1863
"	Russell, R. L......	10th Arkansas.....	"	"	" July 9, 1863
"	Reid, J. D........	17th Tennessee.....	"	Denmark, Tenn....	Macon, Tenn., July 4, 1863
"	Reid, J. G. R......	23d Alabama......	"	Mt. Meeting........	Port Gibson, May 1, 1863
"	Rose, C. A........	44th Tennessee....	Tennessee...	Memphis, Tenn....	At Home, July 30, 1863
"	Rollins, W. N......	7th Tennessee.....	Northern Va.	Rural Hill.........	Gettysburg, July 1, 1863
"	Rhodes, S. P......	27th Mississippi....	Tennessee...	De Soto, Miss......	Lookout M't'n, Nov. 24, 1863
"	Rodgers, M........	27th Mississippi....	"	"	" Nov. 24, 1863
"	Ridding, W. W.....	34th Mississippi....	"	Wyatt, Miss........	" Nov. 24, 1863
"	Rust, A. F........	24th Louisiana.....	"	De Kalb, Miss......	" Nov. 24, 1863
Lieut.-Col..	Roberts, R. B.....	35th Tennessee.....	Northern Va.	....	Oceola,
"	Rockwell, H. L....	2d Georgia........	"	Lumpkin, Ga......	Green Castle, Pa., July 5, 1863
"	Ridding, G. D.....	10th Tennessee.....	Tennessee...	Maberly, Tenn.....	Murfreesboro', Dec. 31, 1862
"	Robb, L. W.......	12th Louisiana Batt.	Mississippi...	New Orleans, La...	Port Hudson, July 9, 1863
"	Robinson, J. D. H...	13th Alabama......	Northern Va.	Eastville, Tenn....	Green Castle, Pa., July 5, 1863
"	Roberts, J. W.....	45th North Carolina,	"	Greysville, N. C....	South Mountain, July 5, 1863
"	Rives, S. T........	14th Tennessee.....	"	Clarksville, Tenn...	Gettysburg, July 3, 1863
"	Ripple, G.........	1st Kentucky Cav..	Tennessee....	Louisville, Ky......	Louisiana, Sept. 4, 1863
"	Rodriguez, O......	12th Louisiana.....	Mississippi...	New Orleans, La...	Port Hudson, July 9, 1863
Captain.....	Reed, J. S........	3d Georgia........	Northern Va.	Edenton, Ga.......	Gettysburg, July 4, 1863
Lieutenant..	Rollings, R. A.....	2d Kentucky......	Tennessee...	Louisville, Ky......	Miss'y Ridge, Nov. 27, 1863
Captain.....	Rawson, A. J......	15th Arkansas.....	....	Ozark, Ark........	
Lieutenant..	Roberts, J........	1st Georgia Cav...	....	Calhoun, Ga......	
"	Rindleamem, ——..	57th North Carolina,	....	Lincolnton, N. C...	
"	Reese, J..........	3d Tennessee......	....	Mossy Creek, Tenn.	

Rank	Name	Regiment	Army	Residence	Where and When Captured
Lieutenant..	Riley, C............	8th Kentucky......		Allensville, Ky.....	
"	Randolph, W. F....	4th Virginia Cav....		Warrenton, Va.....	
Captain.....	Reeves J. W........	17th Tennessee.....		Pulaski, Tenn......	
Lieutenant..	Stames, B. B........	9th Georgia Cav....	Mississippi...	Nolly Wood, La....	Port Hudson, July 9, 1863
Captain.....	Simmes, Pat........	8th Kentucky.......	Tennessee....	Washington, Ky....	Washington, Ky., July 1, 1863
"	Sisson, J. W. R.....	15th Tennessee.....	"	Wiseville, Ky......	Lion Creek, Oct. 9, 1863
Major.......	Swagerty, L. M. C..	16th Arkansas......	Mississippi...	Clarksville, Ark....	Port Hudson, July 9, 1863
Lieutenant..	Sellers, C. C........	13th Alabama......	Northern Va.	Camden, Ala.......	Gettysburg, July 1, 1863
Adjutant....	Shorter, J. M.......	31st Alabama......	Mississippi...	Columbus, Ga.....	Champion Hill, May 16, 1863
Colonel.....	Steedman, J G. W.	1st Alabama.......	"	Alleton, Ala.......	Port Hudson, July 9, 1863
Lieutenant..	Shepherd, H. E.....	43d North Carolina.	Northern Va.	Fayetteville, N. C..	Gettysburg, July 3, 1863
"	Smith, N. S.........	13th North Carolina.	Mississippi...	Leakesville, N. C...	Falling Waters, July 14, 1863
"	Sutton, L. B........	4th Virginia Cav....	Northern Va.	Winston, Tenn.....	Brandy Station, Nov. 21, 1863
"	Sponna, B. G.......	6th Alabama.......	"	Franklin, Ala......	Gettysburg, July 3, 1863
"	Spence, W..........	44th Georgia.......	Mississippi...	Sand Hill, Ga......	Champion Hill, May 16, 1863
"	Stevens, S..........	56th Georgia.......	"	New Orleans, La...	" May 17, 1863
"	Shaw, H. B.........	Bragg's Scout......	Tennessee...	Nashville, Tenn....	Pulaski, La., Nov. 12, 1863
"	Shift, W. M.........	34th Georgia.......	Mississippi...	Waterford, Ga.....	Champion Hill, May 17, 1863
"	Stevens, F. S........	5th Texas Cavalry..	"	Yazoo City, Miss...	Jackson, July 12, 1863
Captain.....	Saunders, R. H.....	2d Miss. Batt.......	"	Deanesville, Miss...	Yazoo City, July 3, 1863
Lieutenant..	Storkes, W. D......	Engineer Corps....	"	Richmond, Va.....	Port Hudson, July 9, 1863
Captain.....	Sessions, J. F.......	18th Mississippi....	Northern Va.	Lexington, Miss....	Gettysburg, July 2, 1863
Lieutenant..	Smith, G. W........	8th Virginia........	"	Spring Hill, Va.....	" July 3, 1863
Captain.....	Simms, Wm........	8th Louisiana......	"	Napoleon, La......	Rappahannock, Nov. 7, 1863
Lieutenant..	Shilley, J. L.........	22d Georgia........	"	Warrenton, Ga.....	Gettysburg, July 3, 1863
"	Stills, J. N..........	34th Mississippi....	Tennessee....	Ripley, Miss........	Lookout M't'n, Nov. 24, 1863
"	Sorrells, T. L........	1st Mississippi Art..	Mississippi...	Yazoo City, Miss...	Port Hudson, July 9, 1863
Captain.....	Sargent, R. D.......	2d Mississippi Art.	"	Vernon, Miss.......	Gettysburg, July 3, 1863
Lieutenant..	Sibley, W. L........	28th Louisiana.....	Tennessee...	Lake Providence, La	Murfreesboro', June 2, 1862
"	Suttle, E. D.........	30th North Carolina.	Northern Va.	Shelby, N. C.......	Gettysburg, July 3, 1863
Lt.-Col......	Smith, J. G. C......	9th Alabama.......	"	Athens, Ala.	" July 2, 1863
Captain.....	Small, E. A.........	11th North Carolina.	"	Edenton, N. C.....	" July 2, 1863
"	Seay, W. A.........	55th Georgia.......	Tennessee...	Greenville, Ga.....	Cumberl'd Gap, Sept. 9, 1863
Lieutenant..	Scales, S. A.........	55th Georgia.......	"	"	" Sept. 9, 1863

Rank.	Name.	Regiment.	Army of	Residence.	Where & When Captured.
Colonel	Smith, D. Howard	5th Kentucky	Tennessee	Georgetown, Ky	Meigs, Ohio, July 5, 1863
Captain	Stubbs, J. T.	1st Alabama	Mississippi	Fort Depont, Ala	Port Hudson, July 9, 1863
Lieutenant	Sanford, H.	1st Kentucky	Tennessee	Overton, Ky	Smithville, June 5, 1863
"	Sharp, J. H.	9th Alabama	Northern Va.	Decatur, Ala	Gettysburg, July 2, 1863
"	Seward, Pat	9th Alabama	"	Guntersville, Ala	" July 2, 1863
Captain	Sharp, W.	4th North Carolina	"	Harrisville, N. C.	" July 2, 1863
Major	Saunders, J. H.	33d North Carolina	"	Chapel Hill, N. C.	" July 3, 1863
Lieutenant	Sheppard, M. L.	23d North Carolina	"	Dry Pond, N. C.	" July 3, 1863
"	Sloan, F. B.	1st Mississippi	"	New Albany, Miss	" July 3, 1863
Captain	Smith, W. W.	17th Virginia	"	Alexandria, Va.	Manassas, July 21, 1863
"	Smith, G. F.	54th North Carolina	"	Hallsbury, N. C.	Rappahannock, Nov. 7, 1863
Lieutenant	Simpson, Wm	17th Virginia	"	Alexandria, Va.	Pick Deep, July 25, 1863
"	Sanford, J. G.	27th North Carolina	"	Winston, N. C.	Rappahannock, Nov. 7, 1863
Captain	Sechler, J. A.	52d North Carolina	"	Chisholm, Cr'k, N. C	" Nov. 7, 1863
"	Stuley, M.	52d North Carolina	"	Weir Gap, Tenn.	Phil'a, Tenn., Oct. 20, 1863
Major	Spratley, G. W.	A Q. M.	Mississippi	Camden, Ala.	Port Hudson, July 9, 1863
Captain	Simpson, G. W.	A. I. G.	"	New Orleans, La	" July 9, 1863
"	Sewell, W. B.	12th Louisiana Art.	"	Greenville, Ala.	" July 9, 1863
"	Sanders, F. A.	2d South Carolina	Northern Va.	Darlington, S. C.	Martinsburg, July, 17, 1863
"	Sherry, W. M.	11th Texas	Tennessee	McKinney, Texas	Tennessee, June 5, 1863
"	Spaulding, R. S.	1st Kentucky	"	Morganfield, Ky	" June 5, 1863
Lieutenant	Snowden, W. P.	11th Mississippi	Northern Va.	Aberdeen, Miss.	Gettysburg, July 3, 1863
"	Smith, R. M.	61st Tennessee	Tennessee	Blountsville, Tenn.	
Captain	Semple, W. F.	30th Tennessee	"	Saundersville, Tenn.	Sumner Co., Sept. 29, 1863
Major	Steward, W. E.	14th Arkansas	Mississippi	——, Maryland	Port Hudson, July 9, 1863
Lieutenant	Stent, J. W.	1st Arkansas	Trans-Miss.	Hebron, Ark.	Big Black, May 17, 1863
Captain	Sullens, S. B.	1st Alabama	"	Pirotalin, Ala.	Port Hudson, July 9, 1863
"	Snead, C.	3d Georgia	Northern Va.	Augusta, Ga.	Gettysburg, July 2, 1863
Lieutenant	Samford, W. J.	46th Alabama	Mississippi	Auburn, Ala.	Champion Hill, May 16, 1863
"	Spence, J.	51st Alabama Cav.	Tennessee	Talladega, Ala.	Shelbyville, June 21, 1863
"	Sharp, R. G.	34th Mississippi	Mississippi	Salem, Miss.	Lookout M't'n, Nov. 24, 1863

Rank	Name	Regiment	Department	Residence	Place and Date
Lieutenant	Sageley, J. A.	4th Tennessee	Tennessee	Brandyville, Tenn.	Liberty, June 5, 1863
"	Smith, A. P.	16th Arkansas	Mississippi	Burrowville, Tenn.	Port Hudson, June 7, 1863
"	Strong, F. J.	13th Alabama	Northern Va.	Rockford, Ala.	Gettysburg July 3, 1863
"	Steele, J. R.	23d Mississippi	Mississippi	Corinth, Miss.	Champion Hill, May 16, 1863
Captain	Stone, W. A. S.	8th Tennessee	Tennessee	Patriot, Tenn.	Benton, Nov. 3, 1863
Lieutenant	Shirrell, W. W.	57th North Carolina	Northern Va.	Lourin Co., N. C.	Gettysburg, July 3, 1863
Captain	Shearer, J. M.	29th North Carolina	Tennessee	Tunnelton, N. C.	Chickamauga, Sept. 19, 1863
"	Sayres, E. B.	Engineer Corps	"	St. Louis, Mo.	" Sept. 19, 1863
"	Sheridan, T. B.	Ball's Missouri Cav.	Trans-Miss.	"	Little Rock, Sept. 10, 1863
Lieutenant	Sandy, F. H.	2d Tennessee	Tennessee	Chattanooga, Tenn.	Lorence, Sept. 9, 1863
"	Shay, John	6th Louisiana	Northern Va.	New Orleans, La.	Rappahannock, Nov. 7, 1863
"	Sparks, J. W.	3d Kentucky Cav.	Tennessee	Louisa, Ky.	McGoffin, Oct. 7, 1863
"	Staunton, W.	52d Tennessee	"	Clifton, Tenn.	Harden co, Tenn, Aug. 3, 1863
"	Swayne, R. D.	5th Louisiana	Northern Va.	New Orleans, La.	Rappahannock, Nov. 7, 1863
"	Sidberry, M.	Hawkins' Scout	Tennessee	Baird's Town, Tenn	Perry Co., Tenn., Oct. 29, 1863
"	Short, W. F.	48th Tennessee	"	Cartsville, Tenn.	Hickman, Tenn., Oct. 20, 1863
Colonel	Smith, Baxter	4th Tennessee Cav.	"	Gallatin, Tenn.	Bluff Co., Tenn., May 20, 1863
"	Shelby, W. B.	39th Mississippi	Mississippi	Brandon, Miss.	Port Hudson, July 9, 1863
Lieutenant	Stephenson, J. T.	2d Missouri	Trans-Miss.	Savannah, Mo.	
Major	Stockdale, J. L.	Beall's Staff	"	Talladega, Ala.	Port Hudson, July 9, 1863
Lieutenant	Sparks, A.	8th Kentucky Cav.	Tennessee	Lexington, Ky.	Cumberl'd Gap, April 17, 1863
"	Stovall, W.	55th North Carolina	Northern Va.	Sandford's Ford, N.C	Falling Waters, July 14, 1863
"	Smith, G. A.	24th Virginia	"	Brown's Mill, Va.	Gettysburg, July 3, 1863
"	Smith, George	7th Virginia	"	Culpeper C. H., Va.	" July 3, 1863
"	Stone, E. M.	7th Virginia	"	Prundesburg, Va.	" July 5, 1863
"	Stublet, G. A.	4th C. S. Cav.	Tennessee	Catsburg, Ala.	Tunnel River, Aug. 10, 1863
"	Sharpton, B. F.	7th North Carolina	Northern Va.	Cold Springs, N. C.	Gettysburg, July 3, 1863
"	Sale, J. J.	53d Virginia	"	Aylett's, Va.	" July 3, 1863
Captain	Sprey, J. G.	1st Arkansas	Trans-Miss.	Columbia, Va.	Doytresville, Sept. 12, 1863
"	Stamfer, H. H.	10th Kentucky	Tennessee	Woodleburg, Ky.	Glenville, July 9, 1863
Lieutenant	Sumner, B.	7th North Carolina	"	Tasm, N. C.	Winchester, July 5, 1863
Captain	Shuck, W. A.	8th Kentucky Cav.	"	Shelbyville, Ky.	Salesville, July 26, 1863
"	Sandram, W. L.	10th Kentucky Cav.	"	Piketon, Ky.	Gladesville, July 7, 1863
Lieutenant	Swadley, W. F.	31st Virginia	Northern Va.	High Town, Va.	Monterey, Va., Aug. 28, 1863

Rank.	Name.	Regiment.	Army of	Residence.	Where & When Captured.
Lieutenant..	Sullivan, N. R.....	Orr's Rifles.......	Northern Va..	Anderson C.H., S.C.	Falling Waters, July 14, 1863
"	Shaler, F. H. B....	2d South Carolina..	"	Columbia, S. C.....	Gettysburg, July 2, 1863
"	Scater, S. M........	40th Virginia.......	"	Morning Grove, Va.	Falling Waters, July 14, 1863
"	Spears, R. D......	14th Arkansas.....	Mississippi....	Newton Co., Ark...	Port Hudson, July 9, 1863
"	Stone, W. C........	12th Arkansas	"	Buck Creek, Ark...	" July 9, 1863
"	Saunders, J. D.....	12th Arkansas.....	"	Holly Springs, Ark.	" July 9, 1863
"	Smith, Morrison....	39th Mississippi.....	"	Jackson, Miss......	" July 9, 1863
Captain.....	Sublett, J. M.......	40th Louisiana......	Tennessee ...	Yazoo City, Miss....	Vicksburg, July 4, 1863
Lieutenant..	Smith, E H........	3d Georgia Cav.....	"	Talbotton, Ga......	Alpine, Ga., Sept. 9, 1863
"	Sacy, J. A.........	Signal Corps.......	Mississippi...	Crawfordsville, Ga..	Port Hudson, July 9, 1863
"	Sayres, J. T........	4th Virginia........	Northern Va..	——, Virginia.......	Gettysburg, July 3, 1863
"	Spangler, C. H.....	28th Virginia.......	"	Old Hickory, Va...	" July 3, 1863
Captain.....	Strikes, T. J........	11th Mississippi.....	Mississippi...	Brookville, Miss....	" July 3, 1863
"	Strickler, G. B......	4th Virginia........	Northern Va..	Lynchburg, Va.....	" July 3 1863
"	Stick, F. E.........	3d South Carolina..	Tennessee....		
Lieut.-Col...	Stockton, W. F.....	7th Florida Cavalry.	"	Quincy, Fla.......	Miss'y Ridge, Nov. 24, 1863
Captain.....	Slicer, T. J.........	1st Florida Cavalry.	"	Tallahassee, Fla....	" Nov. 24, 1863
"	Scales, W..........	14th Tennessee.....	"	Charleston, Mo.....	
Lieutenant..	Stewart, T. J.......	C. S. A............	"	Tarboro', N. C.....	
"	Steptoe, J. M.......	9th Louisiana......	Northern Va..	Lynchburg, Va.....	Rappahannock, Nov. 7, 1863
"	Shipman, J. T......	60th North Carolina.	Tennessee....	Brown's Bluff, N. C.	Miss'y Ridge, Nov. 25, 1863
"	Sheffield, T. W. ..	55th Georgia.	"		
"	Stephenson, J. M. D.	15th Arkansas......			
Captain.....	Smith, R. H........	17th Mississippi.....	Northern Va.	East Port, Miss.....	Brownsville, Nov. 14, 1863
"	Stephens, W. C....	16th Arkansas.....	Mississippi...	Berryville, Ark.....	Port Hudson, July 9, 1863
Lieutenant.	Stubbs, J. J........	39th Mississippi.....	"	Stone Creek, Miss..	" July 9, 1863
Captain	Smith, A. H........	Melvin's Regiment.	Tennessee....	St. Matthews, Ky...	Big Hill, Ky., July 30, 1863
"	Salter, Mike........	3d Kentucky Cav...	Mississippi...	Lancaster, Ky	Newtonville, July 3, 1863
Lieutenant..	Sears, J. H.........	....	Northern Va..	Plainsville, Va.....	
"	Scott, E. B.........	1st Louisiana Cav..	Tennessee ...	Dallas, Texas......	Hansford, Ky., Aug. 1, 1863
Captain	Stubbs, J. T........	1st Alabama Art...	Mississippi...	Fort Deposit, Ala..	Port Hudson, July 9, 1863

Rank	Name	Regiment	Army	Residence	Place & Date
Lieutenant	Stiner, J. F.	21st Arkansas	Mississippi	Augusta, Ark.	Port Gibson, May 16, 1863
Captain	Surat, M.	2d Mississippi	Northern Va.	Rienzi, Miss.	Green Castle, Pa., July 5, 1863
"	Stagg, Lewis	16th Louisiana	Tennessee	Valle Platt, La.	Miss'y Ridge, Nov. 25, 1863
Adjutant	Stedman, S. D.	1st Alabama	Mississippi	Stedman, S. C.	Port Hudson, July 9, 1863
Lieutenant	Selectman, S. K.	3d Battalion Cav.	"	Savannah, Miss.	Big Black, May 16, 1863
Captain	Stent, J. F.	1st Arkansas Batt.	"	Hebron, Ark.	" May 16, 1863
"	Stakes, J. E.	40th Virginia	Northern Va.	Wicomoco Ch., Va.	Gettysburg, July 3, 1863
Major	Stakes, E. T.	40th Virginia	"	"	" July 3, 1863
Lieutenant	Swink, G. W.	8th Virginia	"	Gainesville, Va.	" July 3, 1863
"	Smith, H.	9th Virginia	"	Amherst C. H., Va.	" July 3, 1863
Lieut.-Col	Shannon, D. W.	5th Texas	Trans-Miss.	Novesota, Texas	June 28, 1863
Lieutenant	Smith, A. E.	19th Tennessee	Tennessee	Rhea's Town, Tenn.	Valtona, Nov. 23, 1863
"	Smith, L. B.	Blythe's Misssissippi	Mississippi	Hernando, Miss.	At home, April 22, 1863
"	Stockton, G M.	154th (?) Tennessee	Tennessee	Memphis, Tenn.	West Town, April 30, 1863
Captain	Sherwin, C.	Harmon's Batt.	Mississippi	"	Hernando, April 8, 1863
Colonel	Scales, J. J.	30th Mississippi	Tennessee	Carrollton, Miss.	Chickamauga, Sept. 28, 1863
Lieutenant	Smith, J. S.	14th Tennessee	Northern Va.	Danville, Tenn.	Green Castle, July 4, 1863
"	Speed, C. A.	6th North Carolina	"	South Mills, N. C.	Gettysburg, July 4, 1863
"	Stephenson, J. W.	15th Georgia	"	Connersville, Ga.	" July 4, 1863
"	Shelly, W. A.	14th Tennessee	"	Clarksville, Tenn.	Falling Waters, July 14, 1863
"	See, J. W.	2d North Carolina	"	Greenville, Ga.	Gettysburg, July 5, 1863
"	Saunders, R. R.	45th North Carolina	"	Oak Ridge, N. C.	Green Castle, July 5, 1863
"	Simmons, S. M.	9th Louisiana Cav.	Mississippi	Askya, Miss.	Port Hudson, July 9, 1863
"	Smith, E.	13th North Carolina	Northern Va.	Charlotte, N. C.	Gettysburg, July 3, 1863
"	Speller, S P.	Yelden's Batt.	Trans-Miss	St. Harris, Mo.	Helena, July 4, 1863
"	Stockton, R. H.	2d Missouri	"	Covington, Ky.	Vicksburg, June 15, 1863
"	Shaddock, R. I.	Hawthorne's	"	Lake Village, Ark.	Helena, July 4, 1863
"	Saffarons, T. H.	13th Tennessee Cav.	Tennessee	Nashville, Tenn.	Helly Ferry, July 3, 1863
"	Snow, C. C.	5th Louisiana	Northern Va.	New Orleans, La.	Rappahannock, Nov. 7, 1863
"	Southwick, D. F.	Dent's Battery	Tennessee	Eufaula, Ala.	Miss'y Ridge, Nov. 25, 1863
"	Smith, J. E	9th Mississippi	"	——, Mississippi	" Nov. 25, 1863
"	Smith, W. H.	Hawthorne's Reg't	Trans-Miss	Helena, Ark.	Solet's River, Nov. 7, 1863
"	Sandelle, S W.	3rd Mississippi	Northern Va.	Magnolia, Miss.	Gettysburg, July 5, 1863
"	Sanders, J. W.	21st Mississippi	Mississippi	Cotton Plant, Ark.	Port Hudson, July 9, 1863

Rank.	Name.	Regiment.	Army of	Residence.	Where & When Captured.
Lieutenant..	Shackelford, F.....	22d Arkansas......	Mississippi...	Okalona, Miss......	Port Hudson, July 9, 1863
"	Sloan, J. P........	14th South Carolina.	Northern Va.	Clinton, S. C......	Gettysburg, July 5, 1863
Major.......	Smith, J. C........	12th Arkansas......	Mississippi...	St. Louis, Mo......	Port Hudson, July 9, 1863
Captain	Stewart, M. W.....	12th Arkansas......	"	Arkadelphia, Ark..	" July 9, 1863
"	Stevens, R. M.....	12th Arkansas......	"	Stephens, Ark.....	" July 9, 1863
Lieutenant..	Smith, S. H.......	27th Mississippi...	Tennessee ...	Ellisville, Miss.....	Lookout M't'n, Nov. 24, 1863
Major.......	Stewart, W. E.....	15th Arkansas......	Mississippi...	Madison, Ark......	Port Hudson, July 9, 1863
Lieutenant..	Stearns, B. M.....	15th Arkansas......	"	"	" July 9, 1863
"	Shipps, C. J. J.....	9th Missouri.......	Tennessee...	Oxford, Miss......	Chickamauga, Sept. 20, 1863
"	Smyth, R..........	3d Kentucky Cav...	"	Bowling Green, Ky.	Ohio, July 26, 1863
"	Sandlim, A. W.....	1st Mississippi......	Mississippi...	Mooreville, Miss....	Port Hudson, July 9, 1863
Captain.....	Smith, W. W......	32d Alabama.......	Tennessee ...	Marianna, Ark	Miss'y Ridge, Nov. 25, 1863
Lieutenant..	Smith, W. H......	32d Alabama.......	"	Mt. Sterling, Ala...	" Nov. 25, 1863
Captain.....	Shelton, S. M......	10th Arkansas......	Mississippi...	Springfield, Ark....	Port Hudson, July 9, 1863
"	Strange, W. B.....	49th Alabama......	"	Gainesville, Ala....	" July 9, 1863
Major.......	Street, T. A.......	49th Alabama......	"	Warrenton, Ala....	" July 9, 1863
Captain.....	Stephens, W. C....	16th Arkansas......	"	Berryville, Ark....	" July 9, 1863
Lieutenant..	Stewart, C. E......	43d Mississippi.....	Tennessee ...	Fulton, Miss.......	Chickamauga, Sept. 19, 1863
Captain.....	Shaw, M. B.......	Q. M. 1st Arkansas.	Mississippi...	Grand Lake, Ark..	Port Hudson, July 9, 1863
Lieutenant..	Stephens, J. A.....	2d Mississippi......	Northern Va..	Cherry Creek, Miss.	Gettysburg, July 1, 1863
Captain.....	Seaville, R. M.....	2d Mississippi......	"	"	" July 1, 1863
"	Shilar, J. G........	5th Florida........	"		Died, Dec. 11, 1863
"	Shedden, Alex.....	8th Alabama......	"	Mobile, Ala.......	
Lieutenant..	Sterling, W. R.....	8th Arkansas......	"	"	
"	Skidmore, W. J....	4th Alabama......	"	Alanda, Ala.......	
"	Scott, J. T.........	—— Tennessee Cav	Tennessee ...		Gettysburg, July 5, 1863
"	Sale, J G..........	10th Kentucky.....	"		
"	Sedgwick, L. T....	2d Kentucky.......			Miss'y Ridge, Nov. 27, 1863
Captain	Stick, R. P........			Pine Bluff, Ark.....	
"	Smith, B. R.......	6th North Carolina..	Northern Va.	Charlotte. N. C.....	Gettysburg, July 4, 1863
Lieutenant..	Simpson, W. M....	17th Virginia......	"	Alexandria, Va.....	Manassas Gap, July 31, 1863

Rank	Name	Regiment	Department	Residence	Battle	Date
Lieutenant..	Seay, E. G..........	14th Virginia.......	Northern Va..			
"	Swagner, M. B......	15th Florida........	....	Newport, Fla......		
Captain	Sanders, E. M......	3d Georgia..........	Northern Va..	Pennfield, Ga......		
Lieutenant..	Shelton, W.........	1st Mississippi.....	Mississippi...	Fulton, Miss.......	Port Hudson,	July 9, 1863
Captain	Twipson, John.....	62d North Carolina.	Tennessee ...	Richland Vall'y, N C	Cumberl'd Gap,	Sept. 9, 1863
Lieutenant..	Tate, J. W.........	62d North Carolina.	"	High Top, N. C....	"	Sept. 9, 1863
"	Thomas, John......	8th Florida.........	Northern Va.	Hopville, Fla......	"	Sept. 9, 1863
"	Turnill, E. W......	5th Virginia........	"	Alexandria, La.....	Rappahannock,	Nov. 7, 1863
"	Thomas, H. C......	7th Louisiana......	"	Morristown, Tenn..	Mt. Sells,	June 9, 1863
"	Tapler, L...........	12th Tennessee Cav.	Tennessee ...	Charlotte, N. C....	Gettysburg,	July 5, 1863
"	Titty, James........	34th North Carolina,	Northern Va.	Orange C. H., Va...	"	July 5, 1863
"	Tuck, W. M........	3d Virginia.........	"	Proctor's Creek, Va.	"	July 3, 1863
"	Taylor, J. L........	14th Virginia.......	"	Vanceburg, Ky.....	Ferrington,	Oct. 14, 1863
"	Thomas, R. E......	2d Kentucky Cav...	Tennessee ...			
Captain.....	Thompson, J C....	18th Arkansas......	Mississippi...	Byrd Springs, Ark..	Port Hudson,	July 9, 1863
"	Thomas, S. M......	Boone's Batt. Art...	"	Simmsport, La.....	"	July 9, 1863
Lieutenant..	Thomas, D. P......	13th Tennessee Batt.	Tennessee ...	Waverley, Tenn....	Humphrey,Ten.,	Oct.28, 1863
"	Turner, C. L.......	33d North Carolina.	Northern Va.	Farmersville, N. C..	Gettysburg,	July 3, 1863
"	Turner, W. G......	6th North Carolina.	"	Morgantown, N. C.	Rappahannock,	Nov. 7, 1863
"	Tipps, J C.........	17th Tennessee.....	Tennessee ...	Winchester, Tenn...	Chickamauga,	Sept. 19, 1863
"	Timberlake, F. A ..	7th Tennessee......	Northern Va.	Carthage, Tenn.....	Gettysburg,	July 3, 1863
"	Turnben, B. N.....	C. S. A............	Trans-Miss...	New Orleans, La...	Christian,	Sept. 25, 1863
"	Thomas, P. W......	1st Kentucky Cav..	Tennessee ...	Taylorsville, Ky....	Chickamauga,	Sept. 14, 1863
Captain	Talor, W. J........	13th Alabama......	Northern Va..	Wetumka, Ala.....	Gettysburg,	July 3, 1863
Lieut.-Col...	Thompson, Z.......	7th Alabama Cav...	Tennessee ...	Cotton Gin, Texas.	Shelbyville,	June 27, 1863
Captain.....	Turpin, J. H.......	28th Alabama......	"	Newberne, Ala.....	Stone River,	Dec. 31, 1862
Major-Gen..	Trimble, J. R......	P. A. C. S	Northern Va.	Baltimore, Md......	Gettysburg.	July 3, 1863
Lieutenant.	Triplett, W. B......	18th Virginia Cav...	"	Front Royal, Va....	Hancock, Md..	June 23, 1863
"	Thornton, J. J......	43d Georgia........	Mississippi...	Jefferson, Ala......	Champion Hill,	June 16, 1863
"	Taylor, W. W......	5th Tennessee......	Tennessee ...	....	Henderson,	Oct. 18, 1863
"	Toby, L. M........	1st Arkansas Cav...	Mississippi...	Morristown, Ark...	Champion Hill,	May 16, 1863
Brig.-Gen...	Thompson M. Jeff..	Missouri S. G......	Trans-Miss...	St. Joseph, Mo.....	Pocahontas,	Aug. 22, 1863
Lieutenant..	Todd, M. L........	1st Missouri Cav...	"	Pattersonburg, Mo.	Big Black,	May 17, 1863
"	Tilman, O..........	1st Tennessee Art..	"	Brannon, Texas....	Port Hudson,	July 9, 1863

Rank.	Name.	Regiment.	Army of	Residence.	Where & When Captured.
Lieutenant..	Tramel, F. E......	17th Arkansas......	Trans-Miss...	Fort Smith, Ark....	Port Hudson, July 9, 1863
Captain	Tucker, M. P......	55th Georgia.......	Tennessee ...	Greenville, Ga.....	Cumberl'd Gap, Sept. 9, 1863
"	Taylor, John......	A. Q. M...........	Northern Va.	King George Co., Va	King Geo. co., Aug. 29, 1863
"	Tayloe, J. J.......	Mil. Agt..........	"	King George Co., Va	" Aug. 29, 1863
Lieutenant..	Thorp, P. H.......	13th Virginia Cav...	Tennessee....	Hicksford, Va......	Upperville, Va., June 21, 1863
Captain.....	Tatum, P. A.......	2d N. C. Cav......	Northern Va..	Greensboro, N. C...	
"	Turner, J. C.......	6th North Carolina.	"	Salisbury, N. C.....	Rappahannock, Nov. 7, 1863
Major......	Thompson, J. P....	Morgan's Cav.....	Tennessee ...	Owensboro', Ky....	Owensboro', Ky., May 17, 1863
	Triplett, J. H......	1st Kentucky Cav...	"	Owensboro', Ky....	" May 1, 1863
Lieutenant..	Thippen, J. C......	18th Mississippi....	Northern Va..	Raymond, Miss.....	Gettysburg, July 2, 1863
Adjutant ...	Thornton, J. R.....	12th Arkansas......	Mississippi ...	Camden, Ark......	Port Hudson, July 9, 1863
Captain	Turner, N. J.......	23d North Carolina.	N. Carolina...	Henderson, N. C...	Gettysburg, July 1, 1863
Lieutenant..	Thomas, J. J.......	17th Arkansas	Mississippi...	Washington, Ark...	Port Hudson, July 9, 1863
"	Tomlinson, J. W....	7th Kentucky Cav..	Tennessee ...	Owenton, Ky......	Hamilton July 14, 1863
"	Toca, T............	Miles' Legion......	Mississippi...	New Orleans, La...	Port Hudson, July 9, 1863
Captain.....	Taylor, E. S.......	8th Louisiana......	Northern Va	....	Rappahannock, Nov. 7, 1863
"	Tilman, S. H.......	39th Mississippi....	Mississippi...	Vandoon, Miss.....	Port Hudson, July 9, 1863
Lieutenant..	Tilman, W. J.......	39th Mississippi.....	"	Vandoon, Miss.....	" July 9, 1863
Captain	Thompson, J H....	1st Mississippi.....	Northern Va..	Salem, Tenn.......	Gettysburg, July 3, 1863
Lieutenant..	Thompson, J. H....	4th Kentucky Cav..	Tennessee ...	....	Roane, Ky., April 3, 1863
"	Thompson, E. T....	28th North Carolina	Northern Va..	Judahville, N. C....	Gettysburg, July 5, 1863
"	Tallins, E. A.......	—— Battalion......	Mississippi...	New Orleans, La...	Port Hudson, July 9, 1863
Captain.....	Turney, J. B.......	1st Tennessee......	Northern Va..	Boone's Hill, Tenn.	Gettysburg, July 3, 1863
Lieutenant.	Twitt, W..........	64th Virginia......	Tennessee....	Hickory Flat, Va...	Cumberl'd Gap, Sept. 9, 1863
"	Taba, W K........	64th North Carolina	"	Columbus, N. C....	" Sept. 9, 1863
Captain.....	Taylor, B..........	19th Virginia......	Northern Va..	Charlottesville Va..	Gettysburg, July 3, 1863
Lieutenant..	Tincher, J. N......	6th Virginia Cav....	"	Egypt, Va.........	Fayetteville, Aug. 5, 1863
"	Tucker, O. M......	28th Virginia......	"	Midway, Va.......	Gettysburg, July 5, 1863
"	Taylor, John......	60th Tennessee.....	Mississippi...	Jonesboro, Tenn....	Big Black, May 17, 1863
"	Tibbs, C. H........	2d Tennessee Cav...	Tennessee ...	Clearland, Tenn....	Leavensworth, July 31, 1863
"	Trayner, J. D......	2d Tennessee Cav .	"	Clearland, Tenn....	Flat Lake, Aug. 3, 1863

Rank	Name	Regiment	Army	Residence	Place and Date
Lieutenant..	Taber, George.....	Signal Corps......	Tennessee ...	Gloucester C. H., Va	Chattanooga, Nov. 24, 1863
"	Tredgale, W. R. J. P	23d Alabama.......	Mississippi ...	Pine Hill, Ala......	Port Gibson, May 1, 1863
Captain	Tipton, W. B.......	8th Kentucky Cav..	Tennessee	Washington, Ky....	Salesville, Ohio, July 26, 1863
Lieutenant..	Tindell, W. H......	15th Tennessee Cav.	"	Watery, Tenn......	" July 26, 1863
"	Talley, A. S.......	9th Georgia Batt....	"	Atlanta, Ga.......	Cumberl'd Gap, Sept. 9, 1863
"	Tone L. H.........	45th Tennessee.....	"	Murfreesboro, Tenn.	Lookout M't'n, Nov. 25, 1863
"	Tredgill, J E......	12th Arkansas......	"	....	Died, Dec. 8, 1863
"	Tyan, ——.......	63d North Carolina.			" July 30, 1863
"	Tagle, C. H........	33d Georgia........			" Nov. 6, 1863
"	Turner, A. W.......	14th Virginia.......	Northern Va .	Richmond Hill, Va.	Gettysburg, July 3, 1863
"	Trevillian, C. B.....	4th Virginia........	"	Isspyorna, Va......	" July 3, 1863
"	Tillett, J. N.......	4th N. C. Cav......	"	Shiloh, N C.......	Middleburg, Va., June 19, 1863
"	Thornton, R. W....	56th North Carolina	"	Fayetteville, N. C...	Gum Swamp, May 27, 1863
"	Traywick, A. M....	16th Arkansas......	Mississippi ...	Clinton, Ark.......	Port Hudson, July 9, 1863
Captain.....	Taylor, T. J........	49th Alabama......	"	Mayesville, Ala.....	" July 9, 1863
Lieutenant..	Towns, J. C........	30th Mississippi....	"	Black Hawk, Miss..	Lookout M't'n, Nov. 24, 1863
"	Tuttle, C. E........	1st Alabama........	"	Montgomery, Ala...	Port Hudson, July 9, 1863
"	Thorp, S. R........	2d Kentucky Cav..,	Tennessee ...	Bardstown, Ky.....	Indiana, July 8, 1863
Captain.....	Thrasher, R. M.....	18th Arkansas.....	Mississippi ...	Princeton, Ark.....	Port Hudson, July 9, 1863
Lieutenant..	Taliaferro, J. T.....	18th Arkansas......	"	Florence, Ark......	" July 9, 1863
"	Turner, W. J.......	18th Arkansas......	"	Cotton Plant, Ark..	" July 9, 1863
"	Trammell A. E.....	10th Missouri......	Trans-Miss...	Vienna. Mo.......	Helena, Ark., July 4, 1863
"	Thompson, R C....	7th Missouri........	"	Pineville, Mo......	" July 4, 1863
"	Thompson. J. N....	Hawthorne's Reg't.	"	Manassas, Ark.....	" July 4, 1863
"	Taylor, R. L........	1st Louisiana Batt..	Tennessee ..	London, Miss......	Tennessee, July 30, 1863
"	Tinnad, F..........	10th Missouri......	Trans-Miss...	Patton, Mo........	Clark's Bluff, Ark., July 9, 1863
"	Taylor, John.......	—— S. C. Cav......	Northern Va.	Columbia, S. C.....	White Horn, Va., July 2, 1863
Captain.....	Tucker, J. J........	2d N C. Batt......	"	Wh. Sulp'r Sp'gs, Ga	South Mountain, July 5, 1863
Lieutenant..	Thompson, T. H...	12th Arkansas......	Mississippi ...	Pine Bluff, Ark.....	Port Gibson, May 1, 1863
"	Taylor, J. L........	1st Mississippi P. R.	"	Wallhill, Miss......	Holly Springs, May 3, 1863
Captain.....	Taylor, S. H.......	Ghattin's Staff.....	"	Tassilo, Miss.......	Tussilo, Mo., May 5, 1863
"	Topp, R. C.........	13th Mississippi....	"	Oakland, Miss......	Gettysburg, July 4, 1863
Lieutenant..	Thalhium, P........	9th Louisiana Batt..	"	Baton Rouge, La...	Port Hudson, July 9, 1863
Captain.....	Thompson, J. G....	52d Tennessee.....	"	Dresden, Tenn.....	

RANK.	NAME.	REGIMENT.	ARMY OF	RESIDENCE.	WHERE & WHEN CAPTURED.
Major	Timberlake, J. C.	53d Virginia	Northern Va.	New Kent C. H., Va.	
Lieutenant	Taylor, H. H.	Jackson's Staff	"	Elizabethtown, Ky.	
Captain	Taylor, D. S.	8th Louisiana	"	St. Fandry's, La.	
"	Upchurch, A. J.	55th North Carolina	"		Died Nov. 9, 1863
"	Utley, James F.	2d Louisiana	"	Alexandria, La.	Gettysburg, July 3, 1863
Lieutenant	Underwood, W. R.	4th Missouri Cav.	Trans-Miss	New Kent C. H., Va.	Frederick, Md., July 2, 1863
Captain	Venable, Z. A. P.	10th Arkansas	Mississippi	Springfield, Ark.	Port Hudson, July 9, 1863
Lieutenant	Vann, J. C.	49th Alabama	"	New Hope, Ala.	Port Hudson, July 9, 1863
"	Vaughan, L. L.	18th Virginia	Northern Va.	New Ferry, Virginia	Gettysburg, July 3, 1863
Captain	Van Hoore, J. W.	17th Arkansas	Mississippi	Independence, Mo.	Port Hudson, July 9, 1863
Lieutenant	Vaughn, W. L.	10th Missouri Cav.	Trans-Miss	Waynesville, Mo.	Helena, July 4, 1863
Captain	Vaughn, E. H.	10th Arkansas	"	Quitman, Arkansas.	Port Hudson, July 9, 1863
"	Vasley, W. W.	10th Kentucky Cav.	Tennessee		Died, Feb. 11, 1863
Lieutenant	Vanmeter, W. S.	21st Arkansas	Mississippi	Franklin, Arkansas.	Big Black, May 17, 1863
"	Vaughter, T. H.	52d Georgia	"	Nacoochee, Georgia	Champion Hill, May 16, 1863
Captain	Vaun, J. P.	Bell's Arkansas Reg	Trans-Miss		Died Dec. 24, 1863
Lieutenant	Van Benthuysen, W.	6th Louisiana	Northern Va.	New Orleans, La.	Gettysburg, July 3, 1863
"	Verbal, H. D.	57th North Carolina	"	Salisbury, N. C.	
"	Vanzant, J. A.	52d Georgia	Tennessee	Morgantown, Ga.	Miss'y Ridge, Nov. 25, 1863
Captain	Voight, R.	Miles's Legion	Mississippi	Industry, Texas.	Yazoo City, July 4, 1863
Lieutenant	Vanderun, P.	Ass't Eng'r C. S. N.	"	Savannah, Georgia.	St. Catherine's S'd, Aug. 20, '63
"	Varner, A. W.	27th Virginia	Northern Va.	Lexington, Va.	Gettysburg, July 3, 1863
"	Varner, E.	9th Virginia	"	Petersburg, Va.	" July 3, 1863
"	Vaughn, R. C.	4th Virginia	"	Marion, Virginia.	" July 3, 1863
"	Vermillion, J. A.	9th Virginia	"	Portsmouth, Va.	" July 3, 1863
"	Viner, Benj.	55th Georgia	Tennessee	Rockaway, Georgia	Cumberl'd Gap, Sept. 9, 1863
Captain	Vanlier, R.	Engineer Corps	"	Nashville, Tenn.	Cumberl'd Gap, Sept. 9, 1863
Lieut.-Col	Vaughn, H. H.	10th Arkansas	Mississippi	Quitman, Arkansas.	Port Hudson, July 9, 1863
Lieutenant	Van Prage, H. A.	1st Alabama	"	Eufaula, Alabama.	Port Hudson, July 9, 1863
"	Whittenburg, J. W.	62d North Carolina	Tennessee	Claytonville, N. C.	Cumberland Gap, Sep. 9, 1863
"	Wilson, R. M.	62d North Carolina	"	Webster, N. C.	" Sep 9, 1863

Rank	Name	Regiment	Army	Residence	Place/Date
Lieutenant..	Williams, J. L......	3d Arkansas.......	Tennessee....	Gibsonville, Va.....	Shelbyville, Oct. 7, 1863
Captain.....	Wilkinson, S. C....	18th Alabama......	"	Fosterville, Ala.....	Miss'y Ridge, Nov. 25, 1863
"	White, L. B........	5th Virginia Cavalry	Northern Va..	Norfolk, Va........	Brandy Station, June 9, 1863
Lieutenant..	Weymouth, J. E....	18th Virginia.......	"	Cartersville, Va....	Gettysburg, July 4, 1863
Captain.....	Whiteman, D. C....	9th Tennessee Cav..	"	Clarksville, Texas..	
Lieutenant..	Walker, R.........	39th Mississippi.....	Mississippi...	Westville, Miss.....	Port Hudson, July 9, 1863
"	Waddell, T. W.....	16th Arkansas......	"	Clinton, Arkansas..	" July 9, 1863
Captain.....	Walker, H.........	1st Virginia........	Northern Va..	Cassville, Virginia..	Logan, Va., June 23, 1863
Lieutenant..	Wright, J. M......	2d Texas Cavalry...	Trans-Miss...	Springfield, Texas..	Creek Nation, July 17, 1863
"	Welton, J. E.......	53d Virginia.......	Northern Va.	Farmville, Virginia.	Gettysburg, July, 3, 1863
"	Watts, J. A........	5th Alabama......	"	Roseville, Alabama.	" July 1, 1863
"	Weaver, S. W.....	9th Louisiana......	"	Nassamaury, Va....	" July 3, 1863
"	White, W. W......	3d Virginia........	"	Portsmouth, Va....	" July 3, 1863
Captain.....	Whitehead, J. D....	3d Virginia........	"	Portsmouth, Va.....	" July 3, 1863
"	Wiseman, J. W.....	15th Tennessee.....	Tennessee....	Gallatin, Tennessee.	Tennessee, April 21, 1863
"	Webb, J. E........	18th Arkansas......	Mississippi...	Camden, Arkansas..	Port Hudson, July 9, 1863
"	Wolf, A. J.........	A. Q. M...........	"	Northfork, Ark.....	" July 9, 1863
"	Walden, J. A.......	18th Arkansas.....	"	Carrollton, Ark....	" July 9, 1863
"	White, J. Hook.....	8th Tennessee Cav..	Tennessee....	Price's Creek, Texas	McMinnville, Oct. 4, 1863
Lieutenant..	Winter, F. P.......	10th Louisiana Batt.	Mississippi...	New Orleans, La...	Port Hudson, July 9, 1863
"	Wyatt, J. B........	2d Florida.........	Northern Va.	Quincey, Alabama..	Fredericksburg, June 5, 1863
"	Wood, B. F........	5th Florida........	"	Bristol, Florida.....	Gettysburg, July 2, 1863
"	Walker, H. J.......	13th North Carolina.	"	Charlotte, N. C.....	Martinsburg, July 3, 1863
Captain.....	Walters, W. E.....	Chaplain 2d S. C...	"	Anderson C. H., S.C.	Polk co., Tenn., Nov. 30, 1863
Lieutenant..	Wilkerson, H......	9th Virginia.......	"	Norfolk Va........	Gettysburg, July 3, 1863
"	White, N. C........	8th C. S. Cavalry...	Tennessee...	Danville, Va.......	Shelbyville, June 27, 1863
"	Wallace, John G....	Bell's Arkansas Reg.	Trans-Miss...	Hamburg, Arkansas	Helena, July 4, 1863
Captain.....	White, James......	1st Kentucky Batt..	Tennessee....	Mayesville, Ky.....	Kentucky, June 16, 1863
Lieutenant..	Walsh, E.........	6th Louisiana......	Northern Va.	Richmond, Va......	Rappahannock, Nov. 7, 1863
Captain.....	Warden, Jacob.....	18th Virginia Cav...	"	Baker's Run, Va....	Hardy co., Va., Aug. 22, 1863
Lieutenant..	Warlick, L........	6th North Carolina.	"	Pitt's Grove, N. C...	Rappahannock, Nov. 7, 1863
Captain	Webb, S. G........	8th Louisiana......	"	Munden, La........	" Nov. 7, 1863
"	White, B. F........	6th North Carolina..	"	Mebanesville, N. C..	" Nov. 7, 1863
"	Wray, J...........	3d Virginia Cavalry.	"	Hampton, N. C.....	Brandy Station, Oct. 7, 1863

Rank.	Name.	Regiment.	Army of	Residence.	Where & When Captured.
Captain	Wright, J. W.	20th North Carolina	Northern Va.	Clinton, N. C.	Rappahannock, Oct. 30, 1863
Lieutenant.	Waddell, H. T.	9th Louisiana Cav.	Mississippi	Baton Rouge, La.	Port Hudson, July 9, 1863
Adjutant.	Waterman, P.	12th Louisiana Batt.	"	New Orleans, La.	" July 9, 1863
Captain	Wall, S. F.	9th Louisiana Cav.	"	Tangepohoro, La.	" July 9, 1863
Lieutenant.	Wilson W. W.	8th Florida	"	Quincey, Florida	Gettysburg, July 5, 1863
"	Wing, L. H.	2d Georgia Batt.	Northern Va.	Macon, Georgia	" July 5, 1863
"	Wright, H. C.	30th Louisiana	Mississippi	New Orleans, La.	Port Hudson, July 9, 1863
Lieut.-Col.	Walker, J. S.	12th Arkansas	"	Center Point, Ark.	" July 9, 1863
Captain	Wilson, E. C.	15th Arkansas	"	Camden, Arkansas	" July 9, 1863
"	Watson, G. W. S.	1st Tennessee Cav.	Tennessee	Spencer, Tenn.	Chickamauga, Sept. 19, 1863
Lieutenant.	Webb, J. H.	9th Louisiana	"	Mendon, Louisiana	" Sept. 19, 1863
Captain	Whitly, W. H.	30th Mississippi	"	Soda (?), Mississippi	Lookout M't'n, Nov. 24, 1863
"	Woods, W. B.	2d Tennessee Cav.	"	Warren co., Tenn.	Warren, Sept. 19, 1863
"	Wilson, W. J.	62d North Carolina	"	Forks Pigeon, N. C.	Cumberl'd Gap, Sept. 9, 1863
Lieutenant.	Walke, G. D.	62d North Carolina	"	Rutherfordton, N. C.	" Sept. 9, 1863
Captain	Wetherly, W.	Dobins' Arkansas	Mississippi	Helena, Arkansas	Helena, Oct. 12, 1863
Lieutenant	White, Hugh	Rains's Art.	Tennessee	Knoxville, Tenn.	Cumberl'd Gap, Sept. 9, 1863
"	Wright, W. A.	Wright's Staff	Northern Va.	Augusta, Georgia	Cartersville, July 4, 1863
Captain	Wood, W. J.	18th Tennessee	Tennessee	Woodberry, Texas	Sparta, Tenn., July 20, 1863
"	Ware, F. M.	5th Arkansas	"	Wiltsburg Arkansas	Ohio, July 19, 1863
"	Wash, W. A.	60th Tennessee	Mississippi	Sauceberry, Ky.	Big Black, May 19, 1863
Lieutenant.	Williams, M. B.	62d Tennessee	"	Madisonville, Tenn.	" May 19, 1863
Captain	Willis, L. B.	19th Arkansas	"	Magnolia, Arkansas	" May 19, 1863
"	Watkins, W.	Hawthorne's Ark.	Trans-Miss.	Little Rock, Ark.	Helena, Ark., July 4, 1863
Lieutenant.	Welton, Aaron	18th Virginia Cav.	Northern Va.	Petersburg, Va.	Hardy Creek, June 2, 1863
Captain	Washington, N. C.	Ord. Dep't	Mississippi	St. Louis, Missouri	Port Hudson, July 9, 1863
"	Wiggins, J. H.	—— Artillery	Tennessee	Arkadelphia, Ark.	Shelbyville, June 27, 1863
Colonel	Woods, M. L.	46th Alabama	Mississippi	Montgomery, Ala.	Champion Hill, May 16, 1863
Captain	Wasson, J. W.	21st Arkansas	"	Evening Shade, Ark	Arkansas, Oct. 7, 1863
Lieutenant.	Wammick, J. P.	44th Tennessee	Tennessee	Goodwellsville, Ten.	Murfreesboro', Jan. 4, 1863
"	White, F.	3d Tenn. Cav.	"	Jordan's Valley, Ala.	" May 22, 1863

Rank	Name	Regiment	Army	Residence	Where/When
Lieutenant.	Wallace, J. G.	Bell's Regiment	Trans-Miss.	Hamburg, Arkansas	Helena, July 4, 1863
Captain	Witeman, C. P.	4th Louisiana	Mississippi	Bayou Lear, La.	Port Hudson, July 9, 1863
Ex-Captain	Wagner, J. A.	—— Cavalry	Tennessee	Clarksville, Tenn.	Fayetteville, July 5, 1863
Lieutenant	Webb, T. S.	24th Virginia	Northern Va.	Gogginsville, Va.	Gettysburg, July 5, 1863
Major	Winston, T. R.	45th North Carolina	"	Lakesville, N. C.	" July 4, 1863
Lieutenant.	White, T. H.	14th Tennessee	"	Clarksville, Tenn.	" July 5, 1863
"	Walsh, W. S.	Phillips's Ga. Reg't	"	Savannah, Georgia	" July 2, 1863
"	Wood, N. S.	11th Mississippi	"	Clarksville, Miss.	" July 3, 1863
Captain	Whitehead, G. H.	55th North Carolina	"	Pictolas, N. C.	" July 3, 1863
Major	Winchester, G W.	A. A. G	Tennessee	Gallatin, Tenn.	Miss'y Ridge, Nov. 25, 1863
Lieutenant.	Williams, J. T.	12th North Carolina	Northern Va.	Mount Reroh, N C.	Green Castle, Pa., July 6, 1863
Captain	Wilson, W. H.	Morgan's Cavalry	Tennessee	Somerville, Ky	Kentucky, July 9, 1863
Major	Wilson, J.	A. A. G.	"		Miss'y Ridge, Nov. 25, 1863
Lieutenant.	Willmore, G. F.	10th Kentucky Cav	"	Henderson, Ky.	Kentucky, June —, 1863
Captain	Whitesides, S. A.	48th Tennessee	Mississippi	Columbia, Tenn.	Port Hudson, July 9, 1863
"	Wilson, T. T.	A. A. G.	"	Stony Point, Va.	" July 9, 1863
Lieutenant.	Wilkins, H.	Engineer Corps	Tennessee	—— Georgia	Cumberl'd Gap, Sept. 9, 1863
"	Woodward, J. M.	21st S. C.	Beauregard	Darlington, S. C.	Charleston, S.C., July 10, 1863
"	Wilkins, W. H.	15th Virginia Cav.	Northern Va.	Norfolk, Va.	Culpeper C.H.Va.Sep 13, 1863
Captain	Withers, J. B.	Mosby's Cavalry	"	Warrenton, Va.	Virginia. Sept. 22, 1863
Colonel	Wood, C. W.	—— Militia		Hertford co., N. C.	Hertford co.,N.C.Aug.15,1863
Lieutenant.	Watson, J B	2d N. C. Cavalry	Northern Va.	Tarboro', N. C.	Kelly's Ford,Va., Nov. 7, 1863
"	Weeks, R. R. C.	4th Florida	Tennessee	Ellisville, Florida	Miss'y Ridge, Nov. 25, 1863
"	Wright, S. T.	23d North Carolina	Northern Va.	Dry Pond, N. C.	Gettysburg, July 3, 1863
"	Wicker, Robert	15th Alabama	"	Perats', Alabama	" July 2, 1863
Adjutant	Watson, W. E.	1st Tennessee	"	Winchester, Tenn	" July 1, 1863
Captain	Weathersby, W.	37th Mississippi	Mississippi	Wirtville, Mississippi	Port Hudson, July 9, 1863
Lieutenant.	White, J. J.	"	"	Summit, Mississippi.	" July 9, 1863
Major	Williamson, T. H.	7th Tennessee	Northern Va.	Lebanon, Tenn.	Gettysburg, July 3, 1863
Lieutenant.	Winder, ——	Engineer Corps			Died May 1, 1864
Major	Wilson, M. R	1st Arkansas Batt.	Mississippi	Hamburg, Ark.	Port Hudson, July 9, 1863
Lieutenant.	Wilson, J. B.	39th Mississippi	"	"	" July 9, 1863
"	Wilson, J. M.	3d Georgia Cavalry	Tennessee	Bainbridge, Georgia	Howe's Gap, May 22, 1863
"	Wentworth, J. H.	5th Florida	Northern Va.	Mosely Hall, Fla.	Gettysburg, July 3, 1863

Rank.	Name.	Regiment.	Army of	Residence.	Where & When Captured.
Lieutenant..	Whitley, W. W.....	49th Georgia.......	Tennessee....	Jonesville, Ga......	Gettysburg, July 2, 1863
Captain.....	Williams, J. L......	31st Alabama.......	"	Randolph, Ala......	Ringgold, Ga., Nov. 27, 1863
"	Wood, E. B........	34th Alabama......	"	Marble Valley, Ala.	Miss'y Ridge, Nov. 27, 1863
Lieutenant..	Welch, John.......	40th Virginia.......	Northern Va..	Richmond, Va......	Warsaw, Va, May 4, 1863
"	Whitlock, R. B.....	55th Virginia.......	"	Danville, Va.......	Falling Waters, July 14, 1863
"	Whiting, G. M.....	47th North Carolina.	"	Raleigh, N. C......	Gettysburg, July 2, 1863
"	Woods, W. G......	13th North Carolina.	"	Leesburg, N. C.....	" July 4, 1863
Captain.....	Windsor, F R	5th Virginia Cav...	"	Alexandria, Va.....	Alders, June 7, 1863
Lieutenant..	Windham, J. C.....	40th Mississippi.....	Mississippi...	Paulding, Miss......	Chickasaw Bay'u, May 19, 1863
"	Wallace, D. J......	8th Kentucky Cav..	Tennessee....	Westburg, Ky......	Salesville, Ohio, July 26, 1863
"	Williams, G. S.....	2d Kentucky Cav..	"	Georgetown, Ky...	" July 26, 1863
Captain.....	White, John........	A. Q. M. 5th Ala...	Northern Va.	Catawba, Ala......	Gettysburg, July 5, 1863
"	Wiscoat, ——......	"	"	Greenboro', Ala....	" July 5, 1863
"	Wilson, J. R........	39th Mississippi....	Mississippi...	Summit, Miss.......	Port Hudson, July 9, 1863
Lieutenant..	Williamson, W. T...	1st Alabama.......	"	Greenboro', Ala....	" July 9, 1863
"	Wood, J. R........	3d Alabama Cav....	Tennessee....	Greenport, Ala.....	Shelbyville, June 27, 1863
Major.......	Webb, H	A. A. G...........	"	Nashville, Tenn....	Miss'y Ridge, June 23, 1863
Lieutenant.	Windall, A. L......	8th Tennessee Cav.	"	Monroe, Tenn......	
Captain.....	Williams, W. H....	58th (?) N. C.......	Northern Va..	Franklin, N. C.....	Gettysburg, July 1, 1863
Lieutenant..	Winston, R. H.....	"	"	"	" July 1, 1863
"	Weatherspoon, S...	7th North Carolina..	"	Morrisville, N. C...	" July 3, 1863
Captain.....	Wynn, W. W......	64th North Carolina.	Tennessee....	York River Station.	Cumberl'd Gap, Sept. 9, 1863
Lieutenant..	Wilson, J. S........	55th Georgia.......	"	Bird's Town, Ga....	" Sept. 9, 1863
"	Willah, A	4th Virginia........	"	Gladesville, Va.....	" Sept. 9, 1863
"	Woodward, G. W..	64th North Carolina.	"	Flag Pond, Tenn...	" Sept. 9, 1863
Colonel	Willfolk, G. W.....	....	"	Kentucky..........	Germantown, Dec. 2, 1863
Captain	White, A..........	1st Mississippi Cav..	Mississippi...	Ripley, Miss.......	Hernando, April 6, 1863
Lieutenant..	White, T..........	1st Mississippi Cav..	"	"	" April 6, 1863
"	Whittey, R........	2d Mississippi......	Northern Va.	Lamar, Ala........	Gettysburg, July 3, 1863
Colonel.....	Whitlock, C. H.....	....	Trans-Miss...	Augusta, Ark......	At Home. 1863
Lieutenant..	Williams, J. E......	2d North Carolina...	Northern Va.	Murphy, N. C......	Hanover, June 30, 1863

Rank	Name	Regiment	Army	Residence	Place & Date
Captain	Willis, R. M.	3d Louisiana Cav.	Northern Va.	Talbotton, Ga.	Birdsville, May 17, 1863
"	Wilson, T. B.	2d Missouri	Mississippi	Paris, Mo.	Big Black, May 17, 1863
Lieutenant	White, R. J.	60th Tennessee	"	Laurel Gap, Mo.	" May 17, 1863
"	Whitfield, G. M. T.	48th Georgia	Northern Va.	Swansboro'	Mannassas Gap.
"	Whitfield, B.	1st Tennessee Cav.	Tennessee	Columbia, Tenn.	Murray co., Ten., July 14, 1863
"	Wallace, J. E.	9th Mississippi	"	Buck's M't'n, Miss.	Miss'y Ridge, Nov. 25, 1863
"	Williams, Frank	13th North Carolina	Northern Va.	Mocksville, N. C.	Gettysburg, July 5, 1863
Captain	Wood, ——				Died May, 1862
"	Webb, B. C.	1st Alabama Cav.	Tennessee		Died July 27, 1863
Lieutenant	Williams, J. M.	6th Mississippi			Died Dec. 8, 1863
"	Wells, C. C.	2d Tennessee	Tennessee	Somerville, Tenn.	Somerville, Nov. 27, 1863
"	Weddington, H.	10th Kentucky Cav.	"	Piketon, Ky.	Gladesville, Va., July 7, 1863
Colonel	Webb, R. F.	6th North Carolina	Northern Va.	Flat River	Rappahannock, Nov. 7, 1863
Captain	Williams, H. G.	9th Louisiana	"	Franklinton, La.	" Nov. 7, 1863
"	White, M. B.	14th Virginia Cav.	"	Lewisburg, Va.	Martinsburg, June 14, 1863
Lieutenant	Walton, G. L.	25th Louisiana	Tennessee	Natchez, Miss.	Chickamauga, Sep. 25, 1863
"	Wilkinson, M.	59th Georgia	Northern Va.	Macon, Ga.	Gettysburg, July 3, 1863
"	Watson, J. H.	47th North Carolina	"	Graham, N. C.	" July 3, 1863
"	Whitehead, J. W.	53d Virginia	"	Pittsylvania, C. H.	" July 3, 1863
"	Ward, W. H.	20th North Carolina	"	Whitesville, N. C.	" July 1, 1863
"	Woodson, W. D.	28th Virginia	"	Bonsack's Depot, Va	" July 2, 1863
"	Wellard, S. G.	47th Mississippi	"	Cenatobia, Miss.	" July 1, 1863
"	Workman, O. H.	44th North Carolina	"	Hillsboro', N. C.	Hanover Sta., June 26, 1863
Captain	Wilson, R. C.	14th Tennessee	"	Danville, Tenn.	Falling Waters, July 14, 1863
Lieutenant	White, L. S.	11th Kentucky Cav.	"	Louisville, Ky.	
Captain	Whitfield, J. T.	1st Alabama	Mississippi	Montgomery, Ala.	Port Hudson, July 9, 1863
"	Wheeler, C. N.	Faulkner's Cav.	Tennessee	Pontetoc, Miss.	Hernando, Miss., May 8, 1863
Lieutenant	Walker, D. L.	2d Mississippi	Northern Va.	Veronia, Miss.	Gettysburg, July 1, 1863
Captain	Waller, W S.	Morgan's Cavalry	Tennessee	———, Ky.	Kentucky, May 8, 1863
"	Woodruff, A. R.	Amherst Art.	Northern Va.	Lynchburg, Va.	Gettysburg, July 4, 1863
Lieutenant	Wright, E D.	10th Missouri	Trans-Miss.	Yawly, Mo.	Helena, July 4, 1863
"	Walker, W. L.	10th Missouri	"	Rallo, Mo.	" July 4, 1863
"	Wayland, W. H.	Hawthorne's Reg't	"	Vintage, Ark.	" July 4, 1863
"	Wood, J. B.	10th C. S. Cav.	Tennessee	Vienna, Ga.	Jacksboro', Aug. 27, 1863

Rank.	Name.	Regiment.	Army of	Residence.	Where & When Captured.
Lieutenant..	Warfield, B........	1st Tennessee Cav..	Tennessee....	Williamsport, Tenn.	
"	Wall, T. H. W.....	22d Mississippi.....	Mississippi...	Holly Springs, Miss.	Holly Springs, Sept 8, 1863
"	Wilson, Geo. L.....	7th Kentucky.......		Cadiz, Ky..........	
"	Wilson, G. J.......	Miles' Legion.......	Mississippi...	Barksdale, Miss....	Port Hudson, July 9, 1863
"	Weir, J. H........	40th Alabama......	Tennessee ...	Carrolton, Ala......	Lookout M't'n, Nov 24, 1863
"	Whaling, J. C......	18th Arkansas......	Mississippi...	DeWitt, Ark.......	Port Hudson, July 9, 1863
"	Warren, J. P.......	1st Tennessee......	Northern Va..	Pelham, Tenn......	Gettysburg, July 5, 1863
"	Weaver, W. M.....	18th Mississippi....	Mississippi...	Smithville, Miss....	Port Hudson, July 9, 1863
"	Wells, J. M........	1st Arkansas Batt...	"	Laury Town, Miss..	" July 9, 1863
"	Williams, J. H.....	14th South Carolina.	Northern Va..	Martin's Depot, S. C	Gettysburg, July 5, 1863
"	Williams, L.......	Shaver's Regiment.	Trans-Miss...	Evening Shade, Ark	Laurence Co., Oct. 17, 1863
Captain.....	Walverton, E. H...	1st Arkansas Batt..	Mississippi...	Powhatan, Ark.....	Port Hudson, July 9, 1863
Lieutenant..	West, C. W.......	2d Kentucky Cav...	Tennessee ...	Cynthiana, Ky.....	Salesville, Ohio, July 26, 1863
"	Wallace, Thomas...	6th Kentucky Cav..	"	Somerville, Ky.....	Bardstown, Ky., July 6, 1863
"	Wills, W. H	23d Arkansas	Mississippi...	Midsonville, Ark...	Port Hudson, July 9, 1863
Captain.....	Wilson, W. W.....	15th Arkansas.....	"	DeWitt, Ark.......	" July 9, 1863
Lieutenant..	Watkins, E........	59th Mississippi.....	"	Jackson, Miss......	" July 9, 1863
"	Wilson, M. D......	1st Mississippi......	"	Springdale, Miss...	" July 9, 1863
"	Walker, J. D......	39th Alabama......	"	Gadsden, Ala......	" July 9, 1863
"	Wammac, A. D....	39th Alabama......	"	Stephenson, Ala....	" July 9, 1863
Captain	Westmoreland, S. L.	23d Arkansas......	"	Harrisonburg, Ark.	" July 9, 1863
Lieutenant..	Wilson, A. C.......	16th Arkansas......	"	Cairo Hill, Ark.....	" July 9, 1863
"	Warren, D. J.......	10th Arkansas.....	"	Hebron, Ark.......	" July 9, 1863
"	Ward, J. W.......	28th Alabama......	Tennessee ...	Elston, Ala.........	Miss'y Ridge, Nov. 25, 1863
"	Wing, A M........	32d Alabama.......	"	Jackson, Ala.......	" Nov. 25, 1863
"	Wardlaw, D. S.....	1st Tennessee Cav..	"	Corinth, Miss......	Harden Co., Dec. 21, 1863
Captain.....	Williams, J. A......	1st Tennessee Cav..	"	Camden, Tenn.....	
"	Williams, W. E.....	— Arkansas Batt...	Mississippi...	Memphis, Tenn....	
Lieutenant..	Wright, W. A......	60th Tennessee.....	"	Laurenceburg, Ky..	
Captain: ...	Williams, G. B.....	28th North Carolina.	Northern Va.	Fair Bluff, Ark.....	
Lieutenant..	Wilcoxon, W. R....	66th North Carolina.	"	Jefferson, N. C.....	

Lieutenant..	Wilkinson, J. T....	Bell's Art..........	Northern Va..	Baltimore, Md..,...	
"	Waldrop, E. B......	18th Alabama......	Tennessee...	Elyton, Ala........	
Captain	Williams, M. L.....	9th Louisiana......	Northern Va.		
"	Youngblood, J. W..	Signal Corps.......	Mississippi...	Memphis, Tenn....	Port Hudson, July 9, 1863
Lieutenant..	Young, W. H......	54th North Carolina.	Northern Va.	Oxford, N. C......	Rapid Anne, Va., Nov. 7, 1863
Captain.....	Yeats, J. W.......	1st Mississippi Cav.	Mississippi...	Blackland, Miss....	Blackland, June 26, 1863
Lieutenant..	Young, W. R......	25th North Carolina.	Northern Va.	Lynchburg, Va.....	Gettysburg, July 4, 1863
"	Yarbrough, J. T....	55th Georgia.......	Tennessee...	Ciselhelm, Ga......	Cumberl'd Gap, Sept. 9, 1863
"	Young, R. J.......	38th Alabama......	"	Rehoboth, Ala.....	Miss'y Ridge, Nov. 25, 1863
"	Yarbrough, J.......	10th Kentucky Cav.	"		
Captain.....	Yeats, J. T........	A. Q. M..........	"	St. Joseph, Mo.....	Little Rock, Sept. 10, 1863
Adjutant....	Yousee, J. R.......	3d Louisiana Batt..	"	Gallatin, Tenn......	Tennessee, June 24, 1863
Lieutenant..	Yergin, S. G.......	10th Alabama......	Northern Va.	Gadsden, Ala......	Gettysburg, July 4, 1863
"	Young, A..........	10th Arkansas.....	Mississippi...	Quitman, Ark......	Port Hudson, July 9, 1863
"	York, G. W.......	49th Alabama.....	"	Gadsden, Ala......	" July 9, 1863
"	Young, J. R.......	11th Mississippi....	Northern Va.	Memphis, Tenn.....	Gettysburg, July 3, 1863
"	Yarrington, J. B....	22d N. C. Cavalry...	"		
"	Zeigler, J. R.......	51st Alabama Cav..	Tennessee...	Perota, Ala........	Shelbyville, June 22, 1863

Mortuary List of Prisoners on Johnson's Island,

MAY 1ST, 1862, TO MARCH 3, 1864.

Rank.	Name.	Regiment.	Army of	Residence.	Disease & Date of Death.
Lieutenant	Anderson, C. B.	49th Tennessee	Mississippi	Tennessee	Pneumonia, Aug. 25, 1862
Private	Asberry, J.	Morgan's Cavalry	Tennessee	Kentucky	Typhus Fever, Oct 28, 1862
"	Anderson, W. H.	Poindexter's Cav.		Missouri	" Dec. 18, 1862
Citizen	Ashe, S.			Virginia	Diarrhœa, July 3, 1863
Private	Anderson, J. B.			Missouri	" Feb. 13, 1863
"	Armstrong, W. P.	10th Ky. Cavalry		Kentucky	Fever, Jan'y 21, 1863
"	Allen, A. P.	2d Ky. Cavalry		Kentucky	Dysentery, Oct. 23, 1863
Lieutenant	Arringham, J. O.	22d North Carolina		North Carolina	Fever, Dec. 26, 1863
"	Alexander, T. F.	4th Alabama		Alabama	" Feb. 15, 1864
Captain	Armfield, M. D.	11th North Carolina		North Carolina	Dysentery, Dec. 3, 1863
Citizen	Buckingham, E.			Missouri	Diarrhœa, Nov. 22, 1862
Private	Benn, W.	Marshall's Brigade		Kentucky	" Nov. 24, 1862
Lieutenant	Barrett, J.	— Louisiana Battery		Louisiana	Bronchitis, Nov. 7, 1863
"	Brown, E. W.	9th Louisiana "		Louisiana	Ch. Diarrhœa, Jan'y 19, 1863
Captain	Beecon, J. R.	60th Tennessee		Tennessee	Consumption, Dec. 9, 1863
Lieutenant	Blunt J. B.	55th North Carolina		North Carolina	Fever, Dec. 30, 1863
Colonel	Bausman, C. C.	1st Kentucky Cav.		Kentucky	Erysipelas, Dec 11, 1863
Captain	Barnes, W. C.	15th C. S. A.		Virginia	" Jan'y 8, 1863
Lieutenant	Barty, E.	1st Missouri Cav.		Missouri	Rheumatism, Jan'y 30, 1863
"	Bayne, Frank	2d Florida		Florida	Consumption, Feb. 23, 1863
Private	Barnett, J.	Marshall's Battery		Kentucky	Typhoid Fever, Nov. 9, 1863
Lieutenant	Crow, R. H.	11th Arkansas	Mississippi	Arkansas	Typhus Fever, July 21, 1863
Private	Christian, D.	128th Virginia		Virginia	Ch. Diarrhœa, Oct. 12, 1863
"	Cote, T. M.	— Georgia		Georgia	Typhus Fever, Oct. 16, 1863
Captain	Cauthorn, J. W.	A. D. C. Gen. Price		Virginia	Pneumonia, Nov. 18, 1863
Private	Cole, P.	60th Virginia		Virginia	Diarrhœa, Nov. 22, 1863

Rank	Name	Regiment		State	Cause, Date
Private	Cochran, R.	Poindexter's Cav.		Missouri	Typhus Fever, Dec. 18, 1863
"	Cassius, J.	10th Kentucky Cav.		Missouri	Rubeola, Aug. 21, 1863
Citizen	Clay, D. H.			Kentucky	Typhus Fever, Feb. 24, 1863
Captain	Cummings, G. M.	Price's Staff		Virginia	Rubeola, July 15, 1863
	Copass, R. B.	60th Tennessee		Tennessee	Fever, Aug. 29, 1863
	Carter, J. W.	23d Arkansas		Arkansas	" Sept. 14, 1863
Lieutenant	Collins, J.	10th Kentucky		Kentucky	Erysipelas, Dec. 2, 1863
"	Culman, F. W.	7th Arkansas		Arkansas	Infl. of the bow'ls, Dec. 8, 1863
Private	Crawey, J. W.	19th Virginia		Virginia	Pneumonia, Jan. 14, 1863
Colonel	Campbell, J. A.	37th Mississippi		Mississippi	Hepatitis, Feb. 13, 1863
Lieutenant	Cox, M. H.	15th Louisiana		Tennessee	Rheumatism, Feb. 24, 1863
"	Cooper, F. F.	42d Louisiana		Georgia	Erysipelas, Feb 2, 1863
"	Clark, S. P.	4th North Carolina		North Carolina	Int. Fever, Jan. 1, 1864
Colonel	Clarke, R. S.	8th Kentucky Cav.		Kentucky	Diphtheria, Dec. 31, 1863
	Dodson, J. M.	10th Tennessee		Tennessee	Typhus Fever, Sept. 30, 1863
Private	Dales, J. A.	10th Kentucky		Kentucky	Dysentery, Nov. 23, 1863
Citizen	Deane, P.				Infl. of the bow'ls, Feb. 4, 1863
Lieutenant	Dawson, H. B.	13th Georgia		Georgia	Typhus Fever, Dec. 21, 1863
	Everman, L. H.	7th Kentucky		Kentucky	Typhus Fever, Oct. 30, 1863
Captain	Ezell, F. M.	13th Tennessee		Tennessee	Pneumonia, Oct. 22, 1863
Lieutenant	Evans, R. M.	22d Alabama		Alabama	Fever, Jan. 1, 1864
Private	Emerson, J.	Park's Va. Reg't		Kentucky	Typhus Fever, Dec. 8, 1862
Citizen	Fugary, J.			Kentucky	Fever, Feb. 3, 1863
Captain	Fuller, A. W.	C. S. N.		Tennessee	Gastritis, July 25, 1863
Private	Gray, W. W.	2d Kentucky		Kentucky	Rubeola, June 29, 1863
	Gillispie, Chas.			Virginia	Fever, Sept. 9, 1863
Lieutenant	Graham, ——	2d Texas		Texas	Gunshot wound, Sep. 28, 1863
Private	Gable, H.	5th Kentucky		Kentucky	Typhus Fever, Nov. 2, 1863
Lieutenant	Gush, J. B.	62d North Carolina		North Carolina	Consumption, Oct. 30, 1863
Captain	Gregory, J. M.	9th Virginia		Virginia	——, Nov. 21, 1863
"	Hodgers, J. R.	51st Tennessee	Tennessee	Tennessee	Erysipelas, July 24, 1863
Private	Hardin, J.	10th Kentucky	"	Kentucky	Typhus Fever, Nov. 21, 1863
"	Herring, D.	Poindexter's Cav.		Missouri	" Jan. 16, 1863
"	Hunsucker, J.	—— Cavalry		Missouri	Jaundice, Nov. 4, 1863

Rank.	Name.	Regiment.	Army of	Residence.	Disease & Date of Death.	
Private	Hedge, Robert	Clark's Artillery		Missouri		Feb. 24, 1863
"	Holstein, F. A.	2d Virginia		Virginia	Diarrhœa,	June 3, 1863
	Hudson, W. J.	2d Georgia		Georgia	Enteritis,	Aug. 5, 1863
	Havron, W. A.	51st Georgia		Georgia	Typhus Fever,	Aug. 19, 1863
	Huffstelle, John	1st Arkansas Batt.		Arkansas	Neuralgia,	Sept. 14, 1863
	Hordin, ——	5th North Carolina		North Carolina	Dysentery,	Sept. 30, 1863
	Henry, J. W.	9th Tennessee		Tennessee	Typhus Fever,	Oct. 11, 1863
	Holt, Robert	16th Tennessee		Tennessee	Typhus Fever,	Oct. 10, 1863
Captain	Hardy, J. B.	12th Arkansas		Arkansas	Pneumonia,	Nov. 12, 1863
Lieutenant	Harper, J. R.	4th Florida		Florida	Erysipelas,	Dec. 3, 1863
Captain	Hazzard, J. B.	24th Alabama		Alabama	Fever,	Dec. 31, 1863
Lieutenant	Harper, B. G.	25th Tennessee		Tennessee	Rheumatism,	Jan. 12, 1863
"	High, J. Q.	1st Arkansas Batt.		Arkansas	Erysipelas,	Jan. 12, 1863
"	Hill, J. W.	9th Virginia		Virginia	Fever,	Feb. 3, 1863
	Hatson, N. S.	1st Tennessee		Tennessee	Ch. Diarrhœa,	Feb. 7, 1863
Captain	Hamilton, S.	C. S. Cavalry		Choctaw Nation	Erysipelas,	Feb. 4, 1863
Private	Johnson, W. J.	Poindexter's Cav.		Virginia	Pneumonia,	Nov. 22, 1863
"	Johnson W.	"		Missouri	Typhus Fever,	Dec. 15, 1863
	Jackson, D. C.	12th Virginia		Virginia	Typhus Fever,	Sept. 8, 1863
Captain	Jackson, T. M.	61st Tennessee		Mississippi	Dysentery,	Jan. 1, 1864
"	Jackson, J. A.	38th Alabama		Alabama	Pneumonia,	Dec. 16, 1862
Lieutenant	Johnson, D. L.	48th Tennessee	Tennessee	Tennessee	Fever,	Dec. 2, 1863
"	Kay, R. M.	18th Tennessee	Tennessee	Tennessee	Typhus Fever,	May 25, 1863
Private	Kitchum, ——	15th Batt. Mo. Cav.		Missouri	Diarrhœa,	Dec. 24, 1862
Citizen	Kirtley, W. T.			Kentucky	Fever,	Feb. 3, 1863
	Kinney, John	Stamps's Cavalry		Virginia	Fever,	Nov. 9, 1863
	King, J. M. D.	9th Georgia		Georgia	Gunshot wound,	Nov. 30, 1863
Lieutenant	King, W. J.				Tonsilitis,	Nov. 9, 1863
Captain	Kean, J. M.	12th La. Batt.		Louisiana	Pneumonia,	Nov. 21, 1863
Lieutenant	Kelly, A.	10th Arkansas		Arkansas	Erysipelas,	Jan. 4, 1863
"	Keys, Z. H. O.	1st Mississippi		Mississippi	Dysentery,	Jan. 1, 1864

Rank	Name	Unit		State	Cause	Date
Lieutenant.	Keller, M. D.	22d Tenn. Cavalry		Tennessee	Bronchitis,	Sept. 12, 1864
"	Lyons, M.	65th North Carolina		North Carolina	Typhus Fever,	July 30, 1863
Captain	Lyon, John	53d Virginia		Virginia	Typhus Fever,	Dec. 27, 1863
Lieutenant.	Linzey, N. G.	12th Arkansas		Arkansas	Erysipelas,	Dec. 13, 1863
"	Love, R. C.	1st Mississippi Batt.		Mississippi	Diarrhœa,	March 3, 1864
Captain	Lewis, G. W.	9th Louisiana		Louisiana	Diarrhœa,	Dec. 2, 1863
"	Lewis, W. R.	3d Arkansas		Arkansas	Pneumonia,	Jan. 4, 1863
Lieutenant.	Lane, Z. D.	62d North Carolina		North Carolina	Inflam. Fever,	Jan. 12, 1864
Captain	McWharton, S. A.	3d Mississippi		Mississippi	Typhus Fever,	July 29, 1862
"	Mager, R. E.	30th Tennessee	Tennessee	Tennessee	Dysentery,	Sept. 10, 1862
Citizen	McLane, J. W.			Virginia	Pneumonia,	Nov. 22, 1862
"	McCameg, J.			Missouri	Pneumonia,	Nov. 22, 1862
Private	Miles, S.	Clarke's Mo. Cav		Missouri	Infl'n of brain,	Jan. 7, 1863
"	Moore, S.	Poindexter's Cav		Missouri	Consumption,	Jan. 7, 1863
Citizen	Morrison, E.			Kentucky	Diarrhœa,	Feb. 3, 1863
Private	Mobly, J.	10th Kentucky Cav		Kentucky	Rubeola,	Feb. 4, 1863
Citizen	Manly, M. B.			Kentucky	Typhus Fever,	Feb. 28, 1863
"	McKinney, D.			Kentucky	Typhus Fever,	Feb 24, 1863
Private	Manson, J. S.	Kentucky Cavalry		Kentucky	Pneumonia,	March 14, 1863
"	Myers, R.	Morgan's Cavalry		Kentucky	Cer'bro Sp'l Men.	J'ne 10, 1863
	Mullins, J. W.	1st Mississippi		Mississippi	Consumption,	Sept. 7, 1863
Lieutenant.	Musselman, J. A.	14th Florida		Louisiana	Diarrhœa,	Oct. 20, 1863
"	Monroe, E. A.	62d North Carolina		North Carolina	Typhus Fever,	Oct. 21, 1863
Captain	Meddlebark, J.	4th Georgia		Georgia	Typhus Fever,	Jan. 2, 1863
Lieutenant.	Morgan, F. G.	7th Louisiana		Louisiana	Ch. Diarrhœa,	Feb. 3, 1863
"	McKay, D. H.	46th Alabama		Alabama	Ch. Diarrhœa,	Jan. 1, 1864
Brig.-Gen	Mauzy, ——	Militia		Nashville, Tenn.	Pneumonia,	May 1, 1862
Private	Morris, J.	McBride's Div		Kentucky	Typhoid Fever,	Dec. 25, 1862
"	Norvell, J.			Missouri	Rubeola,	Nov. 21, 1862
Citizen	Neal, J.			Kentucky	Abscess,	Nov. 22, 1862
Lieutenant.	Norwood, W. F.	O. S. C. (?)		South Carolina	Ch. Diarrhœa,	Jan. 11, 1864
Private	Neal, O. P.	Woodward's Cav		Kentucky	Mumps,	Jan. 21, 1863
Captain	Nichol, P.	4th North Carolina		North Carolina	Ch. Diarrhœa,	Feb. 18, 1863
Lieutenant.	Newhart, W.	16th North Carolina		North Carolina	Erysipelas,	Jan. 4, 1864

Rank.	Name.	Regiment.	Army of	Residence.	Disease & Date of Death.
Lieutenant..	Nash, C. B..........	3d Mississippi......		Mississippi.........	Erysipelas, Feb. 15, 1863
Private.....	Oshum, J. W.......	Marshall's Brig.....		Kentucky..........	Typhus Fever, Nov. 28, 1862
Lieutenant..	Orr, E. A. M.......	62d North Carolina..		North Carolina.....	Interm't Fever, Nov. 9, 1863
"	Owens, A..........	57th North Carolina.	Tennessee....	Springfield, N. C...	Pneumonia, Jan. 4, 1863
"	Pierson, S. A.......	30th Tennessee......		Tennessee.........	Typhus Fever, July 6, 1862
Captain.....	Pedue, J. C.				Nov. 11, 1863
"	Peel, N. C..........	18th Arkansas......		Arkansas..........	Pneumonia, Feb. 26, 1863
Private.....	Parks, J...........	16th Virginia.......		Virginia...........	Erysipelas, June 27, 1863
"	Reeves, M..........	1st C. S. Cavalry...		Georgia...........	Typhoid Fever, Oct. 26, 1862
"	Raines, F..........	46th Virginia.......		Virginia...........	" Oct. 14, 1862
Citizen.....	Rhodes, E. P.......			North Carolina.....	Ascites, Dec. 15, 1862
Private.....	Roberts, J. A.......	Johnson's Cav......		Kentucky..........	Rubeola, Feb. 24, 1863
....	Rockham, D........	5th Kentucky.......		Kentucky..........	Pneumonia, Sept. 11, 1863
Lieutenant..	Rickhill, M. B,.....	8th Alabama.......		Alabama..........	Ch. Diarrhœa, Feb. 3, 1863
Captain.....	Riddick, J.........	1st Missouri Cav....		Missouri..........	Camp Fever, Jan 26, 1863
Citizen.....	Smith, D...........	15th Arkansas......		Kentucky..........	Pneumonia, March 6, 1863
....	Stephenson J. M. D.			Arkansas..........	Typhoid Fever, Aug. 21, 1863
Citizen.....	Scruggs, J. E.......			Virginia...........	Dysentery, Nov. 8, 1863
Captain.....	Shuler, B. G........	5th Florida.........		Florida............	Pneumonia, Dec. 11, 1863
Private.....	Shacklett, J. C......			Kentucky..........	Diarrhœa, Feb. 11, 1863
Lieutenant..	Snurk, G. W........	8th Virginia........		Virginia...........	" Feb. 12, 1864
Captain.....	Sullens, S. B.......	P. A. C. S..........		Alabama..........	Rheumatism, Feb. 4, 1863
Lieutenant..	Sherry, C. O.......	10th North Carolina.		North Carolina.....	Erysipelas, Dec. 18, 1863
Private.....	Tarlor, R..........	10th Kentucky.....	Tennessee...	Kentucky.........	Typhus Fever, Oct. 10, 1862
Lieutenant..	Threadgill, J. E.....	12th Arkansas......		Arkansas..........	Diarrhœa, Dec. 8, 1863
Citizen.....	Tuter, J. S.........			Kentucky..........	Typhus Fever, Nov. 22, 1863
....	Talbott, H. T.......	Marshall's Brig.....		Kentucky..........	" Oct. 28, 1863
Captain.....	Tuggle, C. M.......	33d Georgia........		Georgia...........	" Nov. 4, 1863
Private.....	Thompson, W......	4th Virginia........		Virginia...........	Diarrhœa, Nov. 6, 1863
Captain.....	Upchurch, ——.....	58th North Carolina.		North Carolina.....	Dysentery, Nov. 9, 1863
Private.....	Veazy, W. W......	10th Kentucky Cav.		Kentucky..........	Rubeola, Feb. 11, 1863

Rank	Name	Regiment		State	Disease	Date
Lieutenant..	Vaughn, J. B......	Bell's Ark. Reg't....	....	Alabama..........	Fever,	Dec. 24, 1863
Captain.....	Wood, ——......	....	....	Williams Co., Tenn.	Pneumonia,	May 1, 1862
Private.....	Wilson, ——.....	Home Guard......	....	Kentucky.........	Typhus Fever,	Oct 27, 1862
"	White, W........	Woodward's Cav...	....	Kentucky.........	Rubeola,	Feb. 15, 1863
"	Worthington, A....	Marshall's Brig.....	....	Kentucky.........	"	Aug. 2, 1863
....	Williams, L. B.....	63d North Carolina.	....	North Carolina.....	Fever,	Sept. 29, 1863
Lieutenant..	Wills, John........	Farmer's Staff......	....	Florida...........	Fever,	Dec. 2, 1863
....	Welch, H........	4th Mississippi.....	....	Mississippi........	Diarrhœa,	Feb. 4, 1863
....	Weaks, R. R. C....	4th Florida........	....	Florida..........	Camp Fever,	Jan. 20, 1863
....	Wood, J. B........	10th C. S.........	....	....	Ch. Diarrhœa,	Feb. 16, 1863
Captain.....	Webb, D. C.......	1st Alabama.......	....	Alabama..........	Typhus Fever,	July 27, 1863
Private.....	Yarbrough, J......	10th Kentucky Cav.	....	Kentucky.........	Pneumonia,	Feb. 13, 1863

-A-

ABBEY
　G.F., 20
ABERNATHEY
　F.S., 22
ADAIR
　B.H., 19
ADAMS
　D., 19
　E.A., 22(2)
　J.J., 19
　N.K., 21
　R.H., 21
　R.M., 19
　S.F., 21
　W.C., 19
　W.H.H., 19
AGNEW
　J.W., 22
AIKEN
　COL., 1
ALBRIGHT
　G.N., 22
ALCORN
　A.S., 22
　M.S., 19
ALDERSON
　W.H., 21
ALEXANDER
　C.C., 19
　D.G., 19
　J.M., 19
　L.G., 19
　T.F., 100
　T.J., 19
　W.E., 21
　W.J., 21
ALLEN
　A.P., 100
　C.N., 22
　D.W., 21
　H.A., 19
　H.J., 21
　J.J., 21

J.M., 22
J.P., 22
J.W., 22
JOHN, 22
L.B., 21
P.F., 22
R.H., 20
THOMAS J., 20
THOMAS W., 22
W.B., 22
W.E., 19
W.H., 21
ALLENSWORTH
　S.P., 22
ALLERSON
　J.R., 21
　S.R., 21
　W.H., 20
ALLISON
　W.B., 21
ALSTON
　T.B., 21
AMACKER
　O.P., 21
ANDERSON
　A., 21
　C.B., 22, 100
　D.C., 22
　G.P., 21
　J.B., 100
　J.F., 22
　J.H., 21
　JAMES, 22
　L.G., 21
　PAT, 22
　R.M., 22
　S.A., 22
　S.T., 22
　W.H., 100
ANDREWS
　J., 21
　J.S., 21
APPERSON
　W.W., 19
ARBUCKLE

D.A., 21
ARCHER
　A.G., 21
　GEN., 5
　J., 21
　J.J., 19
　J.M., 22
　R.H., 19
ARCHER, BRIG. GEN.
　[JAMES JAY ARCHER],
　　3
ARCHIBALD
　A.B., 22
ARGELL
　J.S., 21
ARMBURG
　W.M., 22
ARMFIELD
　B.F., 22
　M.D., 100
ARMSTRONG
　A.J., 19
　G.W., 19
　S.S., 21
　W.P., 100
ARNETT
　V., 21
ARNOLD
　T.P., 22
ARRINGHAM
　J.O., 100
ARRINGTON
　D., 19
　J.D., 21
　J.V., 21
ASBERRY
　J., 100
ASBURY
　A. EDGAR, 19
　R.R., 19
　S.L., 19
ASH
　V., 19
ASHE
　J.J., 19

S., 100
ASHLEY
　L.R., 21
ASHTON
　JOHN D., 21
ASKE
　S., 21
ASKEW
　R.M.G., 19
ASMASSIN
　M.P., 22
ATKINS
　W.P., 22
ATWOOD
　E., 21
AUSTIN
　A.B., 22
AVANT
　W.R., 19
AYLETT
　WILLIAM R., COL., 12

-B-

BACON
　M., 29
　NATHANIEL, 11
BAILEY
　O.G., 29
　P.R., 25
　W., 27
BAIRD
　W.B., 27
BAKER
　H., 25
　J.H., 24, 25
　S.W., 28
BALDRIGE
　W.F., 25
BALDWIN
　T.T., 25
　W.D., 20
　W.G., 26
BALL
　F.H., 27

R.C., 27
T.J., 20
W.A., 26
BALLENGER
　C.E., 27
BALLENTINE
　W.W., 26
BANAT
　C.L., 24
BANERS
　G.W., 24
BANKS
　J.F., 29
BANNER
　W.O.T., 27
BARKER
　J.L., 27
BARKLEY
　C.W., 25
BARKSDALE
　B., 26
BARNES
　F.C., 26
　N.D., 28
　P., 28
　W., 26
　W.C., 100
　W.F., 28
BARNETT
　J., 100
BARR
　A., 20
BARRETT
　J., 24, 100
　W.L., 23
BARRON
　W.P., 24
BARTHELEMY
　J., 20
BARTLEY
　A.T., 23
BARTON
　A.J., 20
　A.P., 25
　M.W., 28

R.B., 27
W.D., 28
BARTY
　E., 100
BARZIZN
　D.W., 26
BASLON
　F.D., 23
BASSINETT
　F.W., 23
BASSLITTE
　A.H., 23
BATE
　H.C., 25
　MAJ., 3
BATEMAN
　P.H., 28
BATSON
　W.A., 20
BATTLE
　FRANK, CAPT., 3
　GEN., 2
BAUSMAN
　C.C., 100
BAXTER
　G.L., 29
　J.B., 29
　JOHN, 26
BAYLESS
　B.J., 20
BAYNE
　FRANK, 100
BEAL
　GEN., 5
　W.N.R., 27
BEAL, MAJ. GEN.
　[WILLIAM NELSON
　　RECTOR BEALL], 3
BEALL
　J.C.A., 23
BEAN
　P., 28
BEARD
　T.R., 24
BEARDON

    R.M., 27
    W.M.J., 27
BECK
    W.J., 24
BECKTON
    J.G., 27
BEDFORD
    A.M., 26
    F., 26
    P.P., 28
BEECON
    J.R., 100
BEKK
    J.T., 20
BELL
    A.E., 29
    D., 23
    H.M., 24
    J.P., 24
    R.H., 23
    R.S., 24
    S.H., 25
    S.L., 25
BELTON
    W.H., 23
BENN
    W., 100
BENNETT
    W., 29
    W.H., 25
BENSON
    H.H., 29
    J.F., 27
    W.B., 29
BENTLEY
    A.R., 24
    C.F., 28
    T.J., 29
    [BLANK], 24
BENTLY
    C., 20
BENTON
    P.G., 29
BERGEN
    J.M., 28

BERKELEY
    N.M., 26
    W., 26
BERRY
    J.T., 24
BETHEL
    R.L., 20
BETSEL
    A.M., 27
BETTELL
    G.A., 26
BETTS
    T. EDWIN, 27
BEVILL
    J.M., 24
BIBB
    L., 29
BILLINGSLEY
    J.A., 25
BILLS
    J.D., 20
BINGHAM
    ROBERT, 27
BIRD
    W.J., 20
BIRDSONG
    J.C., 29
BIRNEY
    J.L., 24
BISHOP
    W.F., 29
BLACK
    J.A., 27
    J.S., 29
    R.L., 24
BLACKBURN
    J.C., 29
    J.G., 24
    J.W., 29
BLACKMAN
    F.H., 24
BLACKWELL
    C.C., 26
    T.E., 27
BLACKWOLDER

    M., 24
BLACKWOOD
    W.L., 27
BLAIR
    F.L., 25
    FRANK, 1
    JOHN A., 27
BLAKE
    W.J., 29
BLAKENEY
    [BLANK], 29
BLANKENSHIP
    W.A., 23
BLANTON
    Z.A., 23
BLAYDES
    F.M., 20
BLEDSOE
    F.M., 23
BLOODWORTH
    J.H., 20
BLOUNT
    J.B., 27
    T.W., 26
BLUE
    J., 23
    M., 28
BLUNT
    J.B., 100
BOHART
    J.M., 25
BOLLING
    R.P., 27
BOND
    W.R., 26
BONNER
    M., 28
BONTING
    T.J., 24
BOONE
    J.B., 26
BORRUM
    W.J., 29
BOSS
    WILLIAM, 25

BOSTON
    R.B., 27
BOSWELL
    J.C., 20
    W.J., 20
BOTEN
    J.M., 20
BOWEN
    J.C., 28
    J.H., 28
BOWERS
    A.M., 29
    S.C., 25
BOWLES
    G.M., 28
BOWMAN
    A.L., 23
    C.C., 29
BOYD
    J.W., 26, 28
    S.H., 24
    THOMAS, 29
    W.M., 25
BOYLES
    J.R., 28
BRACKEN
    K., 23
BRADBORN
    M.S., 28
BRADFORD
    H., 23
    J.B., 27
    N.G., 28
    W.B., 26, 29
    W.J., 29
BRADLEY
    A., 24
    T.E., 20
BRADSHAW
    W.H., 25
BRADY
    J.B., 28
BRAGG
    J.G., 25
BRANCH

    H.K., 23
    T.J., 27
    W.C., 26
BRAND
    G.C., 29
BRANDEN
    H.C., 24
BRANDON
    W.L., 23
BRANNAN
    H., 24
BRANTLEY
    T.B., 25
BRARER
    W.G., 25
BRASHER
    L.B., 24
BRASWELL
    W.D., 29
BREAR
    J.R., 25
BRECKINRIDGE
    J.C., 26
BREITZ
    E.A., 24
BRENT
    J.L., 29
BREWER
    J.C., 29
BRICE
    H., 27
BRIDGES
    D.L., 28
    G.L., 26
BRINDLEY
    J.P., 25
BRINKLEY
    H.G., 20
BRITTON
    D., 23
    H.C., 25
BROCKENBROUGH
    M., 26
BRONAUGH
    W.T., 23

BRONSON
    MR., 10
BROOKS
    A.M., 23
    A.W.W., 20
    C.O., 25
    S.H., 29
BROUGHTON
    E.P., 23
    G., 25
BROWDER
    D.H., 26
BROWN
    A.J., 20, 25
    B.C., 26
    B.G., 23
    B.L., 25
    C.A.C., 28
    C.H., 29
    D.F., 20
    E.W., 100
    J.B., 23(2)
    J.H., 20
    JACK, 27
    L., 28
    L.M., 23
    N.P., 23
    R.A., 20
    R.G., 26
    S.J., 23
    W.M., 23
    W.W., 25
BRUCE
    H.G., 28
BRUNLEY
    O.R., 26
BRYAN
    GEORGE P., 26
    J.D., 28
    J.W., 27
    N.L., 24
    P.C., 28
BRYANT
    F.M., 27
    G.A., 23

JAMES, 20	W.D., 27	G.R., 31	CARTER	CHAPPELL	M.B., 32
BRYSON	BUTLER	IRA, 31	D.E., 36	F.A., 35	CLAYTON
W.H., 20	A.L., 28	J., 35	G.W., 35, 36	J.H., 31	J.P., 34
BUCHANAN	GEN., 11	J.A., 37, 101	H.S., 35	CHARLES	S.S., 31
J.H., 25	BUTTERMAN	R.C., 32	J.L., 32	J.D., 33	CLEMENTS
BUCKINGHAM	M.E., 29	R.F., 36	J.P., 36	CHENNEY	F.T., 31
E., 100	BYRNE	S.C., 35	J.R., 31	W.R., 30	CLEMONS
BUCKNER	H.H., 25	W.M., 33	J.S., 32	CHERRY	A.M., 36
D.P., 27	J.P., 20	CANATHEY	J.W., 101	G.O., 34	CLEMPSON
BULGER		J.S., 36	P.T., 34	CHESNUT	J.C., 33
W.L., 27	-C-	CANDELL	R.B., 31(2)	A.T., 32	CLEVELAND
BULLOCK		B.E., 30	R.D., 31	CHICHESTER	J.B., 30(2)
ROBERT, 26	CABANISS	H.R.S., 33	T.M., 35	A.M., 30	CLEWELL
BUNHAM	J.S., 32	CANDILL	W.A., 31	[BLANK], 30	F.C., 32
P.B., 24	CAGE	B.T., 30	W.B., 32, 35	CHILCUTT	CLINE
BUNN	F., 32	CANDLE	CARTWRIGHT	J.W., 35	JAMES, 33
G.W., 25	CAHILL	W.M., 36	H.J., 31	CHINNEY	CLOPTON
BURBRIDGE	T.J., 31	CANDLER	CASEY	B.R., 30	H.E., 30
[BLANK], 24	[BLANK], 37	Z.M., 34	W., 37	CHISHOLM	W.E., 30, 34
BURCHELL	CAIL	CANTWELL	CASON	A.C., 31	CLOUD
W.D., 26	A., 34	EDWARD, 35	J.R., 32	B.F., 34	A.S., 35
BURCHFIELD	CALDWELL	CARD	CASSAR	W.R., 34	J.B., 33
H.G., 24	G.S., 35	E.T., 31	C.G., 35	CHRISMAN	COALTER
BURGESS	J.H., 35	CARGILL	CASSIUS	ISAAC, 36	H.T., 35
W.A., 28	J.P., 31	C.N., 33	J., 101	CHRISOLIN	COBB
W.L., 23	J.T., 35	C.W., 36	CASTLEMAN	W.R., 32	G.S., 35
BURKE	O.H.P., 32	CARLONS	B.F., 30	CHRISTIAN	J.E., 34
R.E., 23	CALLIN	W.W., 31	CATTINGHAM	D., 100	L.G., 34
BURKLEY	J.W., 33	CARMICHAEL	J.R., 31	J.M., 32	COCHRAN
[BLANK], 29	CALLOWAGE	T.L., 31	CAUTHORN	T.L., 31, 33	R., 101
BURKS	T.D., 33	CARNAHAN	J.W., 100	W.J., 34	COCKE
C.C., 25	CALLOWAY	J.P., 36	CAUTHORNE	W.S., 33	W.N., 33
H.C., 27	S.D., 36	CARPENTER	[BLANK], 33	WILLIAM, DR., 10	COCKERELL
BURNETT	CALVERT	H., 30	CHADBOURNE	CLAIBORNE	W.M., 33
W.K., 27	J.J., 33	J.C., 30	H.R., 32	W., 37	COCKERHAM
BURROUGHS	THOMAS, 35	CARR	CHAMBERLAIN	CLARK	S.D., 34
J.J., 28	CALVIN	R.B., 32	H.W., 31	J.B., 31, 36	COFER
R.M., 23	H.G., 33	T.F., 32	CHAMBERLAYNE	L.B., 36	J.H., 35
BURRUSS	CAMERON	W.H., 34	J.H., 34	O., 32	COFFER
G.H., 23	F.J., 32	CARRINGTON	CHAMBERS	S.P., 101	R.A., 37
BURTON	CAMP	H., 35	C.E., 30	CLARKE	COFFEY
H.L., 29	J.A., 32	H.A., 37	CHANCEY	R.S., 33, 101	HIRAM, 34
J.F., 24	R.B., 37	CARSON	C., 36	S.P., 33	COFFIN
J.W., 26	CAMPBELL	L.P., 37	CHAPMAN	CLAY	T.E., 34
S.M., 28	A.W., 35	S.P., 34	R.D., 36	D.H., 101	W.N., 34

COGBURN	J.W., 36	R.E., 34	CREATH	JULIAN, 32	T.H., 39
M.S., 36	CONNER	COUCH	H.D., 35	CUMMINGS	W.A., 40
COGGIN	T.B., 32	JOHN, 31	CREEL	G.M., 101	W.B., 38
JERRY, 31	COOK	COUGHTON	S.G., 36	H.R., 35	[CAPT.], 15(3)
COKER	G.G., 36	C.D., 32	CRILE	CUNNINGHAM	DAWSON
W.C., 33	W.B., 36(2)	COULTER	WILLIAM, 35	J.M., 32	C.G., 37
COLDMAN	[BLANK], 37	E.B., 32	CRISP	W.M., 35	H.B., 40, 101
M.D., 31	COOKE	T.W., 30	A.J., 30(2)	CUSHMOND	W.A., 40
COLE	A., 33	COUPLAND	CRITCHER	B.C., 31	DAY
J.M., 30	S.G., 33	T.B., 34	JOHN, 31	CUSSONS	J.W., 39
M.H., 37	COOLEY	COVINGTON	CROCKER	JOHN J., 31	DEAN
P., 100	J.M., 34	W.R., 32	E.W., 35	CUTHBERT	J., 38
S.D., 37	T.L., 34	COWAN	J.F., 35	[BLANK], 37	DEANE
W.W., 37	COON	F.N., 31	J.O.B., 32		P., 101
COLEDON	R.W., 36	COWDEN	CROCKERVILLE	-D-	DEBABABAN
[BLANK], 36	COOPER	W.N., 34	C.C., 35		A.M., 40
COLEMAN	F.F., 101	COWLING	CROFT	DABSON	DEBAREN
A.F., 34	G.G., 34	S.W., 34	D.L., 31	J.V., 39	J.D., 37
C.F., 35	H.M., 34	COX	CROMLEY	DADNEY	DEBASE
F.W., 33	R.A., 33	J.H., 33	R.M., 32	F.T., 39	E.J., 39
H.W., 30(2)	T.F., 37	JOSEPH, 34	CROMWELL	DAILY	DEBERRY
COLES	W.C., 36	M.H., 101	R., 33	J.A., 40	J.B., 38
ISAAC, 32	WILLIAM, 34	M.M., 33	CRONIN	DALES	DECAMP
COLEY	COPASS	W.B., 32	S.D., 32	J.A., 101	T., 40
J.R., 36	R.B., 101	CRACROFT	CROSO	DANIEL	DEGOURNEY
COLGER	R.D., 33	G.K., 36	W.J., 37	J.D., 38	T.F., 39
J.M., 33	COPPEDGE	CRAFFORD	CROSS	DAUGHARTS	DEGRAU
COLLIER	F.T., 36	S.J., 35	H., 34	S.P., 37	W., 37
H., 35	CORBIN	CRAFT	J.F., 30	DAVIDSON	DELTO
J.W., 37	J.M., 36	J.H., 33	J.T., 30	J.B., 37	W.L., 38
T.H., 36	CORDRAY	CRAIG	CROUCH	DAVIS	DENNISON
COLLINS	C.S., 31	A.P., 35	R.C., 32	BAILEY, 37	C.E., 39
H.A., 31	CORKER	CRANE	CROW	CAPT., 12, 13(2),	DENT
J., 101	S.A., 31	R.M., 33	R.H., 100	16(2)	[BLANK], 3
COLLIUM	CORLEY	CRAVENS	CROWE	G.W.C., 39	DENTON
M.V., 36	W.L.J., 33	J.E., 31	G., 35	J.C., 38, 39, 40	E.R., 40
COLTON	COSELAM	CRAWEY	CROWN	J.J., 39	DEPRIEST
JAMES, 36	F.B., 30	J.W., 101	J.B., 33	J.L., 40	C., 39
COMBIE	COSS	CRAWFORD	CULBERTON	J.M., 40	DERRICKS
A.G.M., 33	C.A., 30	J.A., 30(2)	A.L., 31	J.T., 40	J.A., 39
CONDEN	COSTIN	J.H., 33	CULMAN	M.J., 37	DEVAUGHN
C.D., 30	MATT, 34	J.M., 30	F.W., 101	PRES., 10	J.E., 38
CONETOE	COTE	J.R., 30	CULPEPPER	R.G., 37	DEW
F.M., 30	T.M., 100	JAMES, 35	J.A., 30	R.H., 38	T.R., 37
CONNELLY	COTTON	L., 35	CUMMING	S.B., 39	DEWBERRY

109

W., 40
DIBBLE
  SAMUEL, 39
DICK
  R.M., 40
DICKENSON
  J.E., 37
  M.N., 38
  W.J., 39
DICKERSON
  D.V., 39
DICKSON
  E.D., 38
DILLARD
  J.W., 38
  R.G., 38
DILLINGER
  L.A., 40
DILLINGHAM
  W.H., 39
DILLS
  J.R., 37
DISMAKES
  [BLANK], 37
DISON
  H.C., 39
DIXON
  W.W., 40
DODSON
  J.M., 39, 101
  J.N., 38
DOLAN
  W., 40
DONAHUE
  A.J., 40
DONALD
  W.P., 38
DONALDSON
  A.T., 39
  W.J., 38, 40
DONAWAY
  W.F., 37
DONNEGAN
  C.A., 37
DOOLEY

J.E., 39
DORSEY
  A.L., 39
DOSS
  S.P., 38
DOUGHTY
  L.G., 38
DOUGLAS
  H.K., 38
  J.H.T., 37
DOVER
  W., 38
DOWELL
  J.J., 39
DOWNING
  J.S., 38
DRAKE
  R.F., 38
DRAUGHN
  H.H., 40
DREWRY
  S.T., 38
DROIS
  S.T., 39
DUDLEY
  E.V., 39
  J.R., 38
DUFFILL
  F., 39
DUGAN
  J.A., 38
DUGGETT
  A.E., 40
DULIEL
  J.D., 40
DUNAVAN
  J.B., 39
DUNCAN
  H.H., 39
  J., 39
  J.H., 37
  J.T., 38
  J.W., 38
  S.P., 38
DUNHAM

D.L., 39
F., 39
DUNIGAN
  J., 39
DUNN
  B.H., 40
  J.B., 37
  R.J., 38
DUNNER
  W.C., 39
DURALD
  A.V., 40
DURHAM
  J.H., 40
DURPHEY
  T.H.B., 40
DYE
  J.J., 38
DYER
  S.T., 39
  W.S., 38
DYES
  G.A., 37
DYKES
  [BLANK], 38

-E-

EARTHMAN
  J.H., 41
EAST
  W.F., 41
EASTERLING
  W.G., 41
EASTHAM
  A., 41
EDLINS
  O.F., 41
EDWARD
  B., 41
  J., 41
EDWARDS
  J., 41
  W.C., 41
  W.H., 42

EFLAND
  W.S., 41
EGGERS
  J.W., 42
ELAM
  P.R., 41
ELENER
  C.E., 41
ELKINS
  J.M., 41
ELLER
  W., 41
ELLEY
  R.S., 41
ELLIOTT
  B.S., 41
  E.C., 41
ELLIS
  A., 40
  E.J., 41
  H.M., 41
  J.A., 42
  W.N., 41
  W.S., 41
EMAHART
  WM. P., 41
EMERSON
  J., 101
EMRIS
  S.V., 41
ENATE
  E., 40
ENLOE
  L.A., 40
ERVIN
  W.D., 40
ERVING
  H.T., 41
ERWIN
  W.A., 42
ESOIN
  W.T., 41
EUBANKS
  J.B., 41
EUGLIST

T.W., 41
EURE
  M.S., 40
EVANS
  H.M., 41
  J.B., 41
  M.D., 40
  R.M., 101
  S.S., 41
  W.E., 41
EVERETT
  G.W., 41
  T.D., 41
EVERMAN
  L.H., 101
EZELL
  F.M., 41, 101

-F-

FAIN
  N., 42
  W.J., 43
FAIR
  SAMUEL, 42
FALLS
  T.D., 43
FAMDER
  W.R., 44
FANAS
  R.S., 44
FARINHOLT
  B.L., COL., 5, 12
  COL., 6
FARLEY
  J.B., 43
FARNA
  JAMES, 44
FARR
  J.J., 42
  S., 43
FARRENHOLT
  B.L., 44
FARRINGTON
  W.O., 44

FARRIS
  WM., 44
FAULKNER
  J.W., 44
  L.G., 44
FAUMAN
  A.H., 43
FELLOWS
  J.K., 43
  JOHN R., COL., 5
FENWICK
  C.C.H., 43
FERELL
  W.C., 44
FERGUSON
  J.H., 43, 45
  J.W., 44
  R., 44
  RICHARD, 5
FERINER
  R.D., 43
FERRELL
  J.E., 43
FERRING
  W.A., 42
FIDLER
  E.W., 42
FIERSON
  WM., 44
FIGHT
  JOHN A., 44
FINCHER
  J.C., 43
FINKLEN
  J.C., 43
FINLEY
  G., 42
  G.W., 42
  J.H., 44
  J.T., 44
FITE
  COL., 5
FITZGERALD
  P.H., 43
FITZPATRICK

J.B., 43
FLANNAGAN
  W.C., 44
FLETCHER
  J.B., 44
FLOOD
  J.W., 43
FONAGAN
  W.N., 44
FOOT
  W.W., 43
FOOTMAN
  J.W., 42
FORCE
  C.F., 43
FORD
  J.W., 43
  JAMES, 42
  L.D., 44
FORRESTER
  J.T., 42, 43
FORTSON
  J.A., 44
FOSTER
  A.C., 43
  FRENCH, 42
  J.D., 43
  J.M., 43
  J.W., 42
  K.B., 44
  T.H., 42
  T.J., 43
  W.A., 42
FOUNTAIN
  N., 43
FOWLER
  P., 44
FOX
  G.R.R., 42
FRAIME
  M.C., 44
FRANCIS
  T.H., 44
FRANK
  T.F., 43
FRANKLIN
  J.H., 44
  S., 44
FRAVER
  THEOPHILUS, 43
FRAZIER
  A.M., 42
  C.W., 42
  J.W., 42
  S.A., 42
  S.J.A., 5, 34
  SAMUEL JOSIAH ABNER, 1
FREEMAN
  A., 42
  JOHN INZER, 4
FRENCHER
  B.H., 42
FRICK
  W.T.C., 43
FRIERSON
  J.G., 44
FRITH
  C.N., 44
FRY
  B.D., 42
FRYER
  J.H., 42
FUGARY
  J., 101
FULKERSON
  W.B., 43
FULKS
  A.L., 42
FULLER
  A.W., 101
FURAGER
  W.M., 43
FURGERSON
  E.K., 42
  T.B., 43
FURGUS
  W.C., 43
  W.P., 44
FURGUSON
W.W., 43
FURHMAN
  G.P., 42
FURNISH
  L., 42
FURRY
  J.J., 43
FURST
  A., 44

-G-

GABLE
  H., 101
GAILLARD
  R., 46
GALE
  D.D., 47
GALLON
  J.B., 46
GALLOWAY
  J.S., 46
  W., 45
GAMBLE
  ROBERT, 45
GAMMON
  S.R., 46
GAMMOND
  W.M., 48
GARDENHIRE
  FRANK, 1
GARDINER
  N.H., 45
GARDNER
  R.W., 46
GARIG
  WM., 46
GARNETT
  W.N., 45
GARRARD
  A.S., 48
  A.T., 47
GARRETT
  GEORGE, 47
  T.C., 45
GARRING
  G., 47
GARRISON
  A., 48
GASH
  J.B., 48
GASTON
  G.P., 46
GATHRIGHT
  J.R., 48
GAY
  J.S., 47
GENTRY
  L.C., 47, 48
GEORGE
  J.L., 46
  M.J., 47
GERRY
  L.B., 46
GHEE
  J.J., 46
GHOLSTON
  J.O., 48
GIBB
  J.G., 45
GIBBON
  J.W., 48
  W.R., 47
GIBSON
  E., 46
  E., LIEUT., 2
  E.C., 45
  J.R., 47
  J.W., 47
  T.F., 45
GILBERT
  A.S., 48
  E.M., 45
  J.H., 46
  L.E., 48
GILES
  J.R., 45
GILHAM
  G.H., 46
GILL
S.P., 47
GILLESPIE
  W.W., 46
GILLIS
  HUGH, 45
GILLISPIE
  CHAS., 101
GILLOCK
  J.W., 46
GILMER
  J.W., 46
  M., 46
GINEVAN
  M., 45
GIRARD
  E., 47
GIVINS
  L.W., 46
GLASGOW
  W.S., 45
GLASS
  W.P., 45
GLEESON
  T.H., 47
GLENN
  J.B., 47
  W.H., 48
GLOVER
  B.F., 45
  S.H., 45
GODWIN
  A.C., 46
  A.L., 47
GOFF
  E.H., 45
  J.B., 48
GOLD
  J.E., 45
GOLDSBERRY
  W.E., 47
GOLDSBORO
  R.H., 45
GOLDSBY
  W.E., 48
GOODBREAD
J.P.B., 47
GOOGEN
  M.D.H., 47
GORDON
  R.H., 47
GORRICE
  M.M., 45
GORRILL
  R.D., 46
GOWDLETT
  D.T., 47
GOWEN
  W.B., 46
GRABILL
  J.H., 47
GRACE
  W.L., 46
GRAHAM
  A., 45
  S.R., 48
  W.L., 45
  [BLANK], 101
GRANBERRY
  J.G., 48
GRANT
  GEN., 3(3), 9
  J.C., 47
GRASON
  H.C., 47
GRAVES
  J., 48
  J.A., 48
GRAY
  A.H., 46
  C.C., 45
  E.G., 45
  W.W., 101
GRAYSON
  J.W., 48
  W.C., 47
GREEN
  C., 47
  H.H., 47
  H.P., 45
  J.W., 45

R.P., 47
THOMAS, 48
W.A., 48
W.J., 45
GREGORY
  J.M., 48, 101
  W., 45
GRIFFIN
  B., 46
  H.B., 48
  J.R., 47
  S.H., 47
GRIFFITH
  J.R., 47
GRIGGARD
  W.B., 48
GRIGGS
  L.B., 46
  M., 46
GRIGSBY
  L., 46
  M.G., 46
GRIMSHAW
  H., 47
GROGAN
  LIEUT., 5
GUBBINE
  JAMES, 45
GUERRANT
  S.P., 47
GUMA
  JOHN A., 46
GUNN
  W.H., 45
GUNNELLS
  W.M., 47
GURLEY
  T.P., 47
GUSH
  J.B., 101
GUSMAN
  A.L., 45
GUSS
  M.G., 45
GUYTON

D.S., 46
GWIN
  J.T., 48
GWYNN
  H., 46
  W., 45

-H-

HACK
  J.W., 51
HACKWORTH
  N.N., 50
HAGGARD
  R., 51
  W.B., 53
HAGLER
  W.J., 53
HAIL
  T.B., 51
HAILEY
  [BLANK], 52
HAINESS
  A.F., 52
HALE
  J.A., 54
  M.B., 54
  M.C., 51
HALEY
  FRANK, 49
  J.W., 54
  W., 51
HALIBURTON
  W., 50
HALL
  C.W., 55
  J.B., 52
  J.J., 49
  J.W., 53, 54
  JACOB, 54
  R.M., 50
  W.C., 49
  W.J., 52
  [BLANK], 3
HALLARD

J.A., 50
HAMILTON
  A.S., 54
  J.E., 50
  J.W., 54
  R.A., 50
  S., 102
HAMMOND
  [BLANK], 53
HAMPTON
  J.N., 50
HANCOCK
  J.W., 53
HANDLEY
  A.M.J., 53
HANEL
  J.F., 51
HANES
  W.A., 50
HANFORD
  A.W., 49
HANLEY
  J.M., 52
HANNAH
  T.L., 53
HANNANT
  J.A., 50
HANNER
  C.H., 49
HANSBURG
  S.Z., 51
HARBER
  T.B., 52
HARDEN
  W.P., 50
HARDIN
  J., 101
HARDING
  J., 52
  R.A., 54
HARDMAN
  W.H., 48
HARDY
  J.B., 102
  JAMES, 51

W.B., 52
HARE
  F.M., 54
HARGROVE
  J.L., 51
HARMAN
  A.W., 53
HARMON
  A.W., 52
HARPER
  B.G., 102
  G.W., 49
  J.B., 53
  J.R., 102
  R.L., 49
  W.P., 52
HARRING
  J.A., 49
HARRIS
  A.A., 52
  E.B., 51
  G.L., 49
  J.M., 49, 52
  O.C., 52
  S.J., 53
HARRISON
  THOS. R., 52
  W.J., 54
HARRY
  L.E., 53
  S.W., 50
HART
  G.M., 49
  G.W., 49
HARTSELL
  J.J., 48
HARTSFIELD
  W.W., 51
HARTSVILLE
  A.M., 49
HARTZ
  ASA, 5
HARWOOD
  J., 51
  J.S., 54

HASKIN
  C.H., 51
HATCH
  G., 53
HATCHCRAFT
  J.L., 49
HATSON
  N.S., 102
HAVE
  PETER, 49
HAVRON
  W.A., 102
HAWKINS
  H.J., 51
HAYCROFT
  J., 51
HAYER
  S.C., 54
HAYES
  A., 50
  C.W., 53
  J.W., 53
HAYNER
  A.S., 50
HAYS
  J.G., 51
HAYWOOD
  F.J., 49
HAZZARD
  J.B., 102
HEAMSTEAD
  BEALL, 54
HEARD
  C., 48
  COLUMBUS, 54
HEAROD
  B., 49
HEATH
  B., 49
  E.M., 49
  H.N., 54
HEDGE
  ROBERT, 102
HEGGIE
  J.T., 54

HEGWARD
  D.G., 52
HELMS
  W.T., 52
HENDERSON
  F., 52
HENDRICKS
  J.D., 49
  J.L., 54
HENEGARD
  C.S., 52
HENRY
  A.W., 52
  J.W., 102
  P., 54
  S.W., 53
HENSON
  J.R., 54
  W.R., 51
HENTON
  W., 53
HERBERT
  A.M., 51
  J.R., 53
HERD
  J.W., 52
HERLEY
  J.D., 50
HERNDON
  A.S., 53
HERON
  A.J., 51
HERREN
  J.W., 53
HERRING
  D., 101
HESLIP
  J.A., 50
HESTER
  H.T., 51
HEUSON
  L., 48
HICKMAN
  A.H., 52
  J.A., 52

W.D., 54	H., 51	J.M., 50	J.C., 49	IVEY	J.G., 55
HICKS	HOLLEY	HOURSHAN	HUNDLEY	D.L., 55	J.W., 57
F.Y., 49	J.E., 52	W., 48	J.W., 50		L.B., 1(2)
J.D., 53	HOLLINGSWORTH	HOUSTON	HUNSACKER	-J-	M.F., 56
J.R., 49		H.W., 49	J., 50		N.D., 56
L.T., 53	T., 49	JOHN, 55	HUNSUCKER	JACKSON	R.G., 55
HICKSON	HOLLOWMAN	R.M., 54	J., 101	D.C., 102	T.W., 56
M., 50	J.F., 52	T.D., 51	HUNTER	J.A., 56, 102	W., 102
HIGH	HOLMAN	HOWARD	F.C.S., 52	J.M., 56	W.B., 55
J.Q., 54, 102	J.H., 51	C.A., 50	HURLBERT	PHIL, 55	W.H., 56
W.S., 50	HOLMES	J.A., 50	H.A., 53	T., 56	W.J., 55, 102
HILDRETH	P.S., 49	J.C., 50	HURT	T.B., 56	JOHNSTON
[BLANK], 3	HOLSTEIN	J.L., 54	B.H.N., 51	T.M., 57, 102	GEN., 12
HILL	F.A., 102	R., 48	J.H., 52	W.G., 57	J.S., 57
J.T., 53, 54	HOLSTON	R.G., 50	HUTCHINSON	JAQUES	J.W., 57
J.W., 102	T.A., 50	R.J., 49	E.L., 52	J.W., 57	THOS. H., 57
S.P., 51	HOLT	HOWE	H.R., 51	JARRARD	W.S., 57
W.J., 55	A.B., 51	J.T., 51	J.L., 49	C.L., 56	JOINER
HINCH	B., 54	HOWELL	HUZZARD	JARVAS	W.F., 57
T.H., 50	E.A., 49	W.G., 52	J.B., 52	J.A., 57	JONES
HINCHEY	ROBERT, 102	HOWTY	HYDE	JARVIS	A.J., 55
G.H., 49	W.S., 50	J.H., 54	W.A., 53	S.A., 56	B., 56
HIRON	HOLTON	HOYE		JEMISON	BUEHRING H., 56
MR., 16	E.H., 49	M.J.L., 51, 53	-I-	J.B., 56	C.H., 55
HODGE	HOOKER	HUBERT		W.M., 56	CALVIN, 56
J.C., 53	T.B., 54	R.R., 49	ICARD	JENKINS	E.P., 57
J.R., 50	HOOPER	HUDGINS	H.A., 55	B.P., 56	F.M., 55
HODGERS	R.S., 52	J.J., 53	IMBODEN	T.F., 56	G.B., 57
J.R., 101	WARREN, 1	L.M., 49	JAMES, 55	T.M., 56	G.H., 56
HOFFMAN	HOPE	HUDSON	INGE	JENNING	G.S., 56
J., 53	R.A., 53	G.W., 54	J.A., 55	T.L., 57	G.W., 56
J.M., 51	HOPKINS	J., 54	J.E., 55	JENNINGS	H.C., 56
MAJ., 3	F.M., 54	N.J., 50	INGRAM	W.W., 57	H.E., 57
WILLIAM, LIEUT.COL.,	HORD	W.J., 102	J.C., 55	JETT	H.S., 57
	J.C., 50	HUDSPETH	JAMES, 55	E.D., 57	J.A., 57
1	HORDIN	J.B., 53	INMAN	T.C., 56	J.J., 57
HOGAN	[BLANK], 102	HUFFSTELLE	A.A., 55	JOHNS	J.K., 56
ALEX, 48	HORN	JOHN, 102	INZEN	ST. CLAIR, 57	J.M., 55
HOGG	H., 49	HUFFSTUTTLER	J.M., 55	JOHNSON	J.P., 55(2)
GEORGE, 50	HORNER	[BLANK], 53	INZER	A.J., 57	J.R., 56
HOGGES	J.K., 54	HUGHES	JOHN W., COL., 4	B.F., 56	J.S., 57
J.F., 53	HORTON	A.J., 53	IRWIN	B.W., 55	J.W., 57(2)
HOLDER	N., 52	J.T., 51(2)	J.R., 55	D.L., 57, 102	MR., 2
W., 51	W.H., 53	R.J., 51	ISBELL	J.C., 55	O.S., 57
HOLLAND	HOURE	HUMPHRIES	R.H., 55	J.E., 56	R.C., 56

113

S.D., 57
T.B., 56
T.F., 55
T.P., 57
W.B., 55
W.J.F., 57
JORDAN
  A.F., 57
  C.L., 55
  H.F., 55
  J.B., 56
  L.B., 57
  W.C.S., 55
JOYCE
  J.J., 57
JOYNER
  J.S., 55
JULIAN
  R.M., 57
  T.J., 55
JUSTICE
  F., 56
  GEO. F., 57

-K-

KAUTZ
  GEN., 11
KAY
  R., 59
  R.M., 102
KEAN
  J.M., 59, 102
KEANS
  E.D., 59
  W.C., 59
KEAR
  JOHN M., 59
KEELY
  W.J., 59
KEESEE
  J., 59
KEININGHAM
  WM. H., 59
KELLAND

W.W., 59
KELLER
  J.W., 58
  M.D., 103
KELLEY
  B.W., 58
  F.M., 58
  M.L., 58
KELLY
  A., 59, 102
  J.G., 59
  S.A., 59
KELSEY
  J.R., 59
KEMP
  L.H., CAPT., 2
KEMPS
  M.W., 58
KEMPTON
  J.C., 58
KENAN
  T.S., 58
KENARS
  J.G., 58
KENDRICK
  J.M., 58
KENNEDY
  DAN, 1
  R.C., 58
KENNELLY
  W.W., 59
KENNERLY
  H.C., 59
KENT
  B.F., 59
  J.F., 58
  W.C., 58
KERR
  J., 59
KEYS
  J.B., 59
  J.H.O., 58
  Z.H.O., 102
KIDD
  E.M., 58

KIERNAN
  J., 59
KIKEN
  E.R., 59
KILBY
  J.E., 58
KILLEN
  W.E., 59
KIMBROUGH
  FRANK, 59
KING
  A.A., 58, 59
  H.C., 58
  J.M.D., 58, 102
  T.B., 59
  T.J., 59
  W.J., 102
  W.L., 58
KINGCAID
  N.J., 58
KINNEY
  B.F., 59
  JOHN, 102
KINSEY
  JOSEPH, 59
KINZER
  C.S., 58
KIRBY
  B.B., 58
KIRKMAN
  H., 59
KIROFF
  S.E., 58
KIRTLEY
  W.T., 102
KIRWAN
  CAPT., 9
KITCHUM
  [BLANK], 102
KITZMATTER
  L., 58
KLUGH
  W.B., 58
KNICELEY
  H.C., 59

KNIGHT
  T.B., 58
KNITTLE
  H., 58
KNOWLES
  C.C., 58
KNOX
  A.E., 58
KOHNLEY
  A., 58
KUBLER
  G.B., 59
KYLE
  O., 58
  T.J., 59

-L-

LACKE
  S.E., 59
LACKLIN
  J., 60
LAFFOON
  N.S., 60
LAHEY
  J., 61
LAIRD
  J.S., 62
LAMAR
  E.F., 60
LAMPKIN
  E.O., 60
LANDRUM
  J.M., 63
  W.L., 63
LANE
  H.N., 61
  J.M., 62
  P.W., 62
  T.O., 63
  Z.D., 103
LANG
  R.C., 61
LANGLEY
  S.S., 62

LANGTON
  F.B., 61
LANIER
  A.M., 63
  B.W., 63
  J.L., 63
LAPSLEY
  JAMES L., 62
LARD
  J.J., 61
LARGEN
  J., 63
LARKINS
  J.R., 61
LASSITER
  C., 60
LASWELL
  R.M., 63
LATANE
  J.L., 63
  JOHN S., CAPT., 6
  JOHN, CAPT., 7
LATHAM
  L.J., 59
LATIMER
  M.S., 59
LATIMORE
  J.T., 61
LATSPUCK
  W.C., 61
LAUGHLIN
  J.J., 63
LAW
  J.T., 61
LAWEY
  W.L., 61
LAWRENCE
  E.D., 62
  E.H., 62
  H.C., 61
  J.M., 63
  M.N., 60
  R.S., 61
  W.F., 60
LAWSON

W.T., 62
LEACH
  C.E., 63
LEAR
  F.F., 60
LEASCHLER
  GEORGE, 62
LEATHERWOOD
  M.H., 61
LEBALANCE
  A., 60
LEBRETON
  E.S.M., 61
LEE
  B.C., 60
  GEN., 11, 12, 16
  J.A., 61
  J.A.J., 60
  J.T., 61
  J.V., 62
  R.H., 60
  S.M., 63
  T.L., 62
  W., 61
  W.C., 63
  W.E., 60
  W.T.F., 60
  WILLIAM H.F., GEN., 11
LEEMAR
  A.W., 62
LEMON
  GEORGE, 60
LENDERBUCK
  F.M., 60
LENHART
  M., 60
LENTZ
  J.C., 60
LEONARD
  J.R., 62
LEOPHART
  S.L., 62
LESLIE
  S.D., 62

LEWIS	W.G., 63	D.G., 61	C.F., 65	D.M., 64	D.H., 66, 103
A.F., 62	LODGERWOOD	LYLES	M., 69	G.W., 67	McKEE
C.W., 60	WM., 61	A.M., 61	McCAUNN	H.A., 64	S.F., 69
COL., 5	LOFTON	O.P., 62	T.W., 69	J.C., 70	McKENAN
G.W., 61, 103	W.G., 62	S.T., 63	McCAW	M.R., 69	A.S., 71
H.G., 63	LOGAN	LYNN	W.M., 70	R.A., 68	McKENNEY
J.H., 60	G.W., 60	DAVID, 60	McCHESNEY	ROBERT, 71	R.T., 71
J.T., 61	J.A., 62	LYON	W.L., 69	[BLANK], 72	McKENZIE
L.H., 63	M., 61, 63	JOHN, 103	McCHRISTY	McDOWELL	A.A., 70
L.M., 62	LONDON	LYONS	G.W., 69	E.C., 69	A.D., 70
W.P., 63	A., 61	M., 103	McCLARE	McEACHER	McKIBBEN
W.R., 63, 103	LONG	LYSEY	J.J., 66	J.C., 69	R., 64
LIGGIN	B.A., 63	P., 61	McCLARY	McFADGEN	McKILL
JOHN, 61	J.W., 62	LYTTON	L.W., 71	A.M., 67	JAMES, 69
LIGON	L.W., 62	E., 61	McCLELLAND	McFARLAND	McKINNEY
J.S., 62	M.C., 60		J.T., 69	JAMES, 71	D., 103
LILLARD	S.P., 61	-M-	McCLOSKEY	McGAHEE	McKNEW
W.R., 63	LOVE		A.P., 71	W.W.J., 70	M.E., 65
LINDSAY	J.A., 62	McAFEE	McCLUNG	McGARRAH	McKNIGHT
J.A., 63	J.S., 61	T., 64	R.L., 71	S., 70	GEORGE, 65
T.P., 60	R.C., 63, 103	McALLISTER	W.B., 71	McGEEHEE	MAJ., 5
LINZEY	LOVEJOY	W.A., 67	McCONNELL	W.G., 72	McLAIN
N.G., 103	W.H., 60	McALPHINE	CAPT., 12, 13(2), 14	McGENESY	H., 67
LISTER	LOVELL	R.M., 65	J.H., 71	W., 65	McLANE
J.G., 63	H.P., 60	McARTNEY	McCORKLE	McGHEE	J.W., 103
LITAKER	LOWDERMILK	T.B., 69	G.B., 69	C.A., 68	McLANEY
J.F., 60	D.W., 61	McBEE	McCOY	McGILL	L., 71
LITTLE	LUCAS	J.W., 64	W., 69	C.R., 71	McLAUGHLIN
R.J., 62	S.M., 63	S., 69	McCRANE	W.R., 66	H.B., 69
LITTWICH	LUCE	McBOON	S.N., 67	McGINNIS	L.W., 70
J.E., 62	COL., 7, 8	B.F., 71	McCRARY	J.M., 71	McLAUREN
LIVINGSTON	W.H., 60	McBRIDE	M.S., 65	McGRAW	S.H., 70
A.R., 62	LUDLOW	J.R., 64	McCREARY	T.J., 68	McLEAN
T.B., 62	WILLIAM, 63	McBROOKS	A.T., 67	McGREEN	F.J., 69
LLOYD	LUM	J., 72	McCULLOCH	T., 70	N.C., 72
W.D.C., 62	Q.A., 60	McB_____	R., 72	McGRENSEY	T., 71
LOCKE	LUMPKIN	J.B., 64	McCULLOUGH	W., 65	W.L., 67
A.J., 62	E.H., 63	McCAMEG	CAPT., 5	McGURK	McLESTER
B.T., 61	LUNSDALE	J., 103	McCURLEY	J., 66	J.D., 65
M.B., 61	J.V., 62	McCAMPBELL	J.H., 72	McINTIRE	McLUCAN
LOCKETT	LUNSFORD	J.H., 65	McDANIEL	R.M., 70	M.M., 69
B.H., 60	RICHARD, 61	McCANN	H.C., 68	W.R., 69	McMILLER
O.W., 61	LUSHER	D., 70	H.D., 64	McINTURF	W.A., 67
LOCKHART	G.W., 63	DICK, 67	JOHN, 71	J.T., 70	McMULLEY
J.W., 60	LUSK	McCARTY	McDONALD	McKAY	JOHN, 65

115

McMULLIN
  L., 71
McMURRAY
  JAMES, 68
  M., 68
  W.F., 66
McNEELEY
  C.R., 65
  J.R., 65
McRED
  J., 65
McWHARTON
  S.A., 103
McWHISTER
  J.W., 67
MAGEE
  W.G., 65
MAGER
  R.E., 103
MAHAN
  J.T., 67
MAHER
  P.E., 65
MAKELY
  W., 66
MALLORY
  W.S., 70
MALLOY
  D.W., 67
MALONE
  C.B., 70, 71
  H.E., 70
  J.W., 69, 71
  T.H., 64
MANIS
  D.B., 65
MANLY
  M.B., 103
  MATTHEW, 66
MANN
  J.S., 70
MANNING
  J.A., 68
MANSON
  J.S., 103

MARBERRY
  M.P., 67
MARETT
  E.J., 66
MARKHAM
  G.S., 65
MARLAN
  W.A., 65
MARSHALL
  J.M, 71
  J.T., 70
MARTIN
  B.F., 70
  B.Y., 70
  C.P., 64
  J.J., 64
  J.T., 70
  O.P., 65
  P.C., 63
  RALEIGH, LIEUT.COL., 12
  S.J., 67
MASEZ
  L.L., 64
MASON
  H., 68
  J.P., 66
MATCHELL
  T.F., 67
MATHENY
  W.G., 66
MATHERS
  A., 69
MATTHEW
  C.A., 69
  E.W., 67
  W.E., 64
  W.M., 70
MATTHEWS
  J., 66
  L., 69
  W.W., 68
MATTOCK
  C.H., 72

MATTOCKS
  J.W., 72
MAURRAS
  A., 68
MAURY
  E.P.G., 67
MAUZY
  [BLANK], 103
MAXWELL
  G.T., 69
  P., 70
MAYES
  R.E., 67
MAYO
  J.M., 68
  R.E., 68
MEADOWS
  J.D., 66
MEBANE
  W.A., 68
MEDDLEBARK
  J., 103
MEEK
  J.J., 71
MELVIN
  G.W., 66
  J.S., 70
MERCHANT
  A., 69
MERIWETHER
  S.O., 71
MERRILL
  ROBERT, 71
  W.C., 68
MESSICK
  E.H., 69
METHROW
  W.R., 65
METTS
  J.J., 65
MICAN
  A.R., 65
MICHELL
  J.A., 68
MICHIE

H.C., 68
MIDDLEBROOK
  J., 66
MIDDLETON
  J.A., 66
MILES
  L., 70
  S., 103
  W.A., 65, 67
MILLAM
  J.J., 64
MILLER
  A.H., 66
  ALEX, 68
  E.W., 71
  F.M., 71
  J.A., 68
  J.C., 70
  J.H., 65, 68
  JOHN, 63
  JOHN J., 65
  R.T., 71
MILLIKEN
  J.D., 68
MILLS
  J.P., 68
MINER
  WILLIAM, 64
MINNIS
  J.A., 68
MINOR
  "BILL", 3(2)
MINTER
  B.W., 70
MITCHELL
  A., 66
  J.B., 65
  J.C., 66
  W.H., 64
MIZELL
  JOSHUA, 67
MOBLEY
  J.P., 64
MOBLY
  J., 103

MOFFETT
  A.A., 64
MOMFORT
  J.P., 64
MONCURE
  W.P., 68
MONDAY
  T.N., 70
MONLEY
  W.W., 72
MONLY
  A.S., 64
MONROE
  A.J., 68
  E.A., 103
  J.A., 72
MONTGALL
  G.R., 67
MONTGOMERY
  J.N., 66
MOODY
  B.D., 66, 72
  W.C., 65
MOORE
  A.P., 64
  C.W., 67
  H., 67
  H.C., 65
  H.F., 71
  J.B., 66, 69
  J.H., 67
  J.L., 64
  J.P., 65
  J.W., 70
  JAMES, 67
  JOHN, 64
  M.W., 66
  P., 63
  R.L., 68
  S., 103
  S.T., 71
  W.F., 65
  W.J., 67
  W.R., 64

MORGAN
  E.S., 72
  F.G., 103
  GEN., 17
  H.W., 66
  J.E., 71
  J.H., 67
  JOHN, 3, 4
  JOHN, GEN., 4
  P., 64
  T.G., 69
MORNIN
  J.N., 66
MOROSE
  P.J., 71
MORPHIS
  W.J., 70
MORRIS
  B.T., 71
  C.B., 70, 72
  J., 67, 103
  J.F., 68
  J.R., 69, 71
  L., 67
  T.C., 68
  W.G.B., 66
  W.J., 65
  W.L., 63
  W.S., 70
MORRISON
  E., 103
  G.S., 66
  J.F., 72
MOSELEY
  E.B., 64
MOSELY
  ALEXANDER, 64
  J.W., 66
MOSES
  L.L., 71
MOULY
  B.F., 69
MULL
  F.P., 65
MULLINS

B.B., 65, 69	-N-	A.O.P., CAPT., 3	JOHN, 74	OWENS	JOHN, 77
H.H., 69		E.G., 73	O'CONNOR	A., 104	M., 76
J.W., 103	NABURS	H.P., 73	M., 74	E., 74	W.H., 78
MUMPH	C., 73	NITCHELL	T., 73	J.A., 74(2)	PAUL
W., 64	NANCE	H.P., 72	ODORN	J.J., 73	G.W., 75
MUNSON	[BLANK], 72	NIXON	J.G., 73	JOHNNY, 3	PAYNE
S.A., 72	NASH	COL., 3	OFFETT	L.S., 73	WM. H., 75
MURCHISON	C.B., 73, 104	I.O., COL., 3	N.S., 74	R.L., 74	PEAN
K.M., 68	C.C., 72	J.O., 73	OGDEN	V.J., 74	D.B., 75
MURDETT	D.W., 72	NOLAN	W.F., 74	W.V., 74	PEARCE
F.H., 69	NEAL	W.M., 73	OGLESBY		B.F., 76
MURDOCK	J., 103	NOLAND	G.S., 74	-P-	PEARSON
A.G., 67	O.P., 103	P.J., 73	J., 74		J.M., 77
MURPHY	NEILL	NOLINER	OHLSOM	PACETTY	PEDUE
E.D., 67	L.C., 72	JAMES, 72	P.M., 74	LEWIS, 77	J.C., 104
J., 71	W.B., 73	NOLLEY	OLIVER	PAGLER	PEEL
J.B., 66	NELMS	W.F., 73	E.D., 73	W., 78	N.C., 104
J.D., 69	A.M., 73	NOMAN	J.B., 73	PALMER	PEELE
J.J., 67	NELSON	J.S., 73	P.D., 74	B., 77	A.E., 76
J.R., 66	C.A., 73	NORMAN	VICTOR, 73	N.H., 75	PEELER
MURRAY	E., 73	M.H., 72	O'NEAL	PANKEY	A.L., 75
J., 72	J.H., 73	W.M., 72	E.T., 74	S.H., 77	PEELS
T.J., 69	P.D., 73	NORRIS	O'NEIL	PARHAM	W., 75
T.M., 68	NESMITH	J.E., 72	J., 74	S.J., 75	PEGRESS
MURRELL	A., 73	NORTHFIELD	OREA	PARISH	E.D., 77
S.F., 68	NEWHART	M.W., 72	A.J., 73	W.N., 77	PELHAM
MURRICK	W., 103	NORTON	ORILAN	W.R., 75	W., 75
G.A., 68	NEWMAN	W.P., 73	F., 74	PARK	PEMVIS
MURS	A.M., 72	NORVELL	ORR	J.S., 77	H., 77
A.J., 64	A.N., 73	CHARLES, 72	E.A.M., 104	PARKER	PENDERGRAST
MUSE	C.S., 72	J., 103	E.H.M., 74	DAVID, 78	[BLANK], 75
W.B., 65	NEWSOM	NORWOOD	J.P., 73	G.W., 77	PERKINS
MUSGROVE	J.D., 73	J.W., 73	JOHN, 74	J.P., 75, 76	A., 75
J.T., 67	L.J., 73	W.F., 103	OSBORN	P.M., 75	C.A., 75
MUSSELMAN	NEWTON	W.T., 73	E.W., 74	PARKS	PERLE
J.A., 103	A.E., 73	NUCKOLS	J.M., 73	B.F., 76	M.C., 77
J.N., 67	MR., 10	W.L., 72	OSHUM	J., 104	PERRY
MYBS	NICHOL		J.W., 104	M.A., 74	J.A., 77
W.B., 66	P., 103	-O-	OTIS	PASSMORE	JOCK, 77
MYERS	NICHOLAS		N.G., 74	M., 77	R.T., 76
J.W., 66	P., 73	O'BANNON	OWEN	PATE	THOMAS, 75
L.M., 64	W.S., 72	B.C., 74	B.N., 74	W.R., 78	WM. E., 75
P.S., 71	NICHOLS	O'BRIEN	F.A., 74	PATTERSON	PERSON
R., 103	GOV., 5	J., 74	G.W., 74	E.D., 76	S.A., 77
	NICHOLSON	J.E., 74	W.F., 74	PATTON	PETTICON

117

C.H., 75	POND	PROCTOR	RABENAN	A.J., 82	RICH
PETTY	W.W., 76	WM., 75	P.J., 80	RAY	J.E., 80
J., 75	POOLE	PROFFIT	RADER	H., 80	RICHARDS
J.W., 75	J.P., 75	IRA, 76	L.F., 80	REASOR	D.W., 79
PEYTON	POPE	W.A., 76	RAGER	D.S., 78	RICHARDSON
J.H., 78	T.A., 77	PROPST	J., 81	REDBOUT	A., 82
PHARR	PORTER	W., 76	RAINES	W.B., 81	H.B., 79
J.E.W., 76	D., 76	PROVINCE	F., 104	REDDMAN	J., 79
PHELPS	J.N., 75	D., 76	RAISHLER	THOMAS, 80	J.J., 79
C.V., 77	J.W., 78	R.N., 78	C.W., 80	REED	M.C., 79
PHILLIPS	PORTMAN	PROW	RALSTON	D.G., 79	S.H., 81
C.D., 77	S., 76	J.W., 75	GEORGE, 79	ISAAC, 79	T.E., 80
D., 78	POWELL	PRUETT	GEORGE, CAPT., 3	J.B., 79	W.J., 79
D.D., 76	C.H., 76	R.B., 77	RAMSEUR	J.S., 82	W.N., 79
H.R., 75	J.W., 75	PRUITTE	L.M., 78	L., 78	RICKER
J.L., 76	R.M., 77	P.N., 77	O.A., 78	R.L., 79	WINSTON, 79
J.M., 76	T.C., 77	PUBURN	RAMSEY	W.H., 79	RICKHILL
PHILPOT	W.W., 78	W.H.H., 76	D.W., 78	W.J., 79	M.B., 104
B.W., 75	POWER	PUCKETT	RANDALL	REEGUS	RIDDEN
G.B., 76	THOMAS, 76	E.N., 77	J.H., 78	J.M., 79	J.C., 81
PICKETT	POWERS	PULLIAM	S.D., 78	REESE	RIDDICK
G.W., 76	H.N., 78	A.J., 78	RANDOLPH	D.G., 78	J., 104
PIERCE	PRAKER	PUMLEY	H.J., 81	J., 82	[BLANK], 81
CHARLES H., 76	H.C., 77	W.C., 77	T.E., 79	JOSEPH, 80	RIDDING
W.N., 77	PRATOR	PURCELL	W., 82	REEVES	G.D., 82
PIERSON	J.H., 76	A.M., 77	W.F., 83	E.W., 80	W.W., 82
L., 75	PRATT	W.A., 77	W.W., 81	J.W., 83	RIDDLE
S.A., 104	M.E., 75	PURCELLE	RANKIN	M., 104	A.N., 80
PIGMAN	R.H., 77	W.N., 78	J., 81	REID	F.C., 80
W.P., 75	PREBLE	PURVIS	S.C., 81	J.D., 82	RIDLEY
PIPER	JOSEPH, 78	J., 77	W.P., 78	J.G.R., 82	A., 79
G.A., 76	PREIST	J.A., 76	RASS	THOMAS J., MAJ., 2	RIGGS
PITMAN	WM., 74	PUTNAM	A., 80	REPASS	FRANK, 80
J.N., 77	PREVALT	A.W., 77	RASSEAM	S.A., 81	RILEY
W.E., 77	L., 76		W.J., 78	RERSON	C., 81, 83
PITTMAN	PRICE	-Q-	RATICAN	S.N., 80	E.H., 80
J.J., 74	F.L., 77		D.P., 79	REYNOLDS	R.H., 81
PITTS	J.E., 76	QUEEN	RATLIFF	W.G., 81	RINDLEAMEN
J.H., 75	S.R., 75	A.A., 78	J.E., 81	RHODES	[BLANK], 82
PLUNKETT	T.A., 75	QUINN	N.J., 80	D.V., 79	RINGSTAFF
W.A., 76	T.W., 75	J.P., 78	RAWLAND	E.P., 104	H., 81
POINDEXTER	PRINTUB	W.A., 78	R., 81	S.P., 82	RIPPLE
J.E., 78	D.S., 75		RAWLINGS	RICE	G., 82
POLK	PRITCHARD	-R-	T.R., 79	C.R., 79	RIVES
L., 78	C., 76		RAWSON	E., 80	S.T., 82

RIVIS	RODGERS	RUFFIN	F.H., 85	SESSIONS	GEN., 11
H., 80	M., 82	THOMAS, 79	SANFORD	J.F., 83	T.B., 85
ROANE	RODRIGUEZ	RUSH	H., 84	SEWARD	SHERRY
W.L., 78	O., 82	JOHN, 81	J.G., 84	PAT, 84	C.O., 104
ROBB	ROGER	RUSSELL	SARGENT	SEWELL	W.M., 84
L.W., 82	W.J., 82	A.S., 81	JOHN, CAPT., 3	W.B., 84	SHERWIN
ROBERDEAN	ROGERS	L., 79	R.D., 83	SHACKELFORD	C., 87
J.D., 79	A.T., 81	R.L., 82	SAUNDERS	F., 88	SHIFT
ROBERTS	J.C., 79	W.G., 80	J.D., 86	SHACKLETT	W.M., 83
A.W., 79	ROLLINGS	W.R.C., 78	J.H., 84	J.C., 104	SHILAR
E., 80	R.A., 82	RUST	R.H., 83	SHADDOCK	J.G., 88
F.A., 80	ROLLINS	A.F., 82	R.R., 87	R.I., 87	SHILLEY
J., 82	T.R., 82	RUTLEDGE	SAYRES	SHALER	J.L., 83
J.A., 78, 104	W.N., 82	W.W., 80	E.B., 85	F.H.B., 86	SHIPMAN
J.C., 81	ROOT	RYAN	J.T., 86	SHANNON	J.T., 86
J.W., 82	G.J., 81	E., 80	SCALES	D.W., 87	SHIPPS
M.P., 79	ROSE	R.E., 81	J.J., 87	SHARP	C.J.J., 88
R.B., 82	C.A., 82	W.A., 82	S.A., 83	J.H., 84	SHIRRELL
ROBERTSON	ROSENBERGER		W., 86	R.G., 84	W.W., 85
B.F., 81	J.B., 81	-S-	SCATER	W., 84	SHORT
C., 79	ROSS		S.M., 86	SHARPTON	W.F., 85
COL., 3	J.A., 81	SACY	SCOTT	B.F., 85	SHORTER
E.D., 80	J.B., 81	J.A., 86	E.B., 86	SHAW	J.M., 83
W.G., 79	ROTHROCK	SAFFARONS	J.T., 88	H.B., 83	SHUCK
ROBINS	L.H., 80	T.H., 87	SCRUGGS	M.B., 88	W.A., 85
W.E., 82	ROUNTREE	SAGELEY	J.E., 104	SHAY	SHULER
ROBINSON	S.J., 79	J.A., 85	SEARS	JOHN, 85	B.G., 104
C.C., 81	ROWAN	SALE	J.H., 86	SHEARER	SIBLEY
C.S., 79	J.C., 80	J.G., 88	SEAVILLE	J.M., 85	W.L., 83
CAPT., 5, 12, 13,	W.H., 81	J.J., 85	R.M., 88	SHEDDEN	SIDBERRY
15(4), 16	ROWE	SALTER	SEAY	ALEX, 88	M., 85
J.D.H., 82	E.D., 79	MIKE, 86	E.G., 89	SHEFFIELD	SIMMES
JAMES, 79	ROWLAND	SAMFORD	W.A., 83	T.W., 86	PAT, 83
W.J., 80	J.K., 81	W.J., 84	SECHLER	SHELBY	SIMMONS
[CAPT.], 15	ROY	SANDELLE	J.A., 84	W.B., 85	S.M., 87
ROBISON	R.N., 81	S.W., 87	SEDGWICK	SHELLY	SIMMS
E.G., 81	ROYSTER	SANDERS	L.T., 88	W.A., 87	WM., 83
E.M., 81	R.M., 81	E.M., 89	SEE	SHELTON	SIMPSON
J.W., 80	RUCKER	F.A., 84	J.W., 87	S.M., 88	G.W., 84
ROCKHAM	ROBERT, 80	J.W., 87	SELECTMAN	W., 89	W.M., 88
D., 104	W., 80	SANDLIM	S.K., 87	SHEPHERD	WM., 84
ROCKWELL	RUDISILLE	A.W., 88	SELLERS	H.E., 83	SIMS
H.L., 82	J.R., 81	SANDRAM	C.C., 83	SHEPPARD	M.W., CAPT., 3
RODGEDALE	RUDLAND	W.L., 85	SEMPLE	M.L., 84	SISSON
W.A., 82	J.N., 80	SANDY	W.F., 84	SHERIDAN	J.W.R., 83

SKIDMORE
  W.J., 88
SLICER
  T.J., 86
SLOAN
  F.B., 84
  J.P., 88
SMALL
  E.A., 83
SMITH
  A.E., 87
  A.H., 86
  A.P., 85
  B.R., 88
  BAXTER, 85
  D., 104
  D. HOWARD, 84
  E., 87
  E. KIRBY, GEN., 3
  E.H., 86
  FRANK, 2
  G.A., 85
  G.F., 84
  G.W., 83
  GEORGE, 85
  H., 87
  H.A., CAPT., 2
  J.C., 88
  J.E., 87
  J.G.C., 83
  J.S., 87
  JOHN, 11
  L.B., 87
  MORRISON, 86
  N.S., 83
  R.H., 86
  R.M., 84
  S.H., 88
  W.H., 87, 88
  W.W., 84, 88
SMYTH
  R., 88
SNEAD
  C., 84
SNOW
  C.C., 87
SNOWDEN
  W.P., 84
SNURK
  G.W., 104
SORRELLS
  T.L., 83
SOUTHWICK
  D.F., 87
SPANGLER
  C.H., 86
SPARKS
  A., 85
  J.W., 85
SPAULDING
  R.S., 84
SPEARS
  R.D., 86
SPEED
  C.A., 87
SPELLER
  S.P., 87
SPENCE
  J., 84
  W., 83
SPONNA
  B.G., 83
SPRATLEY
  G.W., 84
SPREY
  J.G., 85
STAGG
  LEWIS, 87
STAKES
  E.T., 87
  J.E., 87
STAMES
  B.B., 83
STAMFER
  H.H., 85
STAUNTON
  W., 85
STEARNS
  B.M., 88
STEDMAN
S.D., 87
STEEDMAN
  J.G.W., 83
STEELE
  J.R., 85
STENT
  J.F., 87
  J.W., 84
STEPHENS
  J.A., 88
  W.C., 86, 88
STEPHENSON
  J.M.D., 86, 104
  J.T., 85
  J.W., 87
STEPTOE
  J.M., 86
STERLING
  W.R., 88
STEVENS
  F.S., 83
  R.M., 88
  S., 83
STEWARD
  W.E., 84
STEWART
  C.E., 88
  M.W., 88
  T.J., 86
  W.E., 88
STICK
  F.E., 86
  R.P., 88
STILLS
  J.N., 83
STINER
  J.F., 87
STOCKDALE
  J.L., 85
STOCKTON
  G.M., 87
  R.H., 87
  W.F., 86
STOKES
  CAPT., 12, 13(2)

MAJ., 12, 13
STONE
  E.M., 85
  W.A.S., 85
  W.C., 86
STORKES
  W.D., 83
STOVALL
  W., 85
STRANGE
  W.B., 88
STREET
  T.A., 88
STRICKLER
  G.B., 86
STRIKES
  T.J., 86
STRONG
  F.J., 85
STUBBS
  J.J., 86
  J.T., 84, 86
STUBLET
  G.A., 85
STULEY
  M., 84
SUBLETT
  J.M., 86
SULLENS
  S.B., 84, 104
SULLIVAN
  N.R., 86
SUMNER
  B., 85
SURAT
  M., 87
SUTTLE
  E.D., 83
SUTTON
  L.B., 83
SWADLEY
  W.F., 85
SWAGERTY
  L.M.C., 83
SWAGNER

M.B., 89
SWAYNE
  R.D., 85
SWINK
  G.W., 87

-T-

TABA
  W.K., 90
TABER
  GEORGE, 91
TAGLE
  C.H., 91
TALBOTT
  H.T., 104
TALIAFERRO
  J.T., 91
TALLEY
  A.S., 91
TALLINS
  E.A., 90
TALOR
  W.J., 89
TAPLER
  L., 89
TARLOR
  R., 104
TATE
  J.W., 89
TATUM
  P.A., 90
TAYLOE
  J.J., 90
TAYLOR
  B., 90
  D.S., 92
  E.S., 90
  H.H., 92
  J.L., 89, 91
  JOHN, 90(2), 91
  LIP, 1
  R.L., 91
  S.H., 91
  T.J., 91

W.W., 89
THALHIUM
  P., 91
THIPPEN
  J.C., 90
THOMAS
  D.P., 89
  H.C., 89
  J.J., 90
  JOHN, 89
  P.W., 89
  R.E., 89
  S.M., 89
THOMPSON
  E.T., 90
  J.C., 89
  J.G., 91
  J.H., 90(2)
  J.N., 91
  J.P., 90
  JACK, MAJ., 5
  JEFF, 3
  JEFF, GEN., 5
  M. JEFF., 89
  R.C., 91
  T.H., 91
  W., 104
  Z., 89
THORNTON
  J.J., 89
  J.R., 90
  R.W., 91
THORP
  P.H., 90
  S.R., 91
THRASHER
  R.M., 91
THREADGILL
  J.E., 104
TIBBS
  C.H., 90
TILLETT
  J.N., 91
TILMAN
  O., 89

S.H., 90	TREVILLIAN		J.P., 92	W.S., 97	J.B., 95
W.J., 90	C.B., 91	UNDERWOOD	VEAZY	WALSH	J.H., 97
TIMBERLAKE	TRIMBLE	W.R., 92	W.W., 104	E., 93	W.E., 95
J.C., 92	GEN., 5	UPCHURCH	VENABLE	W.S., 95	WATTS
JOHN, COL., 5	J.R., 89	A.J., 92	Z.A.P., 92	WALTERS	J.A., 93
TIMBERLAND	MAJ. GEN. [ISAAC	[BLANK], 104	VERBAL	W.E., 93	WAYLAND
F.A., 89	RIDGEWAY], 3	UTLEY	H.D., 92	WALTON	W.H., 97
TINCHER	TRIPLETT	JAMES F., 92	VERMILLION	G.L., 97	WEAKS
J.N., 90	J.H., 90		J.A., 92	WALVERTON	R.R.C., 105
TINDELL	W.B., 89	-V-	VINER	E.H., 98	WEATHERSBY
W.H., 91	TUCK		BENJ., 92	WAMMAC	W., 95
TINNAD	W.M., 89	VALLANDINGHAM	VOIGHT	A.D., 98	WEATHERSPOON
F., 91	TUCKER	C.L., 16	R., 92	WAMMICK	S., 96
TIPPS	J.J., 91	VAN BENTHUYSEN		J.P., 94	WEAVER
J.C., 89	M.P., 90	W., 92	-W-	WARD	S.W., 93
TIPTON	O.M., 90	VAN HOORE		J.W., 98	W.M., 98
W.B., 91	TUGGLE	J.W., 92	WADDELL	W.H., 97	WEBB
TITTY	C.M., 104	VAN PRAGE	H.T., 94	WARDEN	B.C., 97
JAMES, 89	TURNBEN	H.A., 92	T.W., 93	JACOB, 93	D.C., 105
TOBY	B.N., 89	VANDERUN	WAGNER	WARDLAW	H., 96
L.M., 89	TURNER	P., 92	J.A., 95	D.S., 98	J.E., 93
TOCA	A.W., 91	VANLIER	WALDEN	WARE	J.H., 94
T., 90	C.L., 89	R., 92	J.A., 93	F.M., 94	R.F., 97
TODD	J.C., 90	VANMETER	WALDROP	WARFIELD	S.G., 93
M.L., 89	N.J., 90	W.S., 92	E.B., 99	B., 98	T.S., 95
TOMLINSON	W.G., 89	VANN	WALKE	WARLICK	WEDDINGTON
J.W., 90	W.J., 91	J.C., 92	G.D., 94	L., 93	H., 97
TONE	TURNEY	VANZANT	WALKER	WARREN	WEEKS
L.H., 91	J.B., 90	J.A., 92	D.L., 97	D.J., 98	R.R.C., 95
TOPP	TURNILL	VARNER	H., 93	J.P., 98	WEIR
R.C., 91	E.W., 89	A.W., 92	H.J., 93	WARRIOR	J.H., 98
TOWNS	TURPIN	E., 92	J.D., 98	MRS., 16	WELCH
J.C., 91	J.H., 89	VASLEY	J.S., 94	WASH	H., 105
TRAMEL	TUTER	W.W., 92	R., 93	W.A., 94	JOHN, 96
F.E., 90	J.S., 104	VAUGHAN	W.L., 97	WASHINGTON	WELLARD
TRAMMELL	TUTTLE	L.L., 92	WALL	N.C., 94	S.G., 97
A.E., 91	C.E., 91	VAUGHN	S.F., 94	WASSON	WELLS
TRAYNER	TWIPSON	E.H., 92	T.H.W., 98	J.W., 94	C.C., 97
J.D., 90	JOHN, 89	H.H., 92	WALLACE	WATERMAN	J.M., 98
TRAYWICK	TWITT	J.B., 105	D.J., 96	P., 94	WELTON
A.M., 91	W., 90	R.C., 92	J.E., 97	WATKINS	AARON, 94
TREDGALE	TYAN	W.L., 92	J.G., 95	E., 98	J.E., 93
W.R.J.P., 91	[BLANK], 91	VAUGHTER	JOHN G., 93	W., 94	WENTWORTH
TREDGILL		T.H., 92	THOMAS, 98	WATSON	J.H., 95
J.E., 91	-U-	VAUN	WALLER	G.W.S., 94	WEST

Heritage Books by James L. Douthat

1832 Creek Census

Alabama Soldiers in the Cherokee War

Augusta County, Virginia Survey Book of James Patton and William Preston, 1752–1755

Burke County, Georgia Records, 1758–1869

Cherokee Reservoir Grave Removals by T.V.A.

Chickamauga Reservoir Cemeteries

Early Wythe County, Virginia Settlers

Early Settlers of Montgomery County, Virginia: 1810–1850 Virginia Census

Fort Loudon Reservoir Cemeteries

Grainger County, Tennessee Various Records, 1796–1848

Hiwassee Reservoir Cemeteries

Jefferson County, Tennessee Will Book 1, 1792–1810

Jefferson County, Tennessee Will Book 2, 1811–1833

Johnson's Island (Federal) Civil War Prison for Confederate Officers, Lake Erie, Ohio

Kentucky Lake Reservoir Cemeteries, Volumes 1–3

Montgomery County, Virginia Will Book I: 1786–1809

Sequatchie Families

Sequatchie Valley Bible Records

Tennesseans in the Cherokee War

Watauga Reservoir Cemeteries

Williamson County, Tennessee Tax Listings, 1800–1801, 1805

www.ingramcontent.com/pod-product-compliance
Lightning Source LLC
Chambersburg PA
CBHW081916180426
43198CB00038B/2792